YO-BWS-152

THE BANK CUSTOMER'S GUIDE TO SAFE AND SMART INVESTING

Jeffrey H. Champlin

IRWIN
Professional Publishing

Chicago • Bogatá • Boston • Buenos Aires • Caracas
London • Madrid • Mexico City • Sydney • Toronto

© Jeffrey H. Champlin, 1996

This publication is designed to provide accurate and
authoritative information in regard to the subject matter
covered. It is sold with the understanding that neither the
author or the publisher is engaged in rendering legal, accounting,
or other professional service. If legal advice or other expert
assistance is required, the services of a competent professional
person should be sought.

From a Declaration of Principles jointly adopted by a Committee
of the American Bar Association and a Committee of Publishers.

Irwin Book Team

Executive editor:	Amy Hollands Gaber
Project editor:	Jean Lou Hess
Assistant manager, desktop services	Jon Christopher
Production supervisor:	Dina L. Treadaway
Senior designer:	Heidi J. Baughman
Compositor:	Douglas & Gayle Limited
Typeface:	11/13 Palatino
Printer:	R. R. Donnelley & Sons

Library of Congress Cataloging-in-Publication Data

Champlin, Jeffrey H.
    The bank customer's guide to safe and smart investing / Jeffrey H.
Champlin.
        p. cm.
    Includes index.
    ISBN 0-7863-0403-0
    1. Investments—United States. 2. Banks and banking—Securities
processing—United States. I. Title.
HG4910.C485 1996
332.6'78—dc20   95–20295

Printed in the United States of America

1 2 3 4 5 6 7 8 9 0 DOC 0 0 0 0 0 0 0 0

Dedicated to:

Linda
Zachary
Heidi
Talia
Brock
Max
Chad
Luke

Acknowledgments

First, I would like to thank my editorial consultant Larry Chambers, author of six excellent books on investing and investments, for his guidance and assistance along with Amy Gaber, executive editor at Irwin Professional Publishing, for recognizing the value of this book and making sure it happened. Second, my thanks to the staff of *Bank Investment Representative:* Gina Lauer, Lyn Fisher, Mark Weese, Doug Gibson, Maren Seamons, Tamara Pluth, Kristin Godsey, Daren Allred, Amy Maestas, Kim Jones, Eric Kohler, and Gil Chapman of the Lexicon Group.

Next, my thanks to Jeff Stanek, editor of the *Annuity Review,* Richard Ayotte, president of American Brokerage Data Services, Inc., and Marilyn Leiker and Susan McClure of Lipper Analytical Services, Inc., for their contributions to the appendix. My thanks to Kent B. Haueter for his encouragement and technical advice.

Also, thanks to Daniel S. Nelsen who started me in this business 13 years ago and who remains the best of friends. Last and most important, I express my warmest thank you to Linda Champlin, the truest of believers and the person I love and admire most.

Preface

This book is a guidebook for you, the bank or savings and loan customer, who for years has used bank accounts to accomplish your financial and savings goals. It's designed to educate you on the safety, risks, and rewards associated with investments now available through your bank. It explains how, why, and when to use investment products and what they are. It will provide you with proven strategies to increase your current income and achieve your long-term financial goals.

The Bank Customer's Guide to Safe and Smart Investing is organized into five parts: Part I reviews the growing and changing financial needs of the bank customer. It navigates you through the complex and confusing world of investing and shows you how to develop a successful investment strategy and where to get solid investment advice.

Part II explains how bank accounts and investments work together and how to put stocks, bonds, and mutual funds to work for you. It provides a reference of what FDIC does and does not insure.

Part III explains how tax-advantaged investments work, how they can increase the after-tax income on your savings, and how to determine if they are appropriate for you considering your tax situation.

Part IV is dedicated to bank customers who are nearing retirement age and need to focus on preparing for retirement. It will provide ways to ensure you fully benefit from retirement plans. It also provides strategies to help ensure that you don't outlive your money.

Part V takes the mystery out of investing by explaining the process of investing through your bank. It also provides a step-by-step guide for implementing your investment plan and tips for remaining on course once you have been investing.

The appendixes contain lists of investment-related resources for bank customers.

Keep in mind, this is not a traditional do-it-yourself book on investing. Instead, it is a guide to help you work effectively with a licensed professional at your local bank who gives investment advice and sells investment products. Together, with the knowledge you get from this book, you and your bank's investment consultant will be able to develop a safe and smart plan for saving and investing. Such a plan will maximize the earning power of your savings, increase your financial independence, and reduce your anxiety in this constantly changing and often intimidating word of economic uncertainty.

Some of the information and ideas contained in this book may be familiar to you, depending on your level of financial experience. If you have little or no experience, you will want to read it from beginning to end. More experienced readers may want to first select those chapters that are of greatest immediate value and return later to other chapters for a review. Therefore, before you begin, a more specific description of the chapters may be helpful.

Chapter 1 puts investing and savings in their proper perspective. It contains an overview of how times have changed and why investments are essential. It outlines what you need to do and know in today's fast-moving investment environment where financial products are more confusing than ever and interest rates are volatile. It shows why banks are a trusted source for investments as well as savings accounts.

Chapter 2 makes an attitude-adjusting distinction between safety and certainty and puts FDIC protection in its proper perspective. This chapter explores the various types of investment risks you could encounter. It shows you how to build a safety net around your personal investment program. You will also learn to coexist with the twin thieves: taxes and inflation.

Help on choosing an investment advisor you can trust is found in Chapter 3. It explains how to know if your bank's investment program is right for you. It provides a method for questioning and evaluating prospective investment advisors to determine if their knowledge, experience, and style are compatible with your needs.

Chapter 4 starts by building basic, easy-to-follow investment strategies that make up your investment foundation. It shows how to beat inflation and demonstrates why diversification is a top priority. The basics of asset allocation—matching investments to satisfy specific needs—are presented.

The Financial Needs Discovery Worksheet is presented in Chapter 5. It will help you through a self-discovery process to determine your needs and goals and assist you in establishing realistic expectations. It will help you, with or without the assistance of your financial advisor, to develop a written investment plan that covers saving for retirement, living through retirement, college savings, elder parent care, tax relief, and so on. It shows how investments and bank accounts can come together in a successful mix to fill your needs.

The last chapter in Part I, Chapter 6, is about putting it all together. It demonstrates how to determine the best time to invest and the value of dollar cost averaging. It focuses on the correct allocation of your money among the investments you need and gives examples of investments that work best at the different stages of your life.

With Chapter 7 begins the first of two parts of the book explaining investment products. In it you will learn the correct uses for many bank accounts and exactly what FDIC does and doesn't cover. You may be in for a surprise in this chapter.

The next two chapters explain stocks and bonds—the two investment vehicles that make up most of the financial-asset-based investments available today. Chapter 8 is about understanding stocks—their types, and their uses and misuses. How to buy and sell stock and the difference between stock dividends and interest is discussed. Chapter 9 covers similar material about bonds. Thoroughly understanding bonds and bond-based investments, the most used and misused investment by bank customers today, is essential.

Chapter 10 focuses on mutual funds, the most popular investments in the United States today. You will see the value and simplicity of using the professional management provided by mutual funds. In this chapter, you will learn exactly what mutual funds are, how they work, what it costs to buy them, and just how safe they are.

In the next three chapters, you will discover tax-advantaged investment products. Chapter 11 discusses municipal bonds, the only tax-free investment. It explains their similarities to and differences with other bonds and helps you determine if they are appropriate for you, considering your tax bracket.

The next two chapters discuss tax-deferred annuities, the second most common investments, next to mutual funds, sold in banks. Chapter 12 explains fixed annuities—why they are a common substitute for CDs, their correct uses, their costs, and how to evaluate their safety. Chapter 13 covers variable annuities. You will learn their advantages over mutual funds and fixed annuities and why many experts consider them the near-perfect investment.

Part IV is for the special needs of soon-to-be retirees and those who have already retired. Chapter 14 focuses on preparing for retirement and examines retirement accounts. It shows why you generally should use retirement accounts to their maximum extent before considering other long-term investments.

Chapter 15 provides special pointers for mature investors age 65 and older who now have a greater need for current income. This chapter shows you how to receive added income from your investments while preserving their safety. You'll learn how to protect your assets against inflation so you can enjoy a comfortable retirement in spite of rising health care costs, nursing homes expenses, and other costs attendant to living a long life.

Part V will help you apply what you've learned. In Chapter 16, you will learn in simple terms what a prospectus is and how to read it. Chapter 17 reveals the real costs of investing: what you get for your money and how much to pay for investment advice. It shows the difference between no-load mutual funds and mutual funds that charge a commission.

Chapter 18 tells you about the mechanics of investing at your bank. It will prevent you from feeling like a fish out of water when it comes to opening an investment account, signing unfamiliar forms, and keeping track of your investments.

Chapter 19 sums up what you've learned. It provides 14 concise steps for a getting started immediately.

Seven valuable tips for staying on course are found in Chapter 20. They will help you stay focused once you have begun your personalized investment plan. They will also help you adjust your plan, with the assistance of your investment advisor, when conditions warrant.

The appendixes contain a listing of the most prominent mutual funds, fixed annuities, and variable annuities available through banks. Chances are, when your bank's investment advisor recommends an investment, the company that offers it will be one listed here. In addition, you will find a list of many marketing companies and broker/dealers that assist banks in providing investment products to you. You may see their names on account forms, business cards, and signs at your bank. They are providing a product or service to your bank's investment program, and regulations often require they be listed on literature or posted on signs.

This book is designed to be read and then referred to whenever you feel unsure about investing. This book delivers what successful investors need: an understanding of all major investment products, techniques, and strategies. By following the book's logical step-by-step process for making safe and smart investment decisions, you'll be in more control, make more money, and have financial peace of mind.

Jeffrey H. Champlin

Table of Contents

Preface   vii

Part I
SAFE AND SMART INVESTMENT STRATEGIES   1

Chapter One
TIMES HAVE CHANGED: WHAT BANK
CUSTOMERS NEED TO KNOW   3
The Harsh Realities of Uncertain Times, 4
Outliving Your Money, 4
The Need to Change Your Plan of Action, 5
Help Is as Close as Your Bank, 7
The Rewards for Starting Now, 8

Chapter Two
SAFETY FIRST   10
Member FDIC, 10
Redefining Safety for the 1990s, 11
The Tax Bite, 12
The Ultimate in Investment Safety, 13
Hiring a Professional Is Safest, 13
Being Deceived and Cheated, 14
Wrong Investments, Wrong Advice, 16

Chapter Three
ADVICE AND ADVISORS: CHOOSING A
BANK INVESTMENT REPRESENTATIVE   17
Investing with and without the Help of a
Professional Advisor, 17

The Bank Investment Representative, 19
Trust, 19
Help with Your Financial Needs, 20
Questions to Ask, 21
Don't Be Confused, 26

Chapter Four
HOW TO BUILD AN INVESTMENT
STRATEGY FOR CHANGE   27
Step 1: Building the Foundation, 27
Step 2: Developing the Growth and Enhance-
         Income Component, 27
Step 3: Lowering Investment Risk while Increasing
         What You Earn, 29
Conclusion, 31

Chapter Five
HOW TO DETERMINE YOUR NEEDS
AND GOALS   32
Finding Out Yourself, 33
Financial Needs Discovery Worksheet, 34
   Step 1: Define Your Financial Goods, 34
   Step 2: Set Your Time Horizon, 35
   Step 3: Consider Your Personal Risk Profile, 36
   Step 4: Find the Investment That Matches Your
           Risk Profile, 37
   Step 5: Check Your Asset Mix, 38
Reaching Your Goals, 41
   Step 6: Rethink Your Investments Periodically, 41

Chapter Six
HOW TO PUT IT ALL TOGETHER   43
Life Stages, 43
   Early Years (20–40), 43
   Middle Years (40–50), 45
   Preretirement Years (50–60), 45
   Retirement Years (60–70), 46
   Late Years (70 plus), 47
Making Your Strategy Work: The Influence of Time
on Investment Risk, 47

Making Your Strategy Work: The Power of
Compounding, 49
Making Your Strategy Work: Systematic Investing/
Dollar Cost Averaging, 50
   Wealth Building, 50
   Reducing Volatility, 50
Summary, 51

Part II
INVESTMENTS AND BANK ACCOUNTS   53

  Chapter Seven
  BANK ACCOUNTS AND FDIC INSURANCE   55
  Short-Term, Mid-Term, and Long-Term Money, 55
    Avoid Two Common Mistakes, 56

Types of Bank Accounts, 56
    Savings Account, 57
    Certificates of Deposit, 57
    Money Market Accounts, 58
    Bank Money Market Deposit Accounts, 59
    Money Market Funds, 59
    U.S. Savings Bonds, 60
  FDIC Insurance, 60
    Background, 60
    Basic Insurance Limit, 63
    Single Ownership Accounts, 63
    Joint Accounts, 64
    Retirement Accounts, 67
    Business Accounts, 68

  Chapter Eight
  UNDERSTANDING STOCKS   70
  Why Stocks? 71
    Common Stock, 71
    Preferred Stock, 71
  How Stock Prices Move, 73
  Trading, 73
    Where Stock Is Traded, 74
    How a Stock Exchange Operates, 75
    How to Measure a Stock's Current Value, 75

Chapter Nine
UNDERSTANDING BONDS   78
Bond Basics, 78
Buying a Bond, 79
   Market Risk, 80
   Credit Risk, 81
Types of Bonds, 81
   Corporate Bonds, 81
   U.S. Government Notes and Bonds, 82
   Zero Coupon Bonds, 83
   Municipal Bonds, 83
   Ginnie Maes, 84
   Bond Terms, 84
   Bond Mutual Funds, 85

Chapter Ten
UNDERSTANDING MUTUAL FUNDS   86
Banks and Mutual Funds, 86
How Mutual Funds Work, 87
Mutual Fund Structures, 87
   Open-End Mutual Funds, 88
   Closed-End Mutual Funds, 88
Major Types of Mutual Funds, 88
   Stock Funds, 89
   Bond Funds, 91
   Money Market Funds, 94
Benefits of Mutual Funds, 94
Costs of Mutual Funds, 97
Other Things You Should Know, 97
   Unparalleled Structural Safeguards, 97
   How These Safeguards Work, 98
   How to Read Newspaper Fund Tables, 99

Part III
TAX-ADVANTAGED INVESTMENTS   101

Chapter Eleven
UNDERSTANDING TAX-FREE MUNICIPAL
BONDS   103
Tax-Free versus Taxable, 103
Tax-Free Bonds Are Not for Everyone, 105

Kinds of Municipal Bonds, 105
Municipal Bond Safety, 106
Credit Risk and Rating Services, 106
Market Risk, 107
Municipal Bond Insurance, 107
Packaged Tax-Free Municipal Bonds, 107
  Tax-Free Unit Investment Trusts, 108
  Municipal Bond Funds, 108
Federally Tax-Free Money Market Funds, 109
  Zero Coupon Municipal Bonds, 109
A Simple Strategy, 110
The Basic Rule of Fluctuation, 111
Summary, 111

Chapter Twelve
UNDERSTANDING FIXED ANNUITIES   112
The Accumulation Phase, 112
The Payout Phase, 113
Buying and Surrendering Your Annuity, 116
Unfamiliar Terms, 118
Benefits beyond Tax Deferral, 118
  Competitive Fixed Interest Rates, 119
  Guaranteed Principal and Interest, 119
  Safety, 119
  Death Benefits/Avoiding Probate, 119
  No Fees, 120
  Bailout Rate, 120
  Bonus Rate, 120
  Liquidity, 120
  Flexibility, 121
Summary, 121

Chapter Thirteen
UNDERSTANDING VARIABLE ANNUITIES   122
Popularity of Variable Annuities, 122
"Variable" Features, 123
  Subaccounts, 123
  Performance of Variable Annuities, 124
  Safety of Subaccounts, 124
  Tax-Free Switching, 125
  Tax-Deferred Stocks, 125

Flexible Deposits, 126
Death Benefit, 127
Withdrawal Options, 128
Costs, 129
Near Perfect, but Not Perfect for Everyone, 130
Summary, 131

Part IV
STRATEGIES FOR SENIORS   133

Chapter Fourteen
PREPARING FOR RETIREMENT   135
Time to Get Serious, 136
Enough Is All You Need, 136
Take Inventory, 139
Social Security, 139
Employer-Sponsored Pension Plans, 140
Personal Savings, 141
Put It All Together, 143
Income Shortfall, 143
Tips for Retirement and Retirement Preparation, 146

Chapter Fifteen
BEYOND RETIREMENT: YOUR
LATER YEARS   151
Safety First, 151
Earning All You Can Safely Earn, 152
"I'm Not Going to Be Around That Long", 153
Use a Variety of Appropriate Investments, 157
Ways to Take Income from Your Investments, 158
Reducing Taxes, 161
Other Important Reminders, 163
Don't Rely on Your Will Alone, 163
Don't Give It All Away, 164
Keep Close to Home, 164

Part V
THE PROCESS OF INVESTING   167

Chapter Sixteen
HOW TO READ A PROSPECTUS   169

Where to Get a Prospectus, 170
Important Highlights of a Prospectus, 170
Beyond the Prospectus, 173

Chapter Seventeen
THE REAL COSTS OF INVESTING 174
The Value of a Professional's Advice, 175
Ways You Are Charged, 175
  Certificate of Deposit, 176
  Fixed Annuities, 176
  Variable Annuities, 176
  Unit Investment Trusts, 177
  Bonds, 177
  Stocks, 177
  Mutual Funds, 178
  The Cost of No Advice, 179
Ways to Reduce the Cost of Investing, 181

Chapter Eighteen
THE MECHANICS OF INVESTING AT
YOUR BANK 184
New Account Applications, 184
Other Applications, 186
  W-9 Form, 186
  Disclosure Forms, 187
  Annuities Applications, 187
Paying for Your Investments, 188
Statements, 188
  Confirmation Statements, 188
  Periodic Account Statements, 189
Customer Complaints and Arbitration, 189

Chapter Nineteen
TIPS FOR GETTING STARTED 191
Tip 1: Act Now, 191
Tip 2: Select an Advisor to Guide and
        Assist You, 193
Tip 3: Complete the Financial Needs Discovery
        Worksheet, 193
Tip 4: Determine Your Risk Tolerance, 193

Tip 5: Set Target Rates of Return, 194

Tip 6: Know Your Products, 194

Tip 7: Use Managed Products, 194

Tip 8: Establish Time Horizons, 194

Tip 9: Avoid Overexposure to Bonds, 195

Tip 10: Avoid Underexposure to Stocks, 195

Tip 11: Ask for a Plan and Investment Recommendations, 195

Tip 12: Start Slow, but Start Now, 196

Tip 13: Worry about Taxes Last, 196

Tip 14: Maximize the Value of Your Retirement Accounts, 196

Remind Yourself, 197

Chapter Twenty
STAYING THE COURSE 198

Tip 1: Expect Your Investments to Fluctuate in Value, 198

Tip 2: Never Act Hastily—Time Is on Your Side, 199

Tip 3: Follow Through and Invest Regularly, 200

Tip 4: Never Chase the "Hot" Tip, 202

Tip 5: Never Fall in Love with Your Own Investments, 202

Tip 6: Keep Accurate Records as You Measure, Not Track, Your Investments, 203

Tip 7: Have an Annual Checkup, 203

Conclusion, 203

Appendixes: Quick References, 205

Appendix A   Mutual Funds Distributed through Banks, 207

Appendix B   Bank Proprietary Mutual Funds, 213

Appendix C   Annuity Providers to Bank Customers, 227

Appendix D   Bank-Related Variable Annuities, 235

Appendix E   Marketers and Broker/Dealers Active in Banks, 237

Index, 243

SAFE AND SMART INVESTMENT STRATEGIES

Chapter One

Times Have Changed
What Bank Customers Need to Know

Y ou are the customer of a bank, S&L, or credit union. In the past, you felt comfortable using savings accounts and certificates of deposit to meet your current and future income needs.

However, today you are contemplating starting an investment program, and you don't feel as comfortable. You have questions. You are not quite sure how investments differ from bank accounts, how they work, or which ones to use. You are becoming overwhelmed because there is so much to know.

Your primary goal is to be safe and smart with your money. In the past, you could be safe and smart by simply buying a CD or adding to a savings account. But times have changed. In today's complex economic environment, you can no longer rely entirely on bank accounts to provide the financial security you need.

You're not expecting to get rich quickly. You're looking for extra earnings, higher income, financial security, or tax advantages. To begin with, you need information you can rely on. This book will help you. It will teach you the basics of the important types of investments, their appropriate uses, and their misuses. By reading it, you will learn how investments work and how to put them to work for you by mixing them with your bank accounts.

This book will help you develop a personalized investment plan. With it you will identify your true financial needs and set achievable goals to satisfy them. You'll gain the knowledge and develop the confidence necessary to work effectively with a financial advisor you can trust to match the right investments to your needs.

This book is an easy-to-understand guide to maximizing the power of your savings dollars safely and wisely, but not overnight. Seeking overnight wealth is neither safe nor smart.

THE HARSH REALITIES OF UNCERTAIN TIMES

Chances are, if you're like most bank customers, your attitude about saving and investing was influenced by the Great Depression. Either you have personal memories of that painful time, or you were born to parents who suffered through the economic uncertainty and despair. In either case, you may harbor the fear of loosing everything.

As a result of this widespread concern, *safety of principal* has remained the most important investment principle for the last 60 years. Consequently, Americans have relied almost exclusively on their banks, backed by the Federal Deposit Insurance Corporation (FDIC), to keep their money safe, sound, and earning interest.

However, times have changed. Banks are as safe as ever, having come successfully through the Savings and Loan Crisis of the late 1980s. But our society's financial landscape has shifted dramatically and it continues to shift further every day. The financial safety net relied on since the Depression is unraveling. Lost is the confidence that governmental social programs will catch you if you fall or that Social Security will adequately provide for your retirement years. Technology is advancing at a dizzying pace, displacing workers and shattering many Americans' confidence in keeping their job and maintaining their standard of living, let alone securing an adequate retirement fund. As a result, it is absolutely clear that your financial independence and economic security is a matter that you must personally tend to. Relying on others is a grave mistake.

Realizing this brings into focus the need to increase the amount of money you are saving and maximize the earning power of your money. Safety of principal is still important, but growth and increased earnings is an absolute must. This need is heightened further when you consider the impact of medical science on your life.

OUTLIVING YOUR MONEY

A woman born in the 1950s who reaches the age of 65 is projected to live until age 87, and a man born the same year is expected to live to age 81. Not only are people living longer, but there are more of them living longer. By the year 2030, the number of Americans age 65 and over will more than double to 65 million, and 10% of the population will be over the age of 75. The fastest growing age group is the 85+ population.

The costs of this longer life is mounting rapidly. A generation ago, a man who retired at 65 could expect to live until age 71 at the most. Today, people are retiring closer to 62 and living into their 80s. Consequently, you or someone you love may spend a quarter to a third of a lifetime in retirement. Can you afford this? Consider that a 5% annual rate of inflation would result in the purchasing power of retirement income being cut in half in 15 years. The chance of outliving your money is great, especially if you're not saving enough or investing wisely.

There's another hitch in this idea of paying for a longer life: the quality of life. Medical science is having a difficult time curing killer diseases like cancer and heart disease, but it is successful at extending the life of the terminally ill. While in most cases a desirable accomplishment, it is extremely costly, and medical costs continue to skyrocket. Imagine the personal resources needed because we're retiring earlier, living longer, and spending many of our final years being kept alive by costly life-extending care. It will be an extremely difficult financial task for everyone, especially those millions of people who are currently spending their resources caring for their parents and who then must save and invest for their own futures.

The greatest financial danger for individuals is outliving their financial resources. No one wants to be old and out of money.

THE NEED TO CHANGE YOUR PLAN OF ACTION

Business as usual is trouble waiting to happen. It's time to rethink your spending habits. It's time to implement an investment strategy that results in a level of financial independence that brings comfort, security, and opportunity to your life. There are two initial steps in a successful plan of action:

1. Save more of what you earn. In other words, don't spend all you make. This isn't a novel concept, but it's a difficult one

for many people to implement. You must save and invest a minimum of 10% of your earned income.

As Americans, we save far too little and much less than citizens in other developed nations. The typical 50-year-old has only $2,300 in financial assets, excluding the primary residence. And 15% of 45- to 65-year-olds are saving nothing at all. A study by the Investment Company Institute, a mutual fund trade group, shows that 83% of all Baby Boomers are not saving for retirement.

You need to examine your lifestyle and shift your attitude and actions away from consumption and toward saving. This isn't easy. For example, it's difficult to save money when your neighbor keeps buying things you can't afford. Yes, we live in a society where what you have determines who you are. If it becomes fashionable to post your bank and investment account statements on your front door, people will save more. Until then, it takes real determination and commitment to do without in the present so you can have financial independence in the future.

The easiest way to increase savings is to pay yourself first. Pay yourself each pay period just like you pay your mortgage, utility bills, and car payment. Always do it; don't get behind, and don't cheat yourself and your future. Even if you're retired and have little or no earned income, you should reinvest a minimum of 10% of your retirement and interest income to hedge against an uncertain future.

2. Invest safely and wisely; don't just save. Does this mean you should no longer use savings accounts, certificates of deposit, and other FDIC-insured bank accounts? Absolutely not. You should still use them but not exclusively. The demands of the present and the future require that bank accounts be balanced with investments that have the ability to earn you higher returns over time. The key is to use the right investments at the right time in the right amounts—to have a well-thought-out investment plan.

No doubt it makes you somewhat nervous to realize that investment products are a must if you want to prosper, or even survive, in today's complex world. You may not be familiar with all the investment terminology. It may seem like a whole new world to you. In fact, if you're like many bank customers, your confidence meter is low when it comes to even discussing investments, let alone placing your money in them. There are so many unknowns, questions, concerns, and confusing concepts that it may almost hurt to think about it. It's not unusual to feel intimidated or uncomfortable about the whole idea and therefore to avoid it. And it's especially common to be concerned about safety, since investments are not FDIC insured.

However, one way to minimize this concern is to have an appropriate mix of bank accounts and noninsured investments. You'll get all the details in the next chapter.

HELP IS AS CLOSE AS YOUR BANK

To review, the two initial steps to change your actions are (1) save more and (2) invest. Invest using proven strategies and a financial plan customized to your needs. It's simple to say, but putting these steps into action on your own may be an overwhelming task. Fortunately, help is as close as your bank. It's best to first seek help from the place you have always trusted with your financial affairs. Your bank has professional investment consultants and financial planners dedicated to serving your investment needs.

As society's financial landscape has changed, so have banks. In fact the banking industry is leading the way. Many banks are now full-service financial centers that provide not only traditional banking services and savings accounts, but investment products as well. Gone are the days when your banker told you a CD would accomplish all your financial goals. Banks have changed with the times. They are committed to providing what you need: bank accounts for some of your financial needs and investments for others.

Bank investment sales are the fastest growing segment of the financial service industry. Over 4,500 of the nation's banks, S&Ls, and credit unions offer investments. By the end of 1997, nearly 8,000 financial institutions will offer investments; that's over 75% of all financial institutions. In a little over a decade, banks have grown to the point that they are distributing 15% of all mutual funds and 33% of all annuities—the two most common investments Americans own. By the end of this decade, banks could well be the dominant provider of investments.

Most bank customers are most comfortable relying on the trained financial consultant at their bank for investment advice. Perhaps it's because banks are dedicated to finding out what you need and helping you develop an investment plan before you invest. It's clear that bank customers like what they are getting. Today, an estimated 10 million American households are investing through their banks.

If you choose, you can also find the help you need from stock-brokers and independent financial planners. You should go where you feel most comfortable and where you know there is someone you can trust. (See Chapter 3, Advice and Advisors.)

There's one thing you want to remember when dealing with your bank: Don't confuse investments with bank accounts. There is a slight possibility this could happen since both are offered at the same location. Your bank's investment consultant, generally called a bank investment representative, will remind you that they are different. Only bank accounts are FDIC insured; investment products of any type are not. (See Chapter 3, Advice and Advisors, and Chapter 7, Bank Accounts & FDIC Insurance.)

THE REWARDS FOR STARTING NOW

Investing may be a new experience for you, but you'll find it rewarding as you move ahead. You'll learn what you need to know through the pages of this book and from the professional investment advisor at your bank. You'll discover that it's much easier than you think and that there is little to fear. And as your confidence grows, you'll gain the satisfaction of being a successful investor and realizing the benefits of an investment plan that brings security to your life.

Your next step is to take a deep breath and get started. The financial world around you will pass you by if you stand still too long. Time is your strongest ally when it comes to investing, so don't waste it. The sooner you invest, the better off you will be. In fact, time is more important than the amount of money you invest.

Consider the following: Suppose that starting at age 20 you invest $2,000 a year for 12 years until you are 32. Then you stop, leaving your investment to grow until you retire. You invest a total of $24,000. Your twin starts investing at age 32, when you stop, and invests $2,000 every year for 33 years until you both retire at age 65. Your twin invests a total of $66,000. You both earn the same 10% annual compound rate of return each year.

Who do you think will have the most comfortable retirement? It's not even close. You will by far, over twice as comfortable in fact. Your $24,000 will grow to more than $1 million ($1,092,627); your twin's $66,000 will grow to less than $500,000 ($488,953). You put in more time; your twin put in more money. Time is more valuable than money.

If you haven't started investing yet, don't let this example discourage you. It's never too late to start. In fact, because time is so important when investing, older bank customers more than younger customers will discover the need to immediately apply the techniques in this book and invest to maintain their assets throughout their life.

So whatever your age, get started now. Because today is usually better than tomorrow, and it's always better than never.

Chapter Two

Safety First

If you're like most bank customers, the safety of your money is first and foremost. Safety, of course, means not losing your money, being certain you have it when you need it. Banks have a long tradition of being trusted because, in the view of the American consumer, they have provided this safety, this certainty. Being providers of safety has been the traditional banker's invaluable franchise. The banking industry has been built on it.

MEMBER FDIC

In 1933, rising out of the Great Depression, a U.S. government agency called the Federal Deposit Insurance Corporation (FDIC) began insuring savings deposits by requiring banks to follow strict investment guidelines and pay an insurance premium to cover any failures. Currently, bank deposits are insured up to $100,000 by the FDIC. (See Chapter 7 for details on what the FDIC does and does not insure.)

The FDIC's oversight has allowed Americans to rest assured, to be certain, their money is secure and free of risk. Over the years since the Great Depression, banks have reinforced this message: "Member FDIC." This message of safety and certainty has become part of society's belief system.

Investments on the other hand, since they are not protected by the FDIC, are viewed as risky. If you're like most Americans, you associate risk with the stock market and the Crash of 1929 that started the Great Depression. When you think of risk, you think of the loss of your principal. It makes you feel uncomfortable. This message of loss of principal has also been reinforced over the last 64 years and is part of our society's belief system.

REDEFINING SAFETY FOR THE 1990s

Today's economic environment is much different than it was 60, 30, or even 10 years ago. It is filled with complexities as well as uncertainties; therefore, our thinking needs to be updated. Today banks are still financially strong, but bank accounts are no longer providers of safety because safety is no longer what it used to be. In the past, safety was certainty, the FDIC-backed maintenance of principal. Bank accounts continue to provide needed certainty, but today safety is the maintenance of purchasing power, something bank accounts don't provide.

What changed the definition of financial safety? Inflation. Inflation seriously erodes your purchasing power, preventing each dollar from buying as much today as it did yesterday. You don't notice from day to day how inflation eats away at your purchasing power, but from month to month, year to year, it goes from eating to devouring.

The rate of inflation has averaged 5.44% a year over the last 20 years. In the late 1970s and early 1980s it soared to double-digit percentages. Even at the relatively modest rate of 5%, your purchasing power will be cut in half in just 15 years. If you're living on a fixed income or all your savings is earning less than the inflation rate, you will suffer a serious reduction in your lifestyle.

The impact of inflation is clearly seen when examining a "basket" of consumer items (Exhibit 2–1).

The risk of loosing out to inflation is greater than the risk associated with investing if you invest prudently. Considering the impact of inflation, an investment strategy that relies entirely on the guarantee of principal will fall short of your needs. Your bank realizes this and has changed with the times. It has responded to your need for safety, by today's definition, by providing investments to go along with its bank accounts.

Your banker knows that bank accounts still play a vital role in your overall saving and investing plan because a large portion of your assets is short-term money that must be available when you need it. But some of your mid- and long-term money must be in investments and incur some risk to achieve a high enough return to be safe from the harmful effects of inflation. You'll learn more in subsequent chapters about the growth and income

EXHIBIT 2–1
"Basket" of Consumer Items

Selected Items	1975*	1980	1985	1990	1994
Food & beverages	$1.00	$1.44	$1.75	$2.19	$2.42
Housing	1.00	1.60	2.12	2.53	2.86
Apparel	1.00	1.25	1.49	1.71	1.89
Transportation	1.00	1.66	2.12	2.41	2.67
Medical care	1.00	1.57	2.39	3.42	4.35
Entertainment	1.00	1.35	1.74	2.14	2.35
Education	1.00	1.46	2.45	3.49	4.44
All items**	1.00	1.53	2.00	2.43	2.76

*What you had to spend because of inflation to obtain the same goods and services that cost you $1.00 in 1975.

**Includes all items in the Consumer Price Index (CPI), the commonly accepted measurement of inflation.

Source: Bureau of Labor Statistics, U.S. Department of Labor.

investments that have always outpaced inflation, when to use them, and how they fit into an overall investment strategy that meets your specific needs while keeping financial risk low.

THE TAX BITE

Besides inflation there is another "thief" to guard against: taxes!

Federal, state, and local taxes reduce the amount of money you get to keep on your savings and investments. When you factor out the 20 to 48% of your interest earnings that you pay in taxes, (depending on your tax bracket and your state and local tax rates), your ability to stay ahead of inflation, or just earn enough interest to live on if you are retired, is seriously reduced. Therefore, you must earn more on your investments or use tax-advantaged investments or both.

You can reduce the impact of taxes through the use of tax-advantaged investments such as municipal bonds that earn tax-free interest, and fixed as well as variable tax-deferred annuities. If you're retired, annuities can even reduce the amount of taxes you pay on your Social Security income.

Maximizing the use of your retirement accounts is another essential part of minimizing the impact of taxes on your savings and investments. These accounts and tax-advantaged investments, like all others, have appropriate and inappropriate uses. Don't rush into using them until you have an understanding of their features and benefits as well as a complete investment strategy. Specific details on tax-advantaged investments and strategies are available from the professional investment advisor at your bank and in Part III of this book.

THE ULTIMATE IN INVESTMENT SAFETY

You've heard it many times before, but it can't be overemphasized. The three keys to safe and smart, and therefore successful, investing are diversify, diversify, diversify. Never put all, or most, of your eggs in one basket. While this advice may sound trite, it is absolutely true.

In investing, too much of a good thing is bad. Balance is critical. Remember, even having all your money in bank accounts has an element of risk: the loss of purchasing power. No investment is the perfect investment; each one fills a different need and reacts differently to interest rate changes, fluctuations in the stock and bond markets, the effects of inflation, and changes in the economy in general. Consequently, a carefully selected and diversified group of investments is the closest you'll get to the perfect and safest investment.

Not only does diversification protect you, it can help you increase your investment income and enhance investment growth while reducing risk. It is the real key to successful investing. Techniques for using diversification as the central method of developing your own investment strategy and examples of effective diversification are the core of Chapters 4 and 6.

HIRING A PROFESSIONAL IS SAFEST

With thousands of investments to choose from, economic trends to evaluate, political ramifications to consider, and your life to live, investing may appear an overwhelming task. It is, if you try and do it alone. It's relatively simple if you hire a professional money management team by investing in what are known as managed investment products. These are investments such as mutual funds, unit investment trusts, and annuities. To be safe, use these managed investment products more often than individual securities such as stocks and bonds. You're safer because you have a professional manager or group of managers investing, monitoring and protecting the value of your assets every business hour of every day.

BEING DECEIVED AND CHEATED

The actual loss of your money due to embezzlement, theft, or fraud is a threat to your financial safety that happens very rarely, but nonetheless is something you should know how to guard against when saving and investing. Of course, your bank is bonded against such events, and the FDIC ultimately insures your accounts. Even so, take some precautions when dealing with your bank, such as never sending cash in the mail or giving cash to a bank employee anywhere except in the bank where you can get a deposit receipt.

It is also essential that you review your account statements to make sure all deposits are accurately recorded and that only *your* withdrawals are listed. Immediately report to a bank officer any discrepancies in your account records.

When dealing with securities (financial investment products such as stocks, bonds, and mutual funds) there are similar safety measures you should be aware of. First, know that the securities you own, that are held for your account by a broker or your bank's brokerage subsidiary, are protected against loss by the Securities Investor Protection Corporation (SIPC). You will see SIPC signs and stickers near the desk of the investment advisor at your bank (see Exhibit 2–2).

SIPC, a nongovernmental entity funded by assessments paid by its members, protects your investment accounts up to $500,000, including up to $100,000 in cash, if a member fails. Most bank investment programs carry additional private insurance that can increase this coverage up to as much as $10 million. A very

EXHIBIT 2–2
SIPC Sign

SECURITIES INVESTOR PROTECTION CORPORATION

important distinction between SIPC protection and FDIC insurance on your bank accounts is this: SPIC does not protect against loss in the value of your investments; your investments can go up and down depending on financial market conditions—federal deposit insurance, on the other hand, protects the amount in your deposit account(s), including accumulated interest in the account, up to $100,000. With investments, you have the risk of your principal and interest declining as well as the potential for growth or increased income.

The same safety basics apply to purchasing investments as to dealing with bank accounts when it comes to not sending cash, making sure you get a receipt, and checking account statements for accuracy.

Fraud and deception are growing problems in our society; however, when it comes to investing these are easily avoided. First and foremost, deal with someone you trust at a financial institution where you feel comfortable. It should be someone you can personally visit at their place of business to transact your business and review your investment accounts. *Never, never* buy investments over the phone from someone you don't know or can't develop a personal relationship with. You might be surprised how often a conservative investor will agonize over and delay the purchase of an appropriate investment and then buy some risky "wild hair" investment over the phone from a stranger with a great story to tell.

If you're contacted over the phone by someone at your bank to talk about investing, fine. But if you don't already know them, visit them and jointly review your financial needs and goals before you invest.

WRONG INVESTMENTS, WRONG ADVICE

Every investment has its place, but that does not mean you need to find a place for it in your investment plan. An investment that doesn't fit your needs can threaten the safety of your overall portfolio. Identify your needs and goals and then match them to appropriate investments. One example of a wrong investment is an investment that ties your money up for years when you need the money for a major purchase in the near future. When you are forced to withdraw your money early, you will probably suffer a loss or a penalty.

You can guard against using the wrong investments by developing your basic knowledge of investments through efforts such as reading this book and other publications dealing with investing. Of course, seeking advice from a professional advisor is a must. **Not seeking advice and going it alone exposes you to a level of risk you will find unsafe.** How to work with and choose an investment advisor is the subject of the next chapter.

Chapter Three

Advice and Advisors
Choosing a Bank Investment
Representative

C hances are that in matters of great importance you turn to
sources you trust the most. This is true in all aspects of life,
whether it be matters of love, health, spirituality, or money. For
someone to be a trusted source, you must feel confident in their
expertise on the subject and feel comfortable with their motives.

Many people rely on books, newspapers, magazines, radio, and
television to educate them in basic money matters. These are excellent sources for the basics of investing and examples of how to
apply that knowledge to your own situation. These are "comfortable" sources because their motives appear clear and not threat-
ening: They are providing information, not selling an investment
product. However, often the media have a less obvious motive:
selling us on the idea that we can do it on our own, using, and
therefore continuing to purchase, their advice.

INVESTING WITH AND WITHOUT THE HELP
OF A PROFESSIONAL ADVISOR

During and after learning the basics of investing, most bank
customers wisely choose to meet personally with an expert to
discuss their own unique situation and to develop an investment plan specific to their needs and goals. Some people,
mostly highly seasoned investors, don't seek advice, but make
decisions on their own.

It is possible to be a successful investor without using a professional advisor, but it requires a lot of time and considerable
resources. It's up to you, but the financial markets have accelerated

to a point where most individual investors cannot keep up with the moment-to-moment market changes (let alone make appropriate investment choices and allocate assets correctly under various market conditions). This problem, coupled with the fact that today's bank customers have limited time to devote to their investment decisions, underscores the value of using an experienced advisor.

Before the stock market decline of 1987, the stock and bond markets were less volatile. There was also far less media coverage, less volume, and less use of such innovations as computer program assisted trading. It was relatively easy for investors to manage their own portfolios in a predictable manner. Investment decisions were not as complicated and confusing as they can be today.

The decline of 1987 and subsequent events proved the value of a professional advisor to individual investors. The stock market had been climbing virtually nonstop since 1982, and mutual funds sales were going through the roof as individuals, mostly first-time investors, clamored to invest in stocks. The largest number of investors entered the market in August 1987, only to have the market decline approximately 25% in October. Within days, individual investors, primarily "do-it-yourself" owners of no-load funds, redeemed their stocks and stock mutual funds, ensuring huge losses. It was a tragic mistake.

Far more investors who had been sold mutual funds by a professional advisor stayed in their investments because their advisors were there to remind them of the long-term nature of stock investments.

Many "do-it-yourself" investors stayed out of the market for the next few years and missed the bull market. Customers who stayed in their mutual funds on the advice of their professional advisor experienced banner years in 1988 and 1989. (The stock market average rate of return was 16.5% in 1988 and 31.4% in 1989.)

When the stock market is rising sharply, every investor in stocks does well. But when the market goes into a downturn as we experienced in 1987 or when there is economic or global uncertainty as we are experiencing today, most investors, left to themselves, tend to flounder. These are times when bold and insightful financial advice is of paramount importance, and that's what a professional advisor can offer.

THE BANK INVESTMENT REPRESENTATIVE

For decades, one consumer survey after another has listed banks as the most trusted source of financial products and advice. Other providers, such as stockbrokers, financial planners, and insurance agents, rank much lower. In most surveys, they rank below accountants, friends, and relatives.

There is no question that the primary reason banks are trusted is because of the FDIC. Banks and bankers are certain to return your money to you when you want it.

However, most traditional bankers know little about investments, financial planning, prudent methods of diversification, and how to maximize the power of your savings through a well-developed investment portfolio. They are trained in making loans, taking deposits, issuing credit cards, and serving customers in other traditional banking functions.

Banks now recognize this and have hired professional investment advisors who have the knowledge and skills you need. Consequently, gone forever are the days of your bank suggesting or inferring that a CD will fill all your investment needs solely because it is backed by the FDIC. Now your individual needs and goals can be met with the appropriate investment products as well as CDs.

These investment experts have the same securities licenses (National Association of Securities Dealers Series 7 or Series 6 licenses) and training as stockbrokers and financial planners. In fact, many are former brokers with traditional Wall Street brokerage firms who switched to a bank because they are customer-first oriented. As mentioned in the last chapter, these brokers-in-the-bank generally use the title of *bank investment representative.*

TRUST

Your bank is extremely careful when hiring its bank investment representatives because your hard-earned trust and the bank's good name are at stake. It steers clear of the slick-talking, hotshot stock-jocks with Rolex watches, gold rings on every finger, and a Lexus parked outside. In hiring investment representatives, your bank uses the same standards of credibility, trustworthiness, and compatibility with the bank environment that it uses when hiring an officer of the bank.

Consequently, bank investment representatives are hybrids, complete with the conservative attributes of a trained banker and the skills and knowledge of an investment broker. This combination is essential; after all, bank investment representatives deal with the bank's most important customers.

They undergo regular training sessions to keep their skills current and are subject to the rules and audits of more regulatory agencies than any other investment provider. It's because of their unique combination of banker and broker that they are currently held to the standards of both the banking and securities industries.

HELP WITH YOUR FINANCIAL NEEDS

What you want is someone to help determine your investment needs. You want help matching the correct investment plan to your unique situation, assistance in reviewing results, and a trusted consultant to be there when you have questions. A bank investment representative should be involved with your portfolio on an ongoing basis. Investing is a process, not a one-time event. Your bank investment representative should be available when you have additional moneys that need investing or when you need to liquidate assets. Your whole financial plan can change, and you'll have decisions to make that will impact choices you've already made. If the economy shifts or there are important personal changes in your life (a death, a birth, children headed for college), you want someone who knows you and your financial picture.

To get what you need, interview your bank investment representative. Ask questions about background, employment history, education history, and how long he or she has been at the bank. Avoid making judgments of investment expertise based on outward appearances of affluence. Many stockbrokers are judged by the kind of car they drive. Someone who would choose a broker by finding out who drove the most expensive car is in trouble. Anyone can lease a car.

You're looking for someone who can be trusted, has a solid background, and is up-to-date. Ask your bank investment representative about the ongoing training he or she undergoes to keep current.

QUESTIONS TO ASK

The following questions can help you assemble the information you need to find an investment advisor you can trust and who can best help you achieve your objectives

What services and products will you provide for me? You want an investment representative who will do more than try and sell you a single product to replace a bank account. You need a bank with an investment program that's full service enough to offer a wide range of investments and investment services.

An investment representative's expertise is in assembling a customer's investment portfolio, not in just selling a product. Therefore, you want an advisor to help with financial strategies for coping with inflation, minimizing taxes, saving for college tuition or retirement, and estate planning. A bank investment representative who uses financial planning techniques may be most appropriate. Fortunately, most bank investment representatives use a financial planning approach to their business.

How will you help me determine my needs and goals? Your advisor should help you establish realistic, long-term investment objectives. In doing so, your expected return and how much money you're willing to risk should be considered along with when you're going to need your funds for a major expenditure. Ask what method will be used to determine your investment objectives. If your advisor is doing the job right, you'll be asked to answer questions on a detailed questionnaire covering topics such as income, assets, family situation, insurance policies, and financial goals. The information is then analyzed by the investment representative to provide an appropriate, individualized financial plan. It's becoming common for this analysis to be done using specialized computer programs. However, that isn't necessary.

What types of customer do you generally serve?   Determine if you match the advisor's typical customer profile. If you are retired, you want someone with experience serving retired investors; if you are a small business owner, you want an advisor with other small business owners as customers, and so on.

You should ask your bank investment representative for references from other professionals, such as bankers, accountants, and lawyers with whom he or she consults on customer affairs.

What kind of accounts do you handle?   Try to determine what types of customers your bank investment representative sees most frequently. Some focus primarily on servicing large institutional investors such as pension funds. Others specialize in "high net worth" individuals, and some devote their business to meeting the investment needs of middle class families. Again, you want someone experienced in serving people like yourself.

Specifically, who will review my financial affairs?   You should always know who is handling your account. At larger banks, one person may initiate customer relationships, while a second individual determines your needs, develops your plan, and sells you investments. In some cases, a third person maintains ongoing customer relations.

If there is going to be more than one person involved, try to meet all the team players before signing on.

How do you monitor my account?   Your advisor should update, monitor, revise, and review your progress toward achieving your financial objectives as often as necessary. Depending on your needs and situation, follow-up sessions may be scheduled monthly, quarterly, or annually. Ask your bank investment representative how frequently you will meet to review your portfolio and how frequently you will receive written account statements.

At a minimum, insist on an annual meeting to measure actual performance against established objectives that you and your bank investment representative set.

Communicate directly with your bank investment representative whenever performance falls below an acceptable level.

Close communication will increase the "comfort level" for both of you.

How would you summarize your investment philosophy? Make sure your advisor's investment philosophy is consistent with your objectives. Ask each potential advisor what their particular investment biases are.

You want to determine if they are biased toward one type of investment over another. You want someone who takes a balanced approach, depending on what you need. It is important to note that bank investment representatives do not manage customers' assets. Instead, their main service is to prepare an investment plan and then to recommend which bank accounts and investments are appropriate. In other words, their purpose is to help you choose an appropriate money manager (i.e., mutual fund, annuities, etc.)

In particular, understand how your bank investment representative balances his or her commitment to preserving your capital with the risks needed to achieve above-average returns. Ask your bank investment representative what process he or she uses to balance risks and rewards. A good way to gauge the level of risk they will employ is to ask what kinds of returns you can expect to make from recommended investments. Excessive risk is being taken if it is suggested you'll consistently earn more than 15% on stock mutual funds and 4% over the going CDs rates on bonds.

Your advisor's investment philosophy should be something you will be comfortable with given your personal investment objectives and your risk tolerance.

What are your educational credentials? While there is no ideal profile for a bank investment representative, you should look for someone who balances basic money management skills with an investing approach that matches your own. Ask your bank investment representative if he or she has a résumé or other written materials summarizing education and experience.

Consider for yourself whether an advisor's academic background conveys a solid foundation of investment knowledge.

Also, be sure to ask how many years your prospective advisor has been an advisor.

How do you keep your investment knowledge current? The complexity of investment management demands a high level of professional competence. Your bank investment representative should keep up to date on the latest financial trends by taking advantage of a variety of professional education resources such as seminars, workshops, professional organizations, and subscription services.

Professional designations such as certified financial planner (CFP), chartered financial consultant (ChFC), certified investment specialist (CIS), certified fund specialist (CFS), licensed investment consultant (LIC) and certified investment management consultant (CIMC) may provide an indication of a professional's competence. At the very least, they demonstrate years of effort to learn the skills of the business. In addition, many of these organizations require adherence to strict ethical standards, which protect investors. You'll find these professional designations displayed in the offices and on the business cards of many bank investment representatives.

What are your sources of investment information? Today's technology allows banks of any size, at any location, to have the information available to advise you properly. Does your advisor's bank have any in-house research capabilities? To what external research or rating services does your advisor subscribe? How does your bank's investment program keep their advisors abreast of the financial market and economic trends?

How are you compensated? You want your bank and your bank investment representative to make money. Doing so ensures they will be in business in the future so you can continue to use their services.

As with most things in life, you get what you pay for when it comes to financial advice. You always pay for advice, either directly by paying a fee or commission or indirectly by suffering the consequences of receiving bad advice.

When receiving "free" advice from someone, consider their motives. These motives include wanting to sell you more advice (newsletters, magazines, books) and wanting to maintain control (many accountants and attorneys). When receiving advice from other investors, friends, or relatives remember that just because an investment was good for them doesn't mean it will be good for you. After all, your needs, wants, fears, objectives, and concerns are unique.

Typically, there are four ways a bank investment representative is compensated: fees, commissions (often called a bonus), salary, or a combination.

Some bank investment programs charge a flat fee for developing an overall investment or financial plan. Depending on the complexity of the plan, fees range from $200 and up for a comprehensive investment plan.

Some bank investment representatives receive a portion of their compensation from the fees described above, but also may receive commissions on investment products they recommend. Using a commission to offset a fee may be entirely appropriate, as long as it is fully disclosed.

However, most common are bank investment representatives who derive their income primarily from commissions. They receive a small part of the funds you invest in a particular product or security. (See Chapter 17, The Real Costs of Investing.) In most cases, an advisor will not charge anything for a financial plan or financial advice. When your advisor does not charge a fee, either for the plan or for its implementation, he or she is likely to be receiving commissions on the investments you purchase. This is good business practice. If you don't like the plan or choose not to implement it, you pay nothing. The investment representative is confident enough in what he or she does to do the work first and then get paid if you buy a recommended investment. If you ask, your bank investment representative will disclose how he or she will be compensated before you order any investments.

Don't be naive when it comes to paying for financial advice and the purchase of investments. However, don't overemphasize this part of the investing process. Your bank's investment program makes money (so do its employees), but the maximum amount that can be charged on each investment is determined by industry regulations that apply to all investment providers.

DON'T BE CONFUSED

It's important to note that each bank's investment program is structured differently depending on its size, state of domicile, and customer demographics. Don't be confused when a bank investment representative is not actually an employee of the bank; he or she might be an employee of the bank's brokerage subsidiary, an outside investment firm contracted to provide investment services for the bank, or in some cases a duel employee of the bank and an outside firm. It really doesn't matter because ultimately the bank investment representative is accountable to bank management, industry regulators, and you.

Selecting a bank investment representative is not something to be taken lightly. You will be entrusting this person with a very important part of your well-being: your financial health. By investing your time before you invest your money, you will be better able to select an appropriate advisor. This professional advisor should be your financial counselor and teacher. Most of all, an advisor you trust should be dedicated to meeting your investment objectives so you can enjoy the financial rewards of investing wisely.

Chapter Four

How to Build an Investment Strategy for Change

I n the past, you have probably had a savings strategy but not an investment strategy. You simply invested in bank savings accounts, CDs, and insured money market funds. The only strategy you needed was to know when to roll over or reinvest your CDs. But today there's more to it. Maintaining your purchasing power is critical; therefore, you need to have a growth component and an enhanced-income component as a part of your investment strategy. Having an investment strategy that will keep your risks low and increase your overall returns will make the transition from saver to investor more comfortable. Following are the steps to building just such a strategy.

STEP 1. BUILDING THE FOUNDATION

Every prudent investment strategy starts with building a conservative foundation. Your foundation includes the portion of your assets designated for your immediate needs and emergency funds and for conservative long-term investments. In short, it is made up of conservative investments and defensive investments that give structure and strength to your financial life. A mix of CDs and savings accounts, fixed annuities, and government bonds are the cornerstones of this foundation.

STEP 2. DEVELOPING THE GROWTH AND ENHANCE-INCOME COMPONENT

Next, you need to begin using those investments that will keep you safe by today's definition: protection of purchasing power.

EXHIBIT 4–1
Stocks, Bonds, CDs, and Inflation

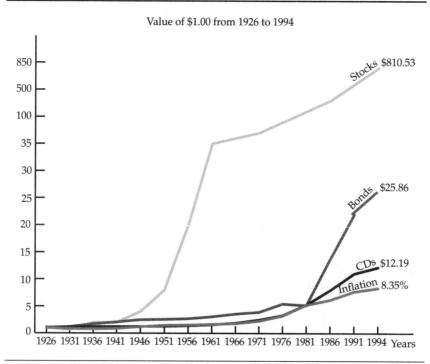

Value of $1.00 from 1926 to 1994

*Stocks: S&P 500 including reinvestment of dividends; bonds: U.S. government bonds with maturity near 20 years; CDs: Represented by U.S. T-bills; inflation: Consumer Price Index.

Source: © *Stocks, Bonds, Bills, and Inflation 1994 Yearbook,*™ Ibbotson Associates, Chicago (annually updates work by Roger G. Ibbotson and Rex A. Singuefield). Used with permission. All rights reserved.

It's these essential investments that will battle the terrors of inflation. These powerful investments are stocks and, to a limited degree, bonds.

Owning stocks is the only way to consistently participate in growth sufficient to outpace inflation. Although the rate of return on bonds generally beats the interest rates paid by bank accounts and has outperformed inflation on many occasions, bonds are not designed to grow in value; they are income vehicles.

Notice in Exhibit 4–1 how large the gap is between what stocks have earned and what CDs have earned. Notice how stocks have outpaced inflation. It's simple, you need to invest part of your money in stocks to avoid the loss of your purchasing power over time (See Chapter 8, Understanding Stocks, and Chapter 9, Understanding Bonds.)

Most stocks and stock-based investments such as stock mutual funds and variable annuities are not designed to pay income. However, they can even though their primary goal is growth. If you need primarily current income, invest in bonds. Adding bonds and/or bond mutual funds to your bank accounts is one way to enhance the overall income you can earn.

STEP 3. LOWERING INVESTMENT RISK WHILE INCREASING WHAT YOU EARN

Two principles for investing have withstood the test of time by reducing risk and increasing what you earn: diversification and asset allocation. The central premise of both of these principles is that investors select from among several types of investment products, providers, and asset categories each with difference risk and return potentials. Using more than one bank is *not* diversification.

Diversification is simply investing in a broad variety of investments so that all of your eggs are not in one basket, so to speak. The idea behind this is that your overall performance should be less volatile than if all your money was in a single investment or the same types of investments. The graphs in Exhibit 4–2 illustrate the power of diversification.

The graph illustrates a single investment of $100,000 that averages an 8% return over 25 years. It also illustrates diversifying the same $100,000 into five $20,000 amounts, representing five investments averaging various rates of return. While three of the five investments showed a lower return than the single investment (including one that lost money), the total for the diversified side was substantially higher.

One type of diversification is to spread your investments in different types of securities such as bonds, stocks, bank accounts, and other short-term investments. Each of these

EXHIBIT 4–2
The Power of Diversification as an Investment Strategy

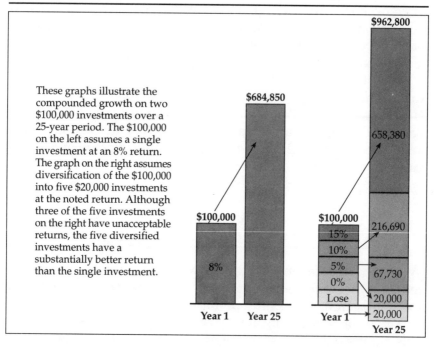

These graphs illustrate the compounded growth on two $100,000 investments over a 25-year period. The $100,000 on the left assumes a single investment at an 8% return. The graph on the right assumes diversification of the $100,000 into five $20,000 investments at the noted return. Although three of the five investments on the right have unacceptable returns, the five diversified investments have a substantially better return than the single investment.

Source: *Bank Investment Representative Magazine.*

investments has different risks and will fluctuate in value during time. Selecting different types of investments will help reduce the risks of owning a single type of investment.

You should also choose different kinds of investments. For example, when it comes to bank accounts, don't just use CDs; use money market accounts and savings accounts. The same applies to mutual funds. Choose stock mutual funds, bond funds, and balanced funds when appropriate. It's a good idea to have several different mutual fund companies as well. The more you diversify, the more you're protected.

Now consider the difference between diversification and asset allocation, the other time-tested principle for decreasing risk and increasing return. It is subtle, often misunderstood, yet significant. Diversification is spreading your money among different investments and investment companies that fall within the same asset categories. Asset allocation is spreading your money among asset categories you choose because their value generally moves in opposite directions to each other. To illustrate this, consider the example of a car buff buying a restored 1933 Chevrolet coupe and a 1932 Ford three-window coupe; buying both would in effect be diversifying. Your investment would be protected if one car went up in value while the other went down. But if the entire classic car market went down, your investment would be in trouble. One way to guard against this would be to buy collector stamps. Why stamps? Because their value moves independently of what happens in the classic car market. The optimal mix would be to buy an asset that always moved exactly opposite to the classic car market if there was one you could identify. The search for an investment the value of which moves opposite to another investment is what has led to the popularity of foreign stocks in recent years. Their values often move opposite to American stocks, allowing investors to hedge against declines.

Research has shown that the asset allocation (how you split your investments up among various asset categories such as stocks, bonds, and cash) has by far the greatest impact on your overall investment performance. According to Ibbotson Associates, more than 91% of your total return is due to the asset allocation of your portfolio. In contrast, when you invest and investment selection account for less than 7%.

CONCLUSION

The strategy to help you make a successful transition into the world of investing is simple: Build a conservative foundation first. Next, develop a growth and income component by owning common stocks for growth; bonds and stocks for enhanced income. Then lower your risk and increase your earnings by diversifying and allocating your money between different asset categories. Your bank investment representative will help you properly allocate your assets to reduce risk and increase returns. Much of it will happen automatically as you select investments to match your needs.

Chapter Five

How to Determine Your Needs and Goals

Y ou now know the importance of maximizing the power of your savings, and you have a basic investment strategy. It's time to determine your financial needs and goals. This is an absolute must before investing. It is vital that your bank investment representative know a lot about you before any recommendations are made or you invest any money. Four things are of primary importance:

1. What you want your money to do for you.
2. Your current financial situation.
3. The level of risk you will tolerate to achieve your goals.
4. The time frame for each goal.

Investment choices are driven by your needs. These needs must be more specific than "to get a higher return." Knowing why higher returns are needed is what helps determine the correct course of action. And action cannot be taken until it is evaluated in concert with your other accounts, investments, and assets and until you have an idea of your risk tolerance.

A retired couple in their mid-70s tells their bank investment representative they have $50,000 to invest and need a higher rate of interest than savings accounts provide. They also say they want to withdraw off the interest to supplement their income. This is all the information they provide.

Filling their needs may seem fairly straightforward: They need a higher return and current income. There are several good investments that can immediately provide what the couple is requesting. However, when their bank investment representative inquires about their life situation, their level of investment experience, their other needs, their other assets, and their time horizons, things change. Facts are discovered that change the initial impression and eliminate the use of several good investments that first come to mind. The husband is seriously ill, and the couple would be ill-advised to commit the money for the long term or tolerate risk to the principal since they will need the $50,000 readily available for medical expenses. They are better off leaving the money in a savings account.

Their need for additional current income can't be filled with the $50,000. However, during the interview process the bank investment representative discovers some information that leads to another solution.

The couple reveals that 10 years ago they purchased a bond mutual fund and are continuing to reinvest all of its income. Their bank investment representative recommends they simply start taking systematic income payments from their existing bond mutual fund to get the added income they need.

In the beginning, the couple didn't feel it was necessary to disclose much about their life situation and other assets. They just wanted a simple answer to their immediate problem of what to do with $50,000 to get more income.

For your own financial health, you need to treat your bank investment representative much as you treat your doctor. You must give a complete picture of your financial condition so as to avoid a misdiagnosis that will damage instead of strengthen you financial health. Your bank investment representative is trained to determine if an investment is suitable for you. In fact, securities regulations requires it be determined suitable before you invest with a bank investment representative.

FINDING OUT YOURSELF

Fully disclosing your needs and current financial condition is not always easy. Perhaps you can't tell your bank investment representative because you don't know yourself, or at least you can't conceptualize and articulate them. This is not uncommon.

When you meet with your bank investment representative, you will be asked a series of questions. Your answers will help you and your bank investment representative understand your financial needs, determine your tolerance for risk, set goals, and design a plan in preparation for the selection of appropriate investments that meet your personal needs.

The following *Financial Needs Discovery Worksheet* will help you determine these facts now and prepare you to communicate them to your bank investment representative. It also contains a section for listing your current assets, accounts, and investments. Although the worksheet is designed in a self-discovery format, you may want to complete it, or at least review it, with your bank representative.

FINANCIAL NEEDS DISCOVERY WORKSHEET

Step 1: Define Your Financial Goals

Do you need monthly income? Are you saving for a house? When do you plan to retire? Identify whether or not your needs are for immediate income, and/or if you want to set aside some assets for future growth. Are you saving for your grandchildren or for your own child's college education, or do you want to supplement your current income? Please take a moment and list your three most important financial goals.

Your Three Most Important Financial Goals

1. _____

2. _____

3. _____

Your choice of investments should always be driven by what you want your money to do for you. You may want your investments to fill very specific needs: provide cash to buy a house or car, pay college costs, or help support your retirement. Or, your goals may be more general, simply to build wealth, for example. On the left side of Exhibit 5–1, find the top three financial goals listed that most closely correspond to your goals or write in your own. Rank them from one to three in order of importance.

EXHIBIT 5–1
Important Financial Goals

Rank	Goal	Short-Term Time Horizon (0–2 yrs.)	Mid-Term Time Horizon (3–5 yrs.)	Long-Term Time Horizon (5+ yrs.)
	Retirement			
	Major purchase: house, car, etc.			
	Build cash reserves			
	Current income			
	Tax-free income			
	School/college expenses			
	Start or buy a business			
	Future medical expenses			
	Protect purchasing power against inflation			
	Vacation			
	Luxury or "fun" money			
	Other:			

Step 2: Set Your Time Horizon

Next, using the same exhibit, assign a time horizon to each goal. If you are saving for a special event, such as buying a house, estimate when you will need the cash to meet your goal. If your objective doesn't have a definite deadline, estimate how long it will continue to be important to you. For instance, if your primary concern is earning income, for how long will you want to continue an income program?

On the right side of Exhibit 5–1, check the time category that best matches the horizon of each of your three goals: short-term (two years or less), mid-term (three to five years), or long-term (more than five years).

Setting time horizons for your goals is critical. Why? Because you should follow a very different strategy when you invest for the short term than when you invest for longer periods. The longer you can leave your money invested, the less you need to worry about liquidity, for example, and the more you can focus on earning a higher return. Risk, return, and timing all go together. As a general rule, the more risk an investment involves, the higher its potential return over time and the more suitable it is for long-term investments.

Step 3: Consider Your Personal Risk Profile

To find how much risk you are willing to tolerate, answer the following questions. Be honest to avoid coming to an incorrect assessment of your risk tolerance. Circle the number of points associated with each answer.

Personal Risk Profile Questionnaire

1. How would you describe yourself when it comes to investing?

	points
Risk avoider	1
Conservative	2
Moderate risk taker	4
Aggressive risk taker	5

2. What would you do if your investments suddenly declined in value by 10%?

	points
Sell them	0
Hold them	2
Buy more	5

3. How important is it to you that the value of your investments stay consistent from quarter to quarter?

Critical	0
Very important	2
Important	3
Not important	5

4. What percentage of investments listed below would you feel more comfortable with over long periods of time?

100% certificates of deposit	0
30% stocks, 70% CDs	2
50% stocks, 50% CDs	3
70% stocks, 30% CDs	4
100% stocks	5

5. Do you need to make regular withdrawals from your investment account?

	points
No	3
Yes	1

6. Do you foresee a major expenditure in the next five years?

	points
No	5
Yes	0

7. What length of time do you feel is appropriate to wait before assessing the performance of your investments?

Less than 1 year	0
1 year	1
2 years	2
3 years	3
5 years	4
Over 5 years	5

8. How much do you expect to make on your investments?

0–4%	0
5–7%	2
7–10%	3
10–12%	4
Above 12%	5

Total score _____

Once you have completed the risk profile questionnaire, take a moment to total the individual scores for each answer. Your total will be between 0 and 38. Your total score will reveal your attitude towards risk. The closer to zero the score, the more risk adverse you are. The higher the score, the more risk you can tolerate.

Plot your range on the scale shown in Exhibit 5–2 and at the same time, note the corresponding category and the level of risk in each category as illustrated as a percentage of stocks vs. fixed investments. For example, if you have a score near zero, and fall in the defensive column, you will probably only feel comfortable with fixed investments.

Step 4: Find the Investment That Matches Your Risk Profile

You can find investments that may be right for you in every time horizon (short-term, mid-term, or long-term) and that correspond to your risk-return category.

EXHIBIT 5–2
Risk/Return Scale

		Risk/Return Scale		
0	5–10	15–20	25–30	35–38

		Risk-Return Categories		
Defensive	Conservative	Balanced	Moderate	Aggressive
100% fixed*	40% stocks	50% stocks	60% stocks	100% stocks
	60% fixed	50% fixed	40% fixed	

*Fixed means bank accounts and bonds.

Use Exhibit 5–3 to see which type of investment best matches your risk-return category. First, on the far left, find the time horizons you feel most comfortable with. Then locate your risk-return category. Where they intersect, you will find a list of investment choices that may fit both your time horizons and your risk-reward category.

Step 5: Check Your Asset Mix

Now that you've seen which investment makes sense based on your time horizons and risk-reward category, you can use Exhibit 5–4 to assess how well your current investments are helping you meet your objectives.

On Exhibit 5–4, list the investments and bank accounts you currently have in each time category. Include IRAs and money invested through employer retirement plans. Then, on the right side of the chart, list your top three goals from Exhibit 5–1 in the appropriate time categories.

After you complete the chart, ask yourself two important questions:

1. Do your current investments match the time horizons of your goals? As a rule, your assets should be concentrated in the same time categories as your major goals. If your investments have longer horizons than your goals, your risk may be too high. If you are using short-term investments to meet long-term goals, you are

EXHIBIT 5-3

Matching Investments to Your Risk Profile

Time Horizon of Goals	Defensive	Conservative	Balanced	Moderate	Aggressive
Short-term 0–2 years	Savings accounts CDs Money market accounts	Savings accounts CDs Money market accounts Treasury bills Tax anticipation notes	Savings accounts CDs Treasury bills & notes Treasury bills Tax anticipation notes	CDs Money market accounts Trading stocks Short-term tax-free bonds Tax anticipation notes	Treasury bills & notes Short-term bonds Stock options
Mid-term 3–5 years	CDs Money market accounts Treasury notes	CDs Money market accounts Treasury notes	CDs Money market accounts Treasury notes Short-term tax-free bonds	CDs Money market accounts Treasury notes Short-term corp. bonds Short-term tax-free bonds	Long-term corp. bonds Long-term tax-free bonds Common stocks
Long-term Over 5 years	CDs U.S. savings bonds Treasury notes & bonds Fixed annuities	CDs U.S. savings bonds Treasury notes & bonds Fixed annuities Utility stocks & funds Real estate Hard assets	CDs Treasury notes & bonds Fixed annuities Variable annuities Utility stocks & funds Real estate GNMAs Gov't securities fund Common stocks Growth & income funds Tax-free bond funds Balanced mutual funds	Variable annuities Real estate Long-term bond funds Common stock International bond funds International stock funds Growth funds Capt. appreciation funds	High-yield bonds & bond funds Small cap stock funds Small company stocks Precious metal stocks/funds Sector funds International stock funds
CAUTION	Inflation will erode your purchasing power.	You may not keep up with inflation.			You may be taking too much risk.

This is not a complete list of investment choices. This chart is only a guide. Your individual circumstances, in consultation with your bank investment representative, should be taken into consideration.

EXHIBIT 5–4
Matching Current Investments, Goals, and Time Horizons

Time Category	Your Current Investments	Appropriate Investments	Your Top Three Goals
Short-term (3–5 years)	$	Savings accounts	
		Money market funds	
		Short-term CDs	
		Short-term bonds	
		Other	
Mid-term (3–5 years)	$	Intermediate bonds	
		Government securities	
		CDs	
		High-income stocks	
		Annuities	
		Other	
Long-term	$	Long-term bonds/mutual funds	
		Long-term CDs	
		Real estate (not including your house)	
		Annuities	
		Common stocks/mutual funds	
		Other	
Your total investments $			

probably earning too low a return on your money. For example, it's common to find bank customers using CDs with 6-month or one-year maturities. It's also common to discover they have done so for up to 10 years. At the very least, they would have been better off earning a higher rate in a long-term CD, and at the very best, other investments.

2. Can you achieve your goals with the amounts you have already invested? If you have enough to meet your goals, you are one of the lucky few. But like most of people, you need more money.

REACHING YOUR GOALS

In Exhibit 5–4, you entered money you currently have saved and invested. Your next step is to estimate how much you will need to reach your goals. Most people underestimate the amount of money they need because it's impossible to know what the future will bring. All you can do is make an educated guess. Obviously, the shorter the time horizon, the easier it will be to make an accurate estimate.

Now, to determine the shortfall subtract the amount you currently have invested from your estimate of what you'll need. The top section of Exhibit 5–5 shows you the amount of money you need to invest today to make up the shortfall if you earn 8% interest compounded monthly on whatever money you invest.

The bottom of Exhibit 5–5 shows how much you can accumulate by investing the same amount each month over various periods of years. You can build a surprisingly large stake by saving regularly, even if you don't have a great deal to invest.

Step 6: Rethink Your Investments Periodically

This investing business is a lifelong process. Since your assets, needs, and goals are always changing as you go through life, you should update your goals by taking out this chart and reworking it once a year and meeting with your bank investment representative to review your goals and investments' performance—sort of an annual checkup. In the end, all the principles described here boil down to four simple rules:

1. Set clear financial goals.

2. Choose investments that provide the combination of risk, reward, and enough time to achieve your goals.

3. Minimize your risk by diversifying as broadly as your resources permit.

4. Use the services of a professional financial advisor you trust.

EXHIBIT 5–5
Amount You Must Invest Today to Reach Future Financial Goals

	Future Financial Goal		
Time Horizon	*$10,000*	*$50,000*	*$100,000*
2 Years	$8,526	$42,630	$85,260
5 Years	$6,712	$33,561	$67,121
10 Years	$4,505	$22,526	$45,052
20 Years	$2,030	$10,149	$20,297

Amount You Can Accumulate through Monthly Investing

	Monthly Investment		
Time Horizon	*$50*	*$200*	*$500*
2 Years	$1,305	$5,221	$13,053
5 Years	$3,698	$14,793	$36,983
10 Years	$9,208	$36,833	$92,083
20 Years	$29,647	$118,589	$296,474

Assumes an 8% interest rate compounded monthly.

Chapter Six

How to Put It All Together

L et's review what you have read about in Part I: how bank accounts and investments work together; the new definition of safety, a basic investment strategy using asset allocation and diversification; and the importance of professional investment advice.

You've determined your needs, set appropriate time horizons, and have a reasonable idea of the investments that are appropriate for you.

LIFE STAGES

Now it's time to apply what you have learned to your current stage in life. Turn to the chart that corresponds with your age (Exhibits 6–1 through 6–4). The charts show examples of how your investments can be allocated based on your age. These charts are just conceptual, so these examples won't apply to everyone. You may have special needs and investment objectives, so you need to speak with your advisor before making your investment decisions.

Please note that only your savings and investment dollars are illustrated in these examples; your emergency money and day-to-day money are not included.

Early Years (20–40)

Investment strategy. Build wealth by investing more of your assets in growth-oriented investments (see Exhibit 6–1). When you are just starting out, your investment time horizon is long, and your primary investment goal should be accumulation

EXHIBIT 6–1
Early Years *(20–40)*

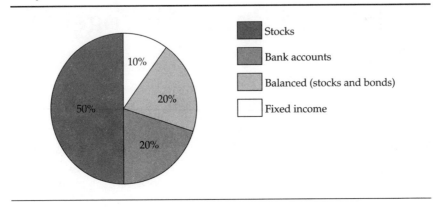

EXHIBIT 6–2
Middle Years (40–50)

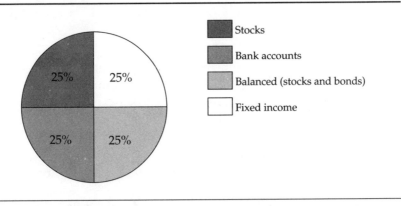

of capital. You do not need to use your investments to enhance your current income. Under these circumstances, stock investments should be a large part of your portfolio. Your diversified portfolio might include 50% in common stock mutual funds with potential for long-term growth and 20% in balanced mutual funds invested in both stocks and bonds. In addition, your portfolio might include 10% in fixed-income securities invested in corporate bonds and 20% in bank accounts.

EXHIBIT 6–3
Preretirement Years (50–60)

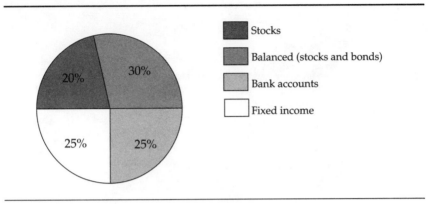

Stocks

Balanced (stocks and bonds)

Bank accounts

Fixed income

Middle Years (40–50)

Investment strategy.   In mid-career, your salary is increasing, but so are your expenses. You may want to include a conservative fixed-income component to preserve capital and provide regular current income if needed (see Exhibit 6–2). Your investment mix for the middle years might include 25% in a stock mutual funds, 25% in balanced stock and bond mutual funds, 25% in high-grade corporate bonds or bond mutual funds, and 25% in bank accounts. If taxes are a problem, variable annuities and tax-free municipal bond funds can be substituted for part of the stock, bonds and in mutual funds.

Preretirement Years (50–60)

Investment strategy.   During these peak earning years, with your children's education complete, you should have a larger pool of assets and may find income taxes increasingly burdensome (see Exhibit 6–3). At the same time, you should start directing your efforts toward securing your retirement. Your investment mix for these years might include 20% in stock mutual funds, 30% in balanced stock and bond mutual funds,

EXHIBIT 6–4
Retirement Years (60–70)

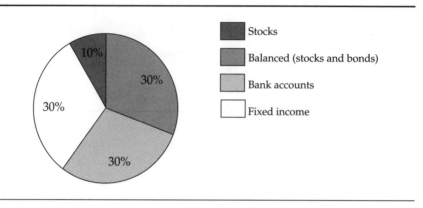

25% in high-grade tax-free municipal bonds or bond mutual funds, and 25% in guaranteed accounts. Fixed and variable annuities are appropriate substitutes for bank accounts and mutual funds.

Retirement Years (60–70)

Investment strategy. As your investing time horizon shortens, you may want to shift more of your stock investments into fixed-income investments (see Exhibit 6–4). A diversified portfolio might include 10% in stock mutual funds, 30% in balanced stock and bond mutual funds, 30% in bonds and bond mutual funds if you need income or in fixed and variable annuities if you don't. Bank accounts could be increased to 30%.

You may want to have some of your bond funds be tax-free municipals if you are in the higher tax brackets.

You'll probably retire during this stage of your life. When you do, your financial goals will center on protecting the assets you have accumulated over the years. In addition, you will focus on generating income to supplement Social Security and pension income.

EXHIBIT 6–5
The Late Years (70 plus)

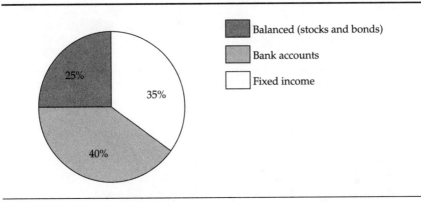

Balanced (stocks and bonds)

Bank accounts

Fixed income

The Late Years (70 plus)

Investment strategy. You been retired for a few years, and your main goal now is to receive income and preserve your capital so you don't outlive your money (see Exhibit 6–5). Your diversified portfolio might include 25% in balanced stock and bond mutual funds that can be accessed for income if necessary, 35% in bonds and bond mutual funds or fixed annuities, and the remaining 40% in bank accounts and short-term government bonds.

MAKING YOUR STRATEGY WORK: THE INFLUENCE OF TIME ON INVESTMENT RISK

None of the strategies just illustrated work effectively if you have such a short time horizon that you are constantly shifting your money around. If your time horizon is short, stay in CDs and saving accounts. Choosing a time horizon is as important as choosing investments. This is because over long periods of time very high returns and very low returns tend to average out (See Exhibit 6–6). This enables you to recoup any losses you may have incurred. Over long periods of time, you can also fully realize the benefits of compounding. You will read more about compounding shortly.

EXHIBIT 6–6
Investment Performance Over Various Holding Periods

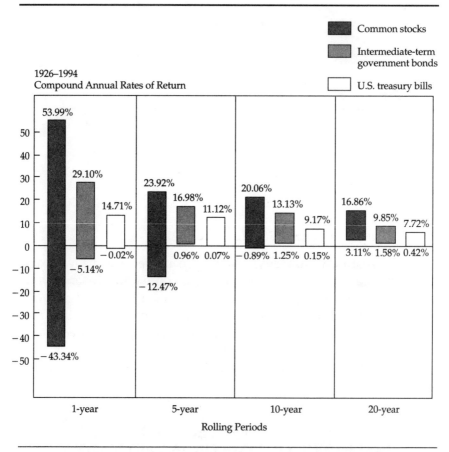

As you can see in Exhibit 6–6, stocks experienced a substantially greater risk and return during this period. *Risk, in this context, means variability, fluctuations in returns.* While annual intermediate-term government bond returns fluctuated between 29 and −5%, stock returns ranged from 54% to −43%, almost three times as much as bonds (36 percentage points versus 97 percentage points respectively). Short-term investments, Treasury Bills, proved the most stable (albeit the lowest yielding), ranging from 0–15%.

EXHIBIT 6–7
The Power of Compounding

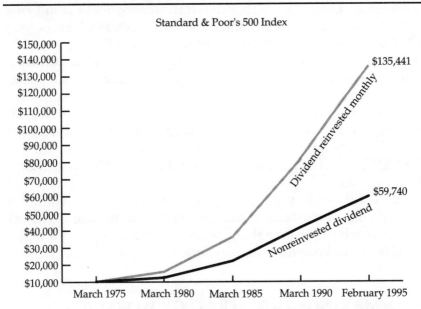

Standard & Poor's 500 Index

The Standard & Poor's 500 is an index comprised of 500 stocks that are accepted as being an accurate representation of the entire stock market.

Source: Lipper Analytical Services, Inc.

Time is your greatest ally. Because the effects of short-term volatility are reduced over time, a longer time horizon affords you greater flexibility in constructing your investment portfolio. In other words, the sooner you start and the longer you stick with it, the more money you will accumulate safely.

MAKING YOUR STRATEGY WORK: THE POWER OF COMPOUNDING

Chances are, you are already familiar with the power of compounded interest because of your bank accounts, but you may not know that the same concept applies to investments. By routinely reinvesting your dividend and capital gains rather than taking them in cash, you are systematically building the value of your account over time and compounding your money. This is reflected in Exhibit 6–7. This illustration shows the result of a $10,000 investment in the Standard & Poor's 500 stock index over a 20-year time period, ending February 28, 1995.

During the 20 years illustrated in Exhibit 6–7, your principal would have increased by more than $49,000, and you would have received almost $13,000 in cash dividends. The total value, therefore, would exceed $72,000, including the original $10,000 investment. However, if your income had been reinvested and not taken in cash, the total value would have grown to more than $135,000. The results are even more dramatic over longer time periods.

The effect of compounding is even more important for fixed-income investments such as bonds, annuities, and bank accounts where principal appreciation is usually not a major component of your long-term return.

MAKING YOUR STRATEGY WORK: SYSTEMATIC INVESTING/ DOLLAR COST AVERAGING

Systematic investing simply means that you make regular additions of a set amount into your investments. This provides two benefits: wealth building and reduced volatility.

Wealth Building

Mutual funds are ideal for systematic investing since they allow you to make smaller incremental investments on a regular basis. This allows you to add to your investment monthly. It is amazing how fast this adds up. As you invest this way, you steadily accumulate more and more shares of the mutual fund.

Reducing Volatility

Besides being a good way to accumulate shares, systematic investing also helps reduce the possibility of making a lump sum

EXHIBIT 6–8
Dollar-Cost Averaging

Month	$ Invested	Share Price	Number of Shares Purchased
1	$300	15	20
2	$300	20	15
3	$300	25	12
4	$300	20	15
5	$300	15	20
6	$300	25	12

Total invested $1,800
Average share price $20.00
Total number of shares purchased 94
Average paid per share $19.14

With dollar cost averaging, your fixed dollars ($300 per month) buy fewer shares as the price per share increases, and more shares as the price per share decreases. In the above example, $1,800 invested systematically bought 94 shares at an average cost of $19.14 per share for a savings of 0.86 per share (or $80.84 total) over the average price per share of $20.

investment at the wrong time, when the price of a fund may be high. Smaller, regular monthly or quarterly investments give you a lower average cost per share over the long term—this concept is called *dollar cost averaging* (See Exhibit 6–8).

SUMMARY

Good job! You've done it. By now you should clearly see how your investment mix works and understand the power of compounding and how income averaging can increase your success. You can see how lengthening your time horizon can almost ensure investment success. It's now time to look at the individual investment products themselves. We'll begin with bank products then move on to individual securities and mutual funds and annuities.

II

INVESTMENTS AND BANK ACCOUNTS

Chapter Seven

Bank Accounts and FDIC Insurance

B ank accounts play an important role in your overall savings and investment plan. But like other financial products, they have their inappropriate as well as appropriate uses. Let's review the basic bank deposit accounts and their appropriate uses, followed by a detailed explanation of what the FDIC insures.

Deposits in traditional bank accounts, such as savings accounts, checking accounts, money market accounts, and certificates of deposit, are insured by the FDIC. Investments, such as mutual funds, annuities, and stocks and bonds, aren't insured, even if you purchase them through your bank.

To ensure that there is no confusion on this matter, government and industry regulators have asked that a statement disclosing this fact be placed on investment literature distributed at banks. An example of such a disclosure statement is: "This investment is not a deposit or obligation of any bank or financial institution. It is not issued or guaranteed by any such institution, the FDIC, the U.S. government, or any government agency, and involves risks, including possible loss of principal."

When you place money in a FDIC-insured bank account, the U.S. government does back your deposit against loss up to $100,000. You can be certain your deposit will be available when you need it.

SHORT-TERM, MID-TERM, AND LONG-TERM MONEY

It is the *certainty* provided by the FDIC that makes bank accounts the ideal place for money that is needed in the short-term and an excellent choice for mid-term money. (Short-term can mean one day to two years. Mid-term means three to five years.)

Bank accounts pay lower interest rates than the returns possible on investments, but that's okay because being *certain* your short-term money is available is more important than the rate you're earning.

Bank accounts are also good for money you will need within three to five years. Investments, however, are best for long-term money— money that isn't needed within five years. Some investments are also appropriate for money in the mid-term category.

Avoid Two Common Mistakes

Don't make the mistake common to many beginning investors in search of high yields or returns and place your short-term money in long-term investments. The *certainty* of having your money when you need it is more important than the possibility of a higher rate.

There is another common mistake when using bank accounts that a safe and smart investor should avoid. It's placing long-term money that should be in investments into bank accounts, which are designed for the short-term or mid-term investment.

This is most often done by default. Since you, as a bank customer, feel comfortable that your money will earn some interest and be insured against loss, it is easier to leave long-term money in bank accounts rather than go to the effort to develop an investment strategy and select the appropriate investments. Avoid this temptation. Leaving long-term assets in bank accounts results in losing the safety that comes from maintaining your purchasing power in the future. Long-term money must be placed in investments in order to maximize its power to grow and provide the financial security you need.

When dealing with investments or bank accounts, the importance of matching needs, goals, and time horizons with the appropriate dollar amounts cannot be overstated.

TYPES OF BANK ACCOUNTS

Selecting a bank account depends on what you need your short-term money to do for you. For example, if you need instant availability, you need a checking account. If you need higher interest and less frequent access, a money market account or certificate of deposit may be the best. Following is a review of the basics of the most common bank accounts.

Please note that these basics vary from bank to bank. Therefore, make sure you inquire at your bank for its deposit account rules and policies.

Savings Account

This is the old standby. A regular savings account allows you to earn modest interest while you accumulate small deposits. There is often a minimum deposit of $100 to open this account. The interest rate may change at your bank's discretion, but usually does so infrequently.

You may make unlimited withdrawals. Your bank may have a minimum balance required during the calendar quarter for you to make withdrawals and transfers without charge. Savings accounts at most banks are recorded on a statement you receive monthly or quarterly. This account is often called a statement savings account. Many banks also continue to offer passbook savings accounts. These savings accounts are posted in the bank's computer and on your personal passbook. You must bring the passbook to the bank when making deposits or withdrawals.

Certificates of Deposit

Certificates of deposit (CDs) are time deposit accounts. A CD allows you to earn interest at a fixed rate on funds you leave on deposit for a specific period of time, called a *term*. Interest rates are fixed for the term and are based on rates in effect at the time you make the deposit. You must make a minimum deposit, normally $2,000 or so, to open a CD. You may choose from terms that range from three months up to several years. Other time deposit accounts, not normally called CDs, are available for terms less than three months.

Unless you specify otherwise, the CD is automatically renewed or "rolled over" by reinvesting your funds when the selected term ends at the maturity date. Both principal and interest are rolled over to another term of equal length as the first term unless you elect to have your interest disbursed. The interest rate on the rolled-over CD is the rate offered on the maturity date for the amount and term of a new CD. If the maturity date falls on a weekend or bank holiday, the maturity date is extended to the next business day. Your funds continue earning interest during the weekend or bank holiday.

You may add to a CD, make a withdrawal, or change the length of the term during the grace period. The grace period normally begins on the maturity date and usually lasts from 2 to 10 days, depending on the term of the account and your bank's policy.

At the bank's discretion, it may allow you to withdraw all or part of your funds at times other than the grace period. Each time you make an early withdrawal of principal, a withdrawal penalty is charged. An early withdrawal penalty may require the bank to reduce your principal.

Interest rates vary and are determined by the amount deposited and the term you choose. Generally, the longer the term, the higher the interest rate.

The bank credits interest to your account at maturity or pays it to you according to the interest disbursement option you select.

You receive an account statement at year-end and at maturity. You also receive notice prior to maturity stating the interest rate that will be paid if the account automatically renews for another term.

Since CDs usually pay the highest of any bank accounts, they are ideal for larger sums of money that can be tied up for periods of time up to five years. And because they are FDIC insured, they can be used as the short-term part of the foundation for your savings and investment portfolio.

Money Market Accounts

Today there are two kinds of money market accounts. Your bank may offer both. There is your bank's own money market accounts that are FDIC insured and money market (mutual) funds that are *not* FDIC insured.

Both types are excellent places for money in transition. Money can be placed in money market accounts or funds while you are waiting to spend it or to put it in a CD or long-term investment.

Bank Money Market Deposit Accounts

A bank money market account allows you to earn interest like a savings account. Normally, you must deposit at least $2,500 to open this account. You pay no monthly service charge for any statement period in which you maintain the minimum balance in your account. Otherwise, there is a small monthly service charge for that period.

Your interest rate and annual percentage yield may change. At the bank's discretion, it may change the interest rate daily. It is compounded daily at the rate in effect for the end-of-day balance. Interest is usually credited monthly when account statements are printed. Checks are usually available for easy withdrawal.

Money Market Funds

Money market funds are offered by banks as an uninsured account with immediate access. With roughly $500 billion of savings parked in them, money market funds managed primarily by mutual fund managers have proven enormously popular. Safety and liquidity are the principal investment goals of most money market funds. A recent SEC ruling requires money market funds to stick to top-rated securities for 95% of their portfolio. Therefore, these funds are safe, even though they are not bank deposits and not FDIC insured. Most funds have a policy of maintaining a net asset value of $1 a share so that investors do not experience price volatility in this investment. Dividend yields or the interest rate being paid do change with the market.

The annualized yield on money market funds is usually slightly but not significantly higher than on bank money market deposit accounts. Cash can be accessed by writing a check against the assets in your fund or by a phone call in most cases. Funds usually pay dividends monthly; you should receive regular statements indicating the amount of your dividends. You can elect to have dividends paid directly to you or automatically reinvested in the fund.

It is usually a convenience advantage to have your money market fund account with the same family of mutual funds you use for other investments. This way it can easily function as a standby depository for money that is earmarked for later spending or for later investment in other funds. However, your bank's money market account can be used for the same purpose and with similar convenience.

U.S Savings Bonds

U.S. savings bonds are not bank accounts, but they available at your bank and offer complete safety, backed by the full faith and credit of the U.S. government. A U.S. savings bond has a guaranteed return and is exempt from state and local tax; the federal tax is deferred until maturity. There are no commissions to buy or sell them.

The Series EE bond is an appreciation-type security available in denominations of $50, $75, $100, $200, $500, and $1,000. The purchase price is one-half the denomination. For example, a $100 bond can be purchased for $50. Years later at maturity, it is worth the $100 dollars. Their interest rates are subject to change twice per year. However, many have a minimum rate they will earn if kept for at least 5 years. To reach full value, it would take over 10 years if the rate averaged 7% per year. Series HH bonds are issued and redeemed at face value, with interest paid semiannually by a check from the Treasury Department. Denominations are $500, $1,000, $5,000, and $10,000. To get the current rates and semiannual market-based rates for series EE bonds and fixed series HH bond rates, call your bank or 1-800-US BONDS.

FDIC INSURANCE

We've reviewed what FDIC does *not* cover. Before we go on, let's review FDIC insurance coverage, what is it, and just what exactly it *does* cover.

Background

What is FDIC?   The Federal Deposit Insurance Corporation (FDIC) is an independent agency of the U.S. government. It was established by Congress in September 1933 to insure bank

EXHIBIT 7–1
FDIC Sign

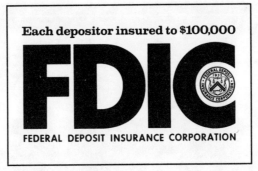

deposits, help maintain sound conditions in the banking system, and protect the nation's money supply in case of financial institution failure.

What types of financial institutions are insured by the FDIC?   The FDIC insures deposits in most, but not all, banks and savings associations. FDIC-insured institutions must display an official sign at each teller window or teller station (see Exhibit 7–1).

Insured savings associations display the official savings association (eagle) sign (not shown). Insured banks display either the official bank (FDIC) sign or the official savings association (eagle) sign.

Credit union deposits are insured up to $100,000 by the National Credit Union Administration (NCUA), a U.S. government agency. Credit unions must display the official NCUA sign (see Exhibit 7-2).

What does federal deposit insurance cover?   Federal deposit insurance protects deposits that are payable in the United States. Deposits that are only payable overseas are not insured. Securities, mutual funds, and similar types of investments are not covered by deposit insurance. Creditors (other than depositors) and shareholders of a failed bank or savings association are not protected by federal deposit insurance.

EXHIBIT 7–2
NCUA Sign

What types of deposits are insured? All types of deposits received by a financial institution in its usual course of business are insured. For example, savings deposits, checking deposits, deposits in NOW accounts, Christmas club accounts, and time deposits are all insured deposits. Cashiers' checks, money orders, officers' checks, and outstanding drafts also are insured.

Certified checks, letters of credit, and travelers' checks, for which an insured depository institution is primarily liable, also are insured when issued in exchange for money or its equivalent or for a charge against a deposit account.

If I have deposits in several different FDIC-insured institutions, will my deposits be added together for insurance purposes? No. Deposits in different institutions are insured separately. If an institution has one or more branches, however, the main office and all branch offices are considered to be one institution. Thus, if you have deposits at the main office and at one or more branch offices of the same institution, the deposits are added together when calculating deposit insurance coverage. Financial institutions owned by the same holding company but separately chartered are separately insured.

How does FDIC determine ownership of funds? The FDIC presumes that funds are owned as shown on the "deposit account records" of the insured depository institution.

If the FDIC determines that the deposit account records of the institution are unambiguous, those records are binding on the depositor. No other records are considered in determining legal ownership. The deposit account records must specifically disclose the existence of any fiduciary relationship (e.g., trustee, agent, nominee, guardian, executor, custodian, or conservator).

Basic Insurance Limit

What is the amount of FDIC insurance coverage?   The basic insured amount of a depositor is $100,000. Accrued interest is included when calculating insurance coverage.

Deposits maintained in different categories of legal ownership are separately insured. Accordingly, you can have more than $100,000 insurance coverage in a single institution if your funds are owned and deposited in different ownership categories.

The most common categories of ownership are single (or individual) ownership, joint ownership, and testamentary accounts. Separate insurance is also available for funds held for retirement purposes—individual retirement accounts (IRAs), Keoghs, and pension or profit sharing plans.

Can I increase FDIC insurance coverage by dividing my funds and depositing them into several different accounts? No. Federal deposit insurance is not determined on a per-account basis. You cannot increase FDIC insurance by dividing funds owned in the same ownership category among different accounts. The type of account (whether checking, savings, certificate of deposit, outstanding official checks, or other forms of deposit) has no bearing on the amount of insurance coverage. Furthermore, social security numbers or tax identification numbers are not used to determine insurance coverage.

Single Ownership Accounts

What is a single ownership account?   A single (or individual) ownership account is an account owned by one person. Single ownership accounts include accounts in the owner's name, accounts established for the benefit of the owner by agents,

EXHIBIT 7–3
Example of Insurance for Single Ownership Accounts

The following example shows the maximum amount of deposit insurance coverage available for the most common types of single ownership accounts.

Depositor	Type of Deposit	Amount Deposited	
A	Savings account	$ 25,000	
A	CD	100,000	
A	NOW account	25,000	
A's Restaurant (a sole proprietorship)	Checking	25,000	
Total deposited			$175,000
Maximum amount of insurance available			$100,000
Uninsured amount			$ 75,000

Source: Federal Deposit Insurance Corporation.

nominees, guardians, custodians, or conservators, and accounts established by a business that is a sole proprietorship.

How is a single ownership account insured?   All single ownership accounts established by or for the benefit of the same person are added together. The total is insured up to a maximum of $100,000 (see Exhibit 7–3).

What about uniform gifts to minors accounts?   Funds given to a minor by this method are held in the name of a custodian for the minor's benefit. Funds deposited for the benefit of a minor under the Uniform Gifts to Minors Act are added to any other single ownership accounts of the minor. The total is insured up to a maximum of $100,000.

Joint Accounts

What is a joint account and how are joint accounts insured?   A joint account is an account owned by two or more persons. Joint accounts are insured separately from single ownership accounts if each of the following conditions are met:

1. All co-owners must be natural persons. This means that legal entities such as corporations or partnerships are not eligible for joint account deposit insurance coverage.

2. Each of the co-owners must have a right of withdrawal on the same basis as the other co-owners. For example, if one co-owner can withdraw funds on his or her signature alone, but the other co-owner can withdraw funds only on the signature of both co-owners, this requirement has not been satisfied. The co-owners do not have equal withdrawal rights. Likewise, if a co-owner's right to withdraw funds is limited to a specified dollar amount, the funds in the account will be allocated between the co-owners according to their withdrawal rights and insured as single ownership funds. Thus, for example, if $100,000 is deposited in the names of A and B, but A has the right to withdraw only up to $5,000 from the account, $5,000 is allocated to A and the remainder is allocated to B. The funds, as allocated, are then added to any other single ownership funds of A or B, respectively.

3. Each of the co-owners must have personally signed a deposit account signature card.

What is the insurance coverage on joint accounts?   No joint account shall be insured for more than $100,000 (see Exhibit 7–4). Deposit insurance for multiple joint accounts is determined by applying the following steps:

1. First, all joint accounts that are identically owned (i.e., held by the same combination of individuals) are added together, and the combined total is insured up to the $100,000 maximum.

2. After step one has been completed, joint accounts involving different combinations of individuals are reviewed to determine the amount of each person's insurable interest (or share) in all joint accounts. Each owner's insurable interest in all joint accounts is added together, and the total is insured up to the $100,000 maximum. Each person's interest in a joint account is deemed equal unless otherwise stated on the deposit account records.

EXHIBIT 7–4
Example of Insurance for Joint Ownership Accounts

Three qualifying joint accounts are owned by A, B, and C, as follows:

Account	Owners	Balance
#1	A and B	$100,000
#2	B and A	25,000
#3	A and B and C	75,000

Step One:

    A and B Combination
        ADD:

Account #1 (A and B)	$100,000
Account #2 (B and A)	25,000
Total deposited:	$125,000

Step one insurable limit is $100,000, so $25,000 is uninsured.

Step Two:

    A's Ownership Interest

1/2 of the insurable balance in A/B combination (accounts #1 and #2)	$ 50,000
1/3 of insurable balance in A/B/C combination (account #3)	25,000
Total of A's insured funds	$ 75,000

    B's Ownership Interest

1/2 of insurable balance in A/B combination (accounts #1 and #2)	$ 50,000
1/3 of insurable balance in A/B/C combination (account #3)	$ 25,000
Total of B's insured funds:	$ 75,000

    C's Ownership Interest

1/3 of insurable balance in A/B/C combination (account #3)	$ 25,000
Total of C's insured funds:	$ 25,000

Summary of Insurance Coverage:

	Insured	Uninsured
A	$ 75,000	$12,500
B	75,000	12,500
C	25,000	0
Total	$175,000	$25,000

Source: Federal Deposit Insurance Corporation.

These steps are always applied with the result that (1) no one joint account can be insured for more than $100,000, (2) multiple joint accounts with identical ownership cannot be insured for more than $100,000 in the aggregate, and (3) no one person's insured interest in the joint account category can exceed $100,000.

What happens when an account fails to qualify for separate insurance in the joint account category?   A deposit account held in two or more names that does not qualify for joint account deposit insurance coverage is treated as being owned by each named owner, as an individual, corporation, partnership, or unincorporated association, according to each co-owner's actual ownership interest. As such, each owner's interest is added to any other single ownership accounts or, in the case of a corporation, partnership, or unincorporated association, to other accounts of such entity, and the total is insured up to $100,000.

Does deposit insurance coverage decrease upon the death of one of the co-owners of a testamentary account?   Yes. Each co-owner is entitled to insurance coverage as to each beneficiary only during the co-owner's lifetime. Upon the death of any one of the co-owners, insurance coverage decreases.

Retirement Accounts

What is the deposit insurance coverage for pension plans and profit sharing plans?   The general rule is that deposits belonging to pension plans and profit-sharing plans receive pass-through insurance. Pass-through insurance means that each beneficiary's ascertainable interest in a deposit—as opposed to the deposit as a whole—is insured up to $100,000.

In order for a pension or profit-sharing plan to receive pass-through insurance, the institution's deposit account records must specifically disclose the fact that the depositor (for instance, the plan itself or its trustee) holds the funds in a fiduciary capacity. In addition, the details of the fiduciary relationship between the plan and its participants and the participants' beneficial interests in the account must be ascertainable from the institution's deposit account records or from the records that the plan (or some person or entity that has agreed to maintain records for the plan) maintains in good faith and in the regular course of business.

How are funds deposited in individual retirement accounts (IRAs) and Keoghs insured?   Until December 19, 1993, IRA and Keogh funds were insured separately from each other and from any other funds of the depositor. Now, IRA and Keogh funds are still separately insured from any nonretirement funds the depositor may have at an institution. But IRA and self-directed Keogh funds will be added together, and the combined total will be insured up to $100,000. IRA and self-directed Keogh funds will also be aggregated with certain other retirement funds: those belonging to other self-directed retirement plans and those belonging to so-called "457 plan" accounts if the deposits are eligible for pass-through insurance. The 457 plans are deferred compensation plans conforming to section 457 of the Internal Revenue Code that are established by state and local governments and not-for-profit organizations. Time deposits made prior to December 19, 1993, do not become subject to the new aggregation rules until the deposits mature, roll over, or are renewed.

Business Accounts

What is the deposit insurance coverage for funds deposited by a corporation, partnership, or unincorporated association?   Funds deposited by a corporation, partnership, or unincorporated association are insured up to a maximum of $100,000. Funds deposited by a corporation, partnership, or unincorporated association are insured separately from the personal accounts of the stockholders, partners, or members. To qualify for this coverage, the entity must be engaged in an independent activity, which means that the entity is operated primarily for some purpose other than to increase deposit insurance.

Accounts owned by the same entity but designated for different purposes are not separately insured. Instead, such accounts are added together and insured up to $100,000 in the aggregate.

Thus, if a corporation has divisions or units that are not separately incorporated, the deposit accounts of those divisions or units will be added to any other deposit accounts of the corporation for purposes of determining deposit insurance coverage.

Funds owned by a business that is a sole proprietorship are treated as the individually owned funds of the person who is the sole proprietor. Consequently, funds deposited in the name of the sole proprietorship are added to any other single ownership accounts of the sole proprietor, and the total is insured to a maximum of $100,000.

Does federal deposit insurance cover Treasury securities? Treasury securities (bills, notes, and bonds) purchased by an insured depository institution on a customer's behalf are not insured by the FDIC. They don't need to be since *they* are backed by the full faith and credit of the U.S. government. However, if a customer's Treasury securities are in a bank's possession at the time of default, they remain the property of the customer. Upon presentation by the customer of a receipt documenting to the FDIC's satisfaction the customer's ownership rights, the FDIC as receiver will give the customer a release that the customer can present to a Federal Reserve Bank or the Department of the Treasury to prove ownership. Alternatively, the FDIC as receiver can hold all Treasury securities and make a distribution upon maturity in the same manner and extent as the closed institution would have done.

For more information about deposit insurance, write to:

Office of Consumer Affairs FDIC
550 Seventeenth Street, NW
Washington, D.C. 20429

Chapter Eight

Understanding Stocks

B efore going into in more detail on the products recommended in the last three chapters, such as mutual funds and annuities, it's important that you have a basic understanding of the core investments that make up today's investment products. These core investments are stocks and bonds. You need to know what types there are, what needs they fill, how they work, the difference between interest and dividends, and how to buy them. Stocks, also called equities, will be covered in this chapter; bonds will be covered in the next chapter.

Let's look at the basics. A stock is a right of ownership in a corporation. The ownership is divided into a certain number of shares; the corporation issues stockholders stock certificates to show how many shares they hold. The stockholders own the company and elect a board of directors to manage it for them.

The money a shareholder exchanges for these shares entitles the shareholder to dividends and to other rights of ownership, such as voting rights.

Prices of stock change according to general business conditions and the earnings and future prospects of the company. If the business is doing well, stockholders may be able to sell their stock for a profit. If it is not, they may have to take a loss if they sell.

Large corporations may have many thousands of stockholders. Their stock is bought and sold in marketplaces called stock exchanges.

The shares of stock represent the value of the corporation. When the corporation has made a profit, the directors may divide the profit among the stockholders as dividends, they may decide to use it to expand the business, or they may do both. Dividends are paid only out of the corporation's profits to the stock shareholders. When profits are used to expand the business, the directors and stockholders may decide to issue more stock representing the new money invested in the business. This new stock will be divided among the old stockholders as stock dividends.

WHY STOCKS?

As an asset category, stocks have historically outperformed all other financial assets. They should be part of every bank customer's investment strategy.

As Exhibit 8-1 plainly shows, stocks have outperformed all other types of financial instruments over time. Now let's examine the basic forms that stock comes in: common and preferred.

Common Stock

Common stock represents true ownership shares in a company. Stockholders share directly in growing company profits through increasing dividends and an appreciation in the value of the stock itself. As the holder of common stock, you are a part-owner in the company issuing the stock. When your bank investment representative uses the term *stock,* he or she normally is referring to common stock. The bulk of stock investments in most mutual funds are common stock. Common stocks are the kind being referred to, almost exclusively, on television and radio stock market reports.

Preferred Stock

Preferred stock, like common stock, represents ownership or equity not debt. The corporation is legally obligated to make interest payments to bondholders (debtholders), but it is not legally required to pay dividends to preferred or common stockholders. These are much less common than common stocks.

Preferred stockholders, however, have a claim on profits that precedes—or is preferred to—the claim of the common stockholder. The preferred stockholder has a right to receive specific dividends (10% of the face value of the preferred share is one example) before the common stockholder can be paid any dividend

EXHIBIT 8–1
Historical Performance of Stocks

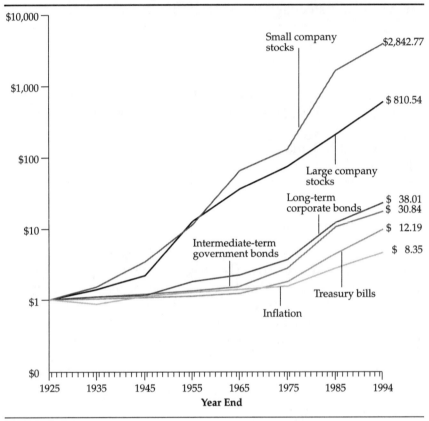

Source: © *Stocks, Bonds, Bills, and Inflation 1994 Yearbook™*, Ibbotson Associates, Chicago (annually updates work by Roger G. Ibbotson and Rex A. Sinquefield). Used with permission. All rights reserved.

at all. But, on the other hand, the preferred stockholder does not have the possibility of making the large gains open to the common stockholder. While the common stockholder may hope for rising dividends and rising stock prices if the corporation prospers, the preferred shareholder will at most receive the specified dividend.

If the preferred stockholders share with the common stockholders in dividends beyond the specified percentage, the stock is called participating preferred.

Preferred stock may also be cumulative. That is, if there are no dividends given in a year, the preferred stockholders must be given double their dividend the next year. This is paid before anything is paid to the common stockholders. It will continue to multiply for as many years as dividends are not paid.

HOW STOCK PRICES MOVE

The stock market is an open auction, where prices are determined by open outcry on the exchange floor. In order to maintain an orderly, supply–demand auction, "specialists" have been designated by the exchanges to handle individual equities. These individuals actually determine stock prices, by matching buy and sell orders delivered by the floor brokers shouting out their customers' orders to buy or sell. The specialist literally changes the prices to match the supply and demand created by the brokers on the exchange floor. In short, the specialist system was created to guarantee that every seller would find a buyer and vice versa. These are the mechanics of how prices move. However, in the long run the value of a stock will be determined by the profitability of the corporation and expectations of future profits.

TRADING

Each year, investors trade billions of shares worth hundreds of billions of dollars. To buy or sell stock, you place an order with your bank investment representative who gets a price quotation by telephone or computer and relays the order to your bank's partner on the floor of the exchange. The partner, a floor broker, negotiates the sale or purchase and notifies your bank's brokerage unit. The transaction may take only a few minutes. You have up to three business days to pay for the stock if you're buying. If you're selling, it takes the same three days to receive the proceeds.

Where Stock Is Traded

To most people, "the stock market" means the New York Stock Exchange (NYSE). The New York Stock Exchange is more than 200 years old. Needless to say, it has come a long way since 24 merchants and auctioneers met at the site of the present exchange to negotiate an agreement to buy and sell the stocks and bonds issued by the new United States government, along with those of a few banks and insurance companies.

It wasn't until 1817 that the exchange adopted an approved constitution, whereby it named itself the New York Stock and Exchange Board. Its dullest day ever was March 16, 1930, when only 31 shares changed hands, and it did not cross the million-share daily threshold until 1986. But as communications became steadily more sophisticated, the exchange began to assume its present form.

There are many other North American exchanges trading stock, from the American Stock Exchange (called the AMEX) on down to the Spokane Stock Exchange. Today you can also take advantage of foreign stock ownership. These stocks are traded on a number of foreign markets. Almost every free country has its own stock exchange representing the country's individual companies that offer public ownership. One thing to know about foreign stock markets is that many of them do not conform to the stringent requirements American stock exchanges have to follow.

In addition, thousands of equities are not traded on any exchange but over the counter. Prices for OTC stocks are readily available through the NASDAQ, an acronym for the National Association of Securities Dealers Automated Quotations system.

There is a distinctive difference between OTC stocks and exchange listed equities, revolving primarily around eligibility requirements. Each stock exchange has listing requirements that must be met before a company may take its place on the exchange floor. For example, before a stock may be listed on the NYSE, the company must have at least one million shares outstanding (available to the public). Those shares must be held by at least 2,000 different stockholders, each of whom owns at least 100 shares. The company must also have earned a pretax profit of at least $2.5 million the year preceding the listing; the pretax profits in the two prior years must have been at least $2 million each year. The AMEX and the regional exchanges have similar (though less stringent) listing requirements, but no such limitations exist for OTC listings.

How a Stock Exchange Operates

Federal and state laws regulate the issuance, listing, and trading of most securities. The Securities and Exchange Commission (SEC) administers the federal laws. Stocks handled by one or more stock exchanges are called listed stocks.

When the stock market is said to be up 10 points, what is usually meant is that the Dow-Jones Industrial Average (DJIA) went up 10 points. The DJIA is based on the average prices paid for 30 blue-chip stocks; it has recorded up-and-down fluctuations of the New York Stock Exchange since 1896. General upward and downward movements of stock prices are symbolized on Wall Street by bulls and bears, respectively.

Because the average is weighted through only 30 companies and because the actual constituents of the average can be (and have been) changed, many market analysts question its validity. The Standard & Poor's 500 Index, the Value Line Composite Index, the NASDAQ, and the New York Stock Exchange Composite Index are more accurate indices and are also more widely followed. These are broader based, which should make them somewhat more accurate in a large market. Since the DJIA consists of only 30 large companies, it may not truly reflect market performance—hence its generic use.

How to Measure a Stock's Current Value

Aside from the price changes you may read about in the newspapers, there are other measures of a stock's current value: price-earnings ratio, dividend payout ratio, and dividend yield. You should have a basic understanding of what these terms mean and how they can be used to explain a stock's value.

Price-earnings ratio. This measures the stock's price divided by the company's earnings per share (or EPS) over the past 12 months. If a stock is trading at $25 and earned $1.25 a share over the past four quarters, its P/E is 20 ($25/$1.25). Value investors look for stocks trading at low P/E, while growth investors don't mind paying for high P/Es if they think the company's profits will be increasing rapidly. Average P/E ratios are also calculated for individual mutual funds. These tell you how the overall portfolio is valued. A growth fund would likely have a higher average P/E than an income-oriented portfolio, for example. You'll learn more about mutual funds in Chapter 10.

Dividend payout ratio.   This is the ratio of a company's indicated annual cash dividend per share to its P/Es. It can range from zero to 100%. A utility that pays out $4 in dividends for each $5 of earnings would have a payout of 80%. The payout is above 50% for the average large industrial company and even higher for the typical utility. The higher the dividend payout, however, the less room there is for dividend increases, since less profit would be available to reinvest for future growth.

Dividend yield.   This measures the annual dividend divided by the stock price. For example, if a utility's dividend is $4 and its stock sells for $50 a share, the yield would be 8%. When P/Es in general are high, yields will be low.

All these factors have some effect on the price of your stock. By understanding what they mean, you get a picture of a stock's current value. This is a simplistic explanation of measuring value; many more factors affect the price changes or movements up or down in your stocks.

One other example is any unforeseen circumstance that may have lessened the earning power of a company and thus lowered the price that people are willing to pay for shares in that company's stock. Prosperous times or better management may increase values. Political and economic events affect the future of companies and cause stock prices to fluctuate. Stock prices often reflect the state of the economy. If business conditions are good, stock prices tend to rise, creating a bull market. If conditions are poor, stock prices drop, causing a bear market.

The key point to remember is that all stocks fluctuate in value and the above circumstances affect their current prices.

If you want equities (stocks) in your portfolio but do not want to do the necessary research and investigation to make a decision on which individual stocks to own, you can simply rely on professional management to pick the stocks for you. The management companies are called mutual fund companies, UITs, or variable annuities. These will be discussed in future chapters. However, if you want to purchase individual stocks, seek advice from your bank investment representative on how to proceed.

Chapter Nine

Understanding Bonds

L ike stocks, bonds are core investments that make up many investment products. An understanding of them is essential, especially for bank customers since bonds and bond mutual funds are the most common investments bank customers own. They are also the investments most likely to be misunderstood and therefore misused.

A recent survey indicates that more than 90% of bank customers are in the dark in this area and that the majority of people who have actually invested in stocks and bonds don't really understand what makes a bond different from other types of investments. And herein lies a danger. Bonds are look-alike products to bank accounts. Consequently, there's a tendency for bank customers to see bonds as bank products that just have a higher yield. Blinded by yield, customers may not take the time to understand the basics of bonds; they may be tempted to load up on them mainly because of current yield. This is the wrong strategy!

BOND BASICS

Let's look at the basics. First, bonds are bought because an investor wants income. Bonds are IOUs. When you buy a bond, you are lending your money, typically to a corporation or government agency. Individual bonds are issued in $5,000 denominations. Interest is paid semiannually and is mailed to the person whose name and address appears on the face of the certificate. A bond has a specific date in the future when it matures and the money is returned to the bondholder. That's the simple mechanics, but what backs the bond? In the case of many bonds, nothing more is behind them than the faith and credit of the companies that issue them. These bonds, usually called debentures, are probably the most common type of debt issued by industrial corporations today. The next most popular type of bond is called mortgage bonds or collateral trust bonds. Public utilities generally issue this type of bond with specific assets as collateral against the loan. Of course, some utilities issue debentures, and some industrial corporations issue collateralized bonds.

The last category of bonds is U.S. government bonds or bonds issued by government agencies such as municipalities. These types of bonds are backed by full faith and credit of the government agencies or municipalities issuing the bond. Obviously, these government bonds are safer than corporate bonds. While these three types of bonds—debentures, collateralized, and government—have different characteristics, they basically share the same structure; they're debt instruments that pay interest until maturity.

BUYING A BOND

When you buy a bond, think of it as lending your money to the issuer of the bond. The issuer agrees to make periodic interest payments to you. You hold the bond, and the issuer repays your principal in full on a certain date, the bond's maturity date. That's pretty simple, right? It is, as long as you don't plan to sell your bond until it matures. Here's where most people get into trouble. They don't realize that bonds are traded. This is the major difference between bonds and CDs. CDs are not traded. Their price does not change. If you "sell" a CD, you have to pay a penalty, usually part or all of the interest you were to receive. Not so with bonds. With a bond, you get whatever it's worth. A bond's price is quoted daily, based on the current or prevailing interest rates.

A bond's stated interest rate is fixed, so if interest rates on other investments of equal quality and length to maturity *soar above* your stated interest rate, your bond drops in value. If interest rates *drop below* your stated interest rate, your bond would rise in value. In other words, the principal value of your bond moves opposite the

EXHIBIT 9–1
Relationship between Interest Rates and Share Price

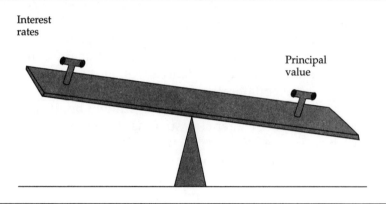

Source: *Bank Investment Representative*, April 1994, p. 45.

way interest rates move in the economy (see Exhibit 9–1 above). However, that background trading activity doesn't really affect your bond unless you decide to sell it. If you keep it, it will still pay the stated interest rate and still repay the entire principal at maturity, as long as nothing has affected the issuer's ability to repay. Like a CD, a bond's interest payments are fixed; the difference is in volatility of its principal value. While your bond's market value can go up or down during its holding period, a CD's value doesn't fluctuate. A CD's principal value always stays the same. If it helps, think of bonds as loans to companies, municipalities, or government agencies with possible daily penalties or bonuses for early withdrawal (in this case, selling).

Market Risk

So what are the risks when you buy a bond? The main risk is that interest rates will change. A bond's current value is directly affected by changes in the interest rates. The effect of higher interest rates on bonds is to lower their price. Conversely, lower rates raise bond prices. The longer the term of the bond, the more the price will be affected by changes in interest rates. This is true whether the bond is issued by the U.S. government, a corporation, or a municipality.

Credit Risk

The rule to remember is this: The price of any bond fluctuates in harmony with the rise and fall of interest rates. This is market risk. The stability of the underlying corporation or agency issuing the bond also affects its value. This is credit risk.

Now, let's talk about the underlying corporation or agency. How do you know if it is solid or weak? There are rating services that independently judge the creditworthiness of the issuer. The three major independent rating services are Moody's, Fitch, and Standard & Poor's. They conduct financial investigations of bond issues on a continuous basis and publish investment-grade ratings ranging from AAA to BBB − (Standard & Poor's), or Aaa to Baa 3 (Moody's), or AAA to BBB (Fitch). Lower-rated bonds such as Ba are considered speculative. Aaa or AAA are considered the highest and safest. Ratings are intended to help you evaluate risk and set your own standards for investment (see Exhibit 9–2).

Remember, strong credit backing does not eliminate market risk; there is still the risk of your bond's value fluctuating because interest rates have changed since you purchased it.

Grades AAA through BBB are considered investment grade. Lower rated bonds and nonrated bonds that involve large amounts of risk to the investor are commonly called junk bonds. Most bank investment representatives will confine their attention to bonds rated A or above. Ratings attempt to assess the probability that the issuing company will make timely payments of interest and principal, and each rating service has slightly different evaluation methods.

TYPES OF BONDS

Now, let's examine the various types of bonds and see how they might fit into your portfolio.

Corporate Bonds

Corporate bonds are issued by corporations of every size and credit quality, from the very best blue-chip companies to small companies with low ratings. Corporate bonds may be backed by collateral.

EXHIBIT 9–2
Bond Safety Ratings

Credit Risk	Moody's	S&P	Fitch
Prime	Aaa	AAA	AAA
Excellent	Aa	AA	AA
Upper medium	A − 1, A	A +, A	A
Lower medium	Baa − 1, baa, ba	BBB +, BBB	BBB
Speculative	Ba	BB	BB
Very speculative	B, Caa	B, CCC, CC	B, CCC, C
Default	Ca, C	DDD, DD, D	DDD, DD, D

Corporate bonds are fully taxable at the federal, state, and local level and pay semiannual interest. Corporate bond yields are higher than that available on CDs or government-issued bonds of similar maturities. The coupon is fixed, and return of principal is guaranteed by the issuer if the investor holds until maturity. If you sell the bond prior to maturity, the bonds will be subject to market fluctuation.

The fully taxable nature of corporate bonds (as opposed to municipals or Treasuries) has an effect on yield. Even when buying a AAA-rated corporate bond, you are buying a security that has more risk than a U.S. government bond. For the risk you are taking, you should receive an additional 1/4 to 1/2% in yield for bonds of like maturities.

U.S. Government Notes and Bonds

The U.S. government issues both Treasury notes (maturites of 2–10 years) and bonds (maturities over 10 years). It also issues Treasury bills (T-bills) with maturities of less than one year. U.S. government securities are considered to have no credit risk, and their rates of return are the benchmark to which all other rates of return in the market are compared. These bonds are auctioned by the government on a regular quarterly schedule or can be purchased through your bank investment representative. Both notes and bonds pay semiannual interest. T-bills, with a maturity of less than one year, pay at maturity.

U.S. government notes or bonds typically have yields 1/2 to 2-1/2% higher than those of T-bills and the same spread lower than a U.S. government bond. Notes are the most likely investment for an individual investor because of the maturity range. The 30-year bond, called the long bond, is actively traded by institutional investors and traders. One benefit of U.S. government securities is that they are exempt from state income tax.

Zero Coupon Bonds

A lot of people used this type of bond for establishing a child's college fund. These hybrid bonds pay no cash interest payments and are sold at a deep discount to their maturity value. The interest accrues as the years go on; and in this way, through the miracle of compounding, a relatively small investment today becomes a large nest egg in the future. The almost prohibitive disadvantage of this investment vehicle for the individual is the IRS position that the appreciation in value is not capital gains to be taxed at lower rates at maturity, but is interest. This means the imputed amount must be added to ordinary income each year for tax purposes. Pension and profit-sharing plans and other nontax-paying entities may find these bonds of interest.

Municipal Bonds

Municipal bonds are investment instruments used to finance municipal governmental activities. These bonds, often called "tax-free bonds," are exempt from federal income taxes. Municipal bonds are totally exempted from federal tax not just tax deferred. In many states, they are also exempt from state and local taxes. Your bank investment representative can tell you if your state allows such an exemption.

There are two basic types of municipal bonds: general obligation bonds and revenue bonds. General obligation bonds are normally backed by the full faith and credit and general taxing power of the issuing authority. These are considered the safest type of municipal bond.

Revenue bonds are secured by specifically pledged revenues and are usually used to finance schools, roads, bridges, public hospitals, waterworks, dams, and so on. Municipal bonds are an excellent investment if you are in a high tax bracket and need income.

Ginnie Maes

Ginnie Maes are government agency securities guaranteed by the Governmental National Mortgage Association (GNMA). Their certificates are backed by pools of home mortgages assembled by mortgage bankers. Principal and interest collected on mortgages are "passed through" to holders of Ginnie Mae securities.

GNMA (or Ginnie Mae) is a government-owned corporation within the Department of Housing and Urban Development. A GNMA pass-through security is one kind of mortgage-backed bond. GNMAs were invented by Wall Street and require a minimum $25,000 investment. They are attractive to investors due to the unconditional backing of the U.S. government and a current yield higher than that of Treasuries. They are different from bonds in that they make payments monthly and each payment includes interest *and* a partial return of principal.

Bonds should be a part of your strategy. Consult with your bank investment representative as to where bonds fit in your overall investment plan.

Bond Terms

Following is a list of terms you should become familiar with before you discuss bonds with your bank investment representative.

Accrued interest: The amount of interest income (coupon income) earned from the date of the last coupon payment to settlement date; all bonds traded plus accrued interest. Bond uses a 360-day or 365-day basis to calculate interest payments.

Coupon rate: The fixed annual interest rate (interest income) stated on the bond.

Current yield: The coupon divided by price, giving a rough approximation of cash flow.

Form: book entry registered, or physical.

Interest payment dates: Dates interest payments are made, usually semiannually.

Maturity date: The date you will be repaid the principal and last interest payment.

Par amount: Face amount of the bond.

Price: Dollar price you paid for the bond. (It's called the offering price, the price you paid to buy the bond; the bid price is the price at which you can sell the bond.)

Rating: For example, A or AA is a solid bond rating. Check the rating sheet listed in this chapter.

Settlement date: The date you pay for your bond and interest starts accruing.

Trade date: The date the bond is purchased in the market.

Yield to maturity: Measure of total return on the bond. This is the yield that should be used when comparing with CDs.

Bond Mutual Funds

Now that you have a basic understanding of individual bonds, your next question should be, Which is best, individual bonds or mutual bond funds?

A good rule of thumb if you have less than $50,000 to invest in bonds is that you're better off in a mutual bond fund (or unit investment trust). Why? Diversification and professional management. It's just common sense: If you have a variety of bonds, the odds are that not all of them are going to have problems.

Bond funds and unit investment trusts are packages of bonds selected by a professional money manager. They will be discussed in detail in the next chapter, Understanding Mutual Funds.

Chapter Ten

Understanding Mutual Funds

Today, one of every four households in America owns at least one mutual fund. This accounts for more than 72 million shareholders with more than $1.6 trillion invested in the mutual fund universe of some 4,000 stock, bond, and money market funds. This is according to the Investment Company Institute, a national mutual fund trade organization. Even though mutual funds are popular, many people still don't understand what mutual funds are and how they work. Some bank customers mistakenly assume that since mutual funds are sold within the four walls of their bank, they are protected by the Federal Deposit Insurance Corporation (FDIC). They're not!

BANKS AND MUTUAL FUNDS

Banks sell the same mutual funds available through brokerage firms and independent financial planners. In addition, over 100 separate banks have their own mutual fund families that are sold exclusively in their respective branch lobbies. (See Appendix B.) Mutual funds of any kind, including a bank's own mutual funds, are not FDIC-insured. Neither are other investments sold in banks, such as stocks, bonds, and annuities. Only traditional bank accounts qualify for FDIC coverage.

There is no insurance coverage from the federal government for mutual fund investors who lose money; your bank is not obligated in any way to return all of what you first invested in an uninsured product. In other words, you face exactly the same risk in buying uninsured products at a bank that you face when making such investments through a brokerage firm, investment company, or insurance company.

This information shouldn't make you feel uneasy about buying mutual funds. In fact, not being insured is what makes a mutual fund an investment you want and need. The risk involved in mutual funds is what makes it possible for you to make higher returns than on guaranteed bank accounts. Unlike a certificate of deposit, which offers a fixed return for a specific period of time, mutual funds may go up substantially in value over time. Of course, this risk also means you can lose part of the money you invest in a mutual fund.

HOW MUTUAL FUNDS WORK

A mutual fund is a company that pools the financial resources of thousands of investors. Instead of just buying a single security, the mutual fund buyer (investor) gets a "basket" holding dozens of stocks or bonds. Mutual funds can help you minimize risk through diversification and also benefit from the expertise of the professional fund manager. Each day, the fund must determine the value of the stocks or bonds in its portfolio. A fund's share price can change from day to day, depending on the daily value of its underlying securities. The overall value of the basket of securities divided by the number of outstanding shares in the mutual fund is the net asset value, or NAV, of each share.

Technically, a mutual fund is an investment company. The investment company makes investments on behalf of its participants, who share common financial goals. Top-performing mutual funds can earn more than 20% annually; over time, 10 to 15% is more typical.

MUTUAL FUND STRUCTURES

A mutual fund can be open-end or closed-end. An open-end fund, the more popular kind, offers new shares continuously to investors and guarantees redemption at net asset value per share. A closed-end fund sells a predetermined number of shares. If investors want to own a closed-end fund after all the shares are sold, they must buy them from existing shareholders via a stock exchange.

Open-End Mutual Fund

Open-end mutual funds generally require minimum dollar amounts to open a new account, ranging from $50 to $3,000. Most funds permit small incremental investments by existing fund shareholders. All open-end funds will redeem shares at their net asset value, which reflects the prices of all their holdings at the end of the day. When mutual funds are discussed in the media, it is almost always open-end funds that are being discussed.

Closed-End Mutual Fund

Even though this type of fund is not as common as the open-end fund, you should understand how it works. A fixed number of shares are issued for a closed-end fund, and the management company does not issue or redeem shares on demand. If you want to sell shares of a closed-end fund, you must sell those shares in the open market to an investor who wishes to buy them. Because this purchase is completed in the marketplace, the price the seller receives may or may not equal the value of the underlying securities in the fund. Buying or selling shares of closed-end funds in the secondary market is like buying or selling a stock. There are a limited number of shares issued. Therefore, supply and demand play a role in the pricing and liquidity of a closed-end fund.

MAJOR TYPES OF MUTUAL FUNDS

The number of funds has grown nearly ten-fold since 1980 when there was approximately 600. There are now mutual funds that suit most investment objectives. Many fund management companies offer a number of different types of funds under one roof, often referred to as a "family of funds." A family might include a growth stock fund, an aggressive growth stock fund, a balanced fund that invests in both stocks and bonds, a tax-exempt bond fund, a money market fund, and perhaps many others. Mutual fund families permit their customers to transfer without a fee or penalty from one fund to another within the family at anytime the customers feel a change is appropriate.

Despite the endless variations, there are really three broad categories of mutual funds: those aimed at providing immediate taxable or tax-free income (bond funds); those oriented toward long-term growth or appreciation (stock funds); and those that provide modest interest rates with easy access (money market funds). A fund's objectives will be stated at the opening of the prospectus, indicating whether the fund emphasizes high or low risk, stability or speculation.

Stock Funds

Stock mutual funds, also called equity funds, simply invest in stocks. Their primary purpose is to grow in value, to appreciate. Stock mutual funds are categorized by the types of stocks in which they invest. The following are the various types of stock funds.

Growth funds. These stock funds emphasize growth. Dividend payouts will be low. These funds stress capital appreciation rather than immediate income. Aggressive growth funds invest in smaller, lesser-known companies, giving them room for enough upward movement to perform spectacularly during a bull market.

Aggressive growth funds. As the name implies, these funds are invested for maximum capital gains and capital appreciation. They are highly volatile and speculative in nature. The old adage "potential high risk, potential high return" describes this kind of fund.

Balanced funds. These funds stress three main goals: income, capital appreciation, and preservation of capital. This fund balances holdings among bonds, convertible securities, and preferred and common stocks. Since it is diversified into both bond and stock markets, a balanced fund is appropriate for bank customers who can only afford one fund.

Convertible funds. This fund invests in convertible securities. The bonds and preferred stocks can be exchanged for a specific number of a company's common shares. This is a hybrid security, at times acting like a stock and at other times acting like a bond. Its performance should be similar to that of a balanced portfolio, with a greater emphasis on income than the typical stock investment.

Growth and income funds.   Combining stocks and bonds, this type of fund captures modest income from bonds and stocks that pay dividends, growth of principal from stocks in companies that's profits are increasing, and growth from a long-term rise in the stock market.

Income funds.   If you're seeking safety and income, rather than capital appreciation, this is the right group. Income funds invest in corporate bonds or government-insured mortgages; if they own any stocks at all, they are usually preferred shares.

Index funds.   An index fund is a mutual fund whose portfolio mirrors that of a broad-based market index such as the S&P 500 index. Unlike other mutual funds in which the portfolio manager and a team of analysts scour the market for the best securities, an index fund manager simply invests to match the performance of an index.

Utility funds.   Utility funds invest in stocks in utility companies around the country. Like bonds, utility stocks generate high income. Utilities are defensive investments because utilities are profitable even during difficult times.

Gold funds.   A gold fund is a cost-effective way to participate in the possible increase in the price of gold. Some funds invest only in South African stocks owning shares of mining firms. The downside is that gold can be highly volatile.

Global funds.   U.S. international and global funds focus their investments outside the United States. The term *international* typically means that a fund can invest anywhere in the world except the United States. The term *global* generally implies that a fund can invest anywhere in the world, including the United States.

Hybrid funds.   Hybrid funds invest in a mixture of different types of securities. Most commonly, they invest in bonds and stocks. These funds are usually less risky and volatile than funds investing exclusively in stocks. Hybrid mutual funds are typically known as balanced or asset-allocation funds. Balanced funds generally try to maintain a fairly constant percentage of investment in stocks and bonds. Asset-allocation funds tend to adjust the mix of different investments according to the portfolio manager's expectations.

Specialty funds.   Specialty funds invest in stocks in specific industries such as banking, technology, health care. They will only perform well if the industry does well.

Bond Funds

A bond mutual fund is nothing more than a large group of bonds carefully selected by the fund's money manger. Most bond funds invest in bonds of similar maturity (the number of years to elapse before the borrower must pay back the money you lend). The names of most bond funds include a word or two that provide clues about the average length of maturity of their bonds.

For example, a *short-term* bond fund concentrates its investments in bonds maturing in the next few years. An *intermediate-term* fund generally holds bonds that come due within 7–10 years. The bonds in a *long-term* fund usually mature in 20 years or so. In contrast to an individual bond, which you buy and hold until it matures, a bond fund is always replacing bonds in its portfolio to maintain its average maturity objective. *In other words, the bond fund never matures.* You must sell your shares at their current value to get your money out.

One major advantage of a bond mutual fund over individual bonds is that most bond funds pay dividends monthly, whereas individual bonds pay out only semiannually. The main purpose for investing in a bond fund is to receive income. However, a bonus in times of declining interest rates is that bond funds can appreciate in value. In times of rising interest rates they decline in value (see pages 79–80).

Bond mutual funds are categorized by the kind of bonds they invest in. There are two basic types of bond mutual funds: taxable and tax-exempt.

Taxable bond funds

Corporate bond funds.   These funds invest primarily in investment-grade corporate bonds that are rated triple-B or higher. They may also hold Treasury securities and short-, intermediate-, or long-term bonds.

U.S. government bond funds.   These funds invest primarily in U.S. Treasury and agency securities.

Mortgage-backed securities funds.   Mortgage-backed bond funds invest primary in mortgage-backed securities such as Ginnie Maes. The income they produce is a combination of interest and return of principal.

High-quality corporate bond funds.   These funds are restricted to corporate bond issues rated single-A or better. They may also own Treasury securities.

High-yield corporate bond funds.   These funds invest primarily in lower-rated, higher-yielding corporate bonds, which are also called "junk bonds."

Global-bond funds.   Global-bond funds invest in foreign as well as U.S. bonds. Portfolios that invest virtually all of their money in overseas obligations are more properly called *international bond funds.*

Tax-exempt bond funds

Municipal bond funds.   These funds invest in tax-free bonds and pass through the tax-free income to shareholders. Although the interest these funds generate is tax-free, any possible gains from price appreciation would be fully taxed.

National municipal bond funds.   These tax-free bond funds hold municipal bonds issued in a number of states and offer broad geographic diversification.

Single-state municipal bond funds. These tax-free bond funds limit themselves to a specific state. The advantage of single-state bonds is that they enjoy a double tax exemption (state and federal). Some even enjoy a triple tax exemption, assuming they hold local bonds in cities and counties that impose personal income taxes on the state residents.

Insured-municipal bond funds. These are municipal bond funds whose obligations are insured by an outside underwriter for timely payment of interest and principal. If the issuer defaults on interest or principal payments, the insurance company steps in and meets the obligation.

Unmanaged bond funds

Unit investment trusts Another investment that is akin to a mutual fund is a unit investment trust (UIT). The two ways to buy large groups of packaged bonds are bond funds or unit investment trusts. Bond funds are managed; unit investment trusts are unmanaged. A bond fund is always replacing bonds in its portfolio to maintain its average maturity objective; a unit investment trust is not.

A UIT is an unmanaged portfolio of bonds or notes with a fixed maturity. It is not technically a mutual fund because it isn't managed. There are as many kinds of UITs as there are bonds: corporate, government, and municipal, in all maturities.

Since the UIT is not managed but the assets are fixed, you can evaluate the UIT by looking at the securities it owns. Evaluate the possibilities of credit and market risk carefully because, although a professional manager did select the bonds initially, there is no manager to protect against credit deterioration in any of the bonds composing the UIT.

As long as the investor plans to hold the UIT to maturity, there is little interest-rate risk. That risk could come into play if an investor had to sell his or her shares prior to maturity. The interest rate is fixed and can be paid as often as monthly. There is no management fee.

Think of a unit investment trusts as a closed-end type of bond fund. The total portfolio of the fund is divided into units of approximately $1,000 each, so you can buy in multiples of $1,000, although the usual minimum investment is $5,000. The portfolio of the trust remains fixed—no new bonds added, no switching of issues—so that the interest payout—monthly, quarterly, or semiannually, at the option of the holder—remains constant.

The advantage of a unit investment trust is that, unlike a bond fund, it matures. This could make unit investment trusts attractive to bank customers who want to be sure principal will be paid back in full but who do not have sufficient funds to buy a diversified portfolio of bonds.

Money Market Funds

Money market funds are the safest type of mutual funds if you are worried about the risk of losing your principal. Money market funds are like bank savings accounts in that the value of your investment does not fluctuate.

Money market funds have several advantages over bank savings accounts. The best ones have higher yields. If you're in a higher tax bracket, you have the option of using tax-free money market funds. No savings account pays tax-free interest. Most money market funds come with free check-writing privileges. (The only stipulation is that each check must be written for a minimum amount—$250 is common.) Money market funds are suitable for money that you can't afford to let fluctuate. **Note: Money market mutual funds are not insured by the federal government.**

BENEFITS OF MUTUAL FUNDS

Full-time professionals. When you invest your savings in a mutual fund, you are hiring a team of professional investors to make complex investment judgments for you and to handle the complicated trading, record keeping, and safekeeping responsibilities for you. People whose full-time profession is money management will sift the thousands of available investments to choose those that, in their judgment, are best suited to achieving the investment goals of the fund, as spelled out in its prospectus.

Given their access to research analysis and computerized support, professional management can help identify opportunities in the markets the average investor may not have the expertise or access to identify. As economic conditions change, the professionals also may adjust the mix of the fund's investments to adopt a more aggressive or defensive posture.

Diversification. The importance of diversifying your investments is so that your savings are not unduly exposed to any one kind of risk. Diversification is one important characteristic that attracts many investors to mutual funds. By owning a diverse portfolio of many stocks and/or bonds, investors can reduce the risk associated with owning any individual security. A mutual fund is typically invested in 25–200 or more securities. Proper diversification ensures that the fund receives the highest possible return at the lowest possible risk, given the objectives of the fund.

Low initial investment. Each mutual fund establishes the required minimum amount it takes to make initial and subsequent investments. A majority of mutual funds have low initial minimums, some as low as $50.

Liquidity. One of the key advantages of mutual funds stems from the liquidity of this investment. You can sell your shares at any time. Mutual funds have a "ready market" for their shares in that they must buy shares back on demand. Additionally, as a shareholder, you will directly receive any dividend or interest payments earned by the fund; payments are usually made on a quarterly basis.

Audited performance. All mutual funds are required to disclose through their prospectus historical data about the fund: returns earned by the fund, operating expenses and other fees, and the fund's rate of trading turnover. The Securities and

Exchange Commission (SEC) audits these disclosures for accuracy. It's like having a guard dog watching the guy who is watching your money.

Automatic reinvestment compounding.   One of the major benefits of mutual funds is that dividends can be reinvested automatically and converted into more shares. The result is a compounded investment combined with a forced saving plan.

Switching.   Switching, or exchange privilege, is offered by many of the larger funds through so-called *family* or *umbrella plans.* Switching from one fund to another accommodates changes in investment goals as well as changes in the market and the economy. Switching from one fund to another in the same family is considered a sell and a buy for purposes of taxation, but you don't pay new commissions when you switch.

Low transaction costs.   When an individual buys 300 shares of a $30 stock ($9,000 investment), he is likely to get a commission bill for about $204, or 2.3 percent of the value of the investment. A mutual fund, on the other hand, is more likely to be buying 30,000 to 300,000 shares at a time! Their commission costs often run in the vicinity of one tenth of the commission you would pay at a discount broker. The commission savings means higher returns for you as a mutual fund shareholder. You do pay a commission to buy mutual funds, but you don't pay directly for each transaction the mutual fund manager makes (see Chapter 17, The Real Costs of Investing).

Flexibility in risk level.   You can choose among a variety of different mutual funds to select those that accept a level of risk you're comfortable with and that meet your personal and financial goals.
- *Stock funds.* If you want your money to grow over a long period of time, you may want to select funds that invest more heavily in stocks.
- *Bond funds.* If you need current income and don't want investments that fluctuate as widely as stocks in value, you may choose more conservative bond funds.

- *Money market funds.* If you want to be sure that your invested principal does not drop in value because you may need your money in the short term, you can select a money market fund.

No risk of bankruptcy. No mutual fund has ever failed and probably won't in the future. The way they are structured, their liabilities can never exceed their expenses. Their share value can fluctuate, but this variation doesn't lead to the failure or bankruptcy of a mutual fund company. In fact, since the Investment Company Act of 1940 was passed to regulate the mutual fund industry, no fund has ever gone under.

Custodian bank. The specific securities in which a mutual fund is invested are held at a custodian, a separate organization independent of the mutual fund company. The employment of a custodian ensures that the fund management company can't embezzle your funds and use assets from a better-performing fund to subsidize a poor performer.

COSTS OF MUTUAL FUNDS

There are cost associated with buying a mutual fund. Fees paid at the time of purchase are called commissions. Fees paid at the time of withdrawal are called contingent deferred sales charges. In addition, there are management and operating fees. The costs of investing in mutual funds will be reviewed in Chapter 17.

OTHER THINGS YOU SHOULD KNOW

Unparalleled Structural Safeguards

Why has the mutual fund industry remained remarkably scandal-free for more than a half century? Because of the unparalleled structural safeguards built into the industry. Think of these safeguards as a series of federally mandated checks and balances that govern how fund shareholders' money is received, invested, and held—and the requirement that every fund make extensive, regular reports to its shareholders.

No other financial industry requires so much disclosure to share-holders. These safeguards were begun in 1940, by a landmark piece of legislation called the Investment Company Act of 1940.

How These Safeguards Work

Consider the typical bank mutual fund transaction today. You could live in Denver and write a check for $1,000 at a local bank to purchase a mutual stock fund. The mutual stock fund is located 4,000 miles away in New York City. You have never met with anyone from the mutual stock fund and don't even know anyone living in New York City, but you do know the people who work at your local bank. You learned about this particular mutual fund from your bank's investment representative.

Your dealings with the mutual fund company will be exclusively at the bank. First, you should receive the mutual fund prospectus and an application form from your bank representative before investing. You will fill out the form, and your bank investment representative will place the order on your behalf. (Once you have established an account, you can place an order to your bank investment representative over the telephone.)

A money manager of a mutual fund has no direct access to his or her investors' cash. The fund manager only decides how to invest shareholders' money. It's the custodian who controls the underlying securities, allowing them to be traded or exchanged with other institutional investors only after getting proper documentation from the manager. The upshot of independent custody is that it's very hard for a fund manager to take the money and leave.

The Investment Company Act adds other layers of investor protection as well. Independent accountants must regularly audit every fund. A fund's board of directors, the modern-day trustees, is supposed to negotiate prudent contract terms with the fund's service providers and generally oversee the operation, and the SEC has the power to inspect funds and bring enforcement action against those that break the rules.

In addition, mutual fund firms have legions of compliance lawyers—essentially, in-house cops—paid to make sure that portfolio managers, traders, and others follow the rules.

Do fund managers have a code of conduct? Yes. Under SEC rules, funds are also required to have codes of conduct for fund managers. The codes require advance reporting of personal securities transactions so that there can be no conflict of interest between a manager's personal trades and what he or she does with a fund's securities.

How to Read Newspaper Fund Tables

The first column in Exhibit 10–1 is the abbreviated fund's name; several funds listed under the same heading indicate a family of funds.

The second column, Sell, is the net asset value (NAV) price per share that you now know how to figure. The NAV is identified as the amount per share you would receive if you sold your shares (less any deferred sales charges, if any). So on any given day, you can determine the value of your holdings by multiplying the NAV by the number of shares you own.

The third column, Buy, is the offering price, sometimes called the asking price. This is the price you would pay if you purchased shares that day. The buy price is the NAV plus any sales charges. If it is a no-load fund "NL" will appear in this column. The buy price is the same as the NAV.

The fourth column shows the change in NAV from the day before.

Regardless of your investment goal—steady income, growth, or a combination—mutual funds, combined in a strategic manner to match your goal and objectives, can help supplement your bank account earnings.

EXHIBIT 10–1
Mutual Fund Quotation Table

	Sell	Buy	Chg		Sell	Buy	Chg		Sell	Buy	Chg
AAA Mutual				*Flyer Trust*				*MMT Group*			
Bond	23.96	24.70	+.07	Bluchp	8.25	8.55	+.01	AsianStk	17.49	18.46	−.05
Growth	15.11	15.86	−.02	Growth	12.85	13.63	+.05	EmgMkt	10.13	10.61	+.09
Income	12.61	13.38	−.12	GlBnd	7.24	7.58	−.01	EuroGr	7.27	7.49	+.04
TxFree	7.27	7.49	+.01	HiYld	5.70	5.97	…	FxdInc	13.84	NL	+.02
				Intl	10.13	10.61	−.02	RealEst	20.11	NL	−.19
ABC Funds				MngdGro	9.11	9.54	−.02	Social	19.04	NL	−.12
AggGrth	10.30	10.73	+.31	NYMun	13.61	14.44	+.05	Value	6.55	NL	−.03
Balance	7.65	8.12	+.08	Select	7.73	8.09	+.01				
Growth	17.49	18.46	−.01	Stock	8.09	8.47	…	*MidAtlantic*			
GovtSec	32.38	34.36	+.22	TxExmpt	9.34	9.91	−.03	Bond p	10.55	10.55	+.04
HiYld	11.13	11.65	+.04	Utilty	10.60	11.10	−.03	GloBnd p	9.56	9.56	−.01
PrcMet	18.56	19.69	−.03	WldFnd	10.40	10.95	+.01	GovtSec p	15.12	15.12	+.05
								HiYld p	14.51	14.51	−.01

These funds are ficticous and are for examples only.

P A R T

III

TAX-ADVANTAGED INVESTMENTS

Chapter Eleven

Understanding Tax-Free Municipal Bonds

A municipal bond, commonly called a tax-free or tax-exempt bond, is an investment instrument used to finance municipal governmental activities. The primary purpose for investing in any bond is to earn interest income. Municipal bonds are used to earn tax-free interest income. You pay no federal income tax on the interest generated by a municipal bond or bond fund. Municipal bonds are the only investments paying interest that are tax-exempt, not just tax deferred. They are also exempt from state income taxes in many states. (Ask your bank investment representative about your state.)

There are more than $500 billion worth of municipal bonds outstanding. That is a testimony to the important role played by these instruments in financing the needs of state and local governments. Additionally, years of high taxes have made municipal bonds an integral part of the portfolios of millions of private investors and thousands of large institutional investors.

TAX-FREE VS. TAXABLE

If you need current income, bonds are excellent investments. But how do you know if you should purchase a tax-free municipal bond instead of a taxable bond or taxable bank account?

Many people believe that investing in municipal bonds is only for the wealthy. This is not true. In 1987, for the first time, the IRS included on the 1040 form a line entry for tax-exempt interest earnings. Recent figures based on this information show that approximately one-third of municipal bond investors earned less than $50,000 a year, and more than 18% earned less than $30,000 a year.

The answer to the question of whether to buy taxable or tax-free municipal bonds is this: Buy the one that allows you to retain the most income after you subtract the amount you pay in taxes. It's a matter of comparing taxable and tax-free yields and applying some simple mathematics.

Let's compare some yields. Remember that municipal bonds pay less interest than corporate bonds or bank accounts with the same maturity date, but the interest they pay is tax free.

You should look at retention rates. That's the amount you get to keep after the IRS takes its cut. You find your retention rate by subtracting your marginal tax rate from 1.00. If your marginal tax bracket is 28%, you subtract .28 from 1.00 to find your retention rate of .72. That means you get to retain, or keep, 72% of the interest you earn on a taxable investment.

If the amount of money you retain after taxes from a taxable investment is greater than the interest you earn on a tax-free bond, buy the taxable investment. If you keep more in your pocket from a tax-free bond than a taxable investment after taxes, buy the tax-free bond.

There is another way of looking at the same question. That's by using a measurement called the "equivalent taxable yield." The equivalent taxable yield is the amount you would have to earn on a taxable investment for it to yield after taxes the same amount as a tax-free bond you are considering.

To find the equivalent taxable yield, the amount you would need from a taxable investment to offset the advantage of tax-free income, divide your retention rate (.72 in our example) into the tax-exempt municipal bond yield.

The formula for figuring equivalent tax yield is

$$\text{Equivalent taxable yield} = \frac{\text{Tax-free yield}}{1.00 - (\text{Federal} + \text{State tax})}$$

If a tax-free bond is earning 4%, for example, and you are in the 28% tax-bracket, the formula would be

$$5.55 = \frac{4.00}{.72 \, (1.00 - .28)}$$

EXHIBIT 11–1
Tax-Exempt Bond Funds (Sample Taxable Equivalent Table)

Tax-Exempt Yield	Investor's Marginal Tax Bracket				
	15.0%	28.0%	31.0%	36.0%	39.6%
4.0 %	4.71	5.56	5.80	6.25	6.62
6.0	7.06	8.33	8.70	9.38	9.93
8.0	9.41	11.11	11.59	12.50	13.24

Example: To an investor in a combined (state and federal) marginal tax bracket of 36%, a 6% tax-exempt bond is the same as a 9.26% rate on a taxable investment.

By applying this formula, you learn that you need a taxable investment yielding 5.55% to equal a tax-free bond yielding 4.00%. Exhibit 11–1 shows what you would have to earn on a taxable account at various tax brackets to keep as much interest as if you bought a tax-free bond paying various yields.

TAX-FREE BONDS ARE NOT FOR EVERYONE

Don't be lured by the idea of paying less taxes and make the mistake of investing in bonds that produce tax-free income unless you're in a high enough tax bracket to benefit. Taxable bonds may end up yielding more even after taxes than what you would earn on tax-free investments. Generally, if you are in the 15% federal tax bracket you are better off using taxable accounts for interest income than using tax-free bonds. If you are in the higher tax brackets, you are a good candidate. Just apply the formula above to be sure.

It's common to not know offhand what tax bracket you fall in. Exhibit 11–2 will help you determine your tax bracket.

KINDS OF MUNICIPAL BONDS

There are two different kinds of municipal bonds: general obligation (GO) bonds and revenue bonds. Principal and interest payments on the bonds are made from either taxes or user fees.

EXHIBIT 11–2
1995 Federal Income Tax Brackets and Rates

Singles Taxable Income	Married, Filing Jointly	Federal Tax Rate
Less than $23,350	Less than $39,000	15.0%
$ 23,335–$ 56,549	$ 39,900–$ 94,249	28.0%
$ 56,550–$117,949	$ 94,250–$143,599	31.0%
$117,950–$256,499	$143,600–$256,500	36.0%
Over $256,500	Over $256,500	39.6%

Note: Taxable income levels adjust annually based on the Consumer Price Index. To determine your taxable income, find the "Taxable Income" line (line 37) on your last year's 1040 form. Other categories may apply (i.e., head of household, corporate, trust.)

Interest is paid every six months. GOs are used to raise money for general-purpose projects. The issuing municipality backs the bonds by their "full faith and credit and taxing power." Revenue bonds are issued by different entities that perform public functions: electric utilities, airports, hospitals, universities, and the like. These bonds pay principal and interest from the operation of a specific income-producing facility.

MUNICIPAL BOND SAFETY

Like taxable bonds, municipal bonds can be affected by credit risk and market risk. Credit risk can be reduced substantially by relying on the evaluations of rating services.

Credit Risk and Rating Services

Just as with corporate bonds, the two major independent rating services—Moody's and Standard & Poor's—also cover municipal bonds. Investment-grade ratings range from AAA to BBB− (Standard & Poor's), or Aaa to Baa3 (Moody's). Lower-rated bonds are considered speculative. In addition, many banks and investment firms maintain staffs of professional municipal research analysts to provide input regarding the credit and market attributes of municipal bonds. Ratings are intended to help you evaluate risk and set your own standards for investment. The rule of thumb, however, is to never buy a bond with a rating lower than A, unless you want to speculate.

Market Risk

The ratings tell us something about the bonds' quality and ability to pay timely payments of interest and its principal when it matures. Of course, strong credit backing does not eliminate market risk. The price of municipal bonds fluctuates somewhat in harmony with the rise and fall of interest rates in general. If interest rates go up, the market value of your bond goes down. If interest rates go down, the market price goes up. (See Exhibit 9–1, Chapter 9.) So when it comes to selling your municipal bond before maturity, keep in mind that price fluctuations can produce opportunities for capital gains or losses.

Municipal Bond Insurance

A growing number of bonds carry private insurance against the risk of default. This insurance does not protect against losses due to selling before maturity (market risk). While insured bonds usually carry a lower yield than uninsured issues, they are almost always rated AAA or Aaa. The three major municipal bond insurance firms providing comfort to individuals buying the bonds are the Municipal Bond Insurance Association (MBIA), Financial Guaranty Insurance Company (FGIC), and American Municipal Bond Assurance Co. (AMBAC). Municipal bonds, like all other investments, are *not* covered by the FDIC.

PACKAGED TAX-FREE MUNICIPAL BONDS

Municipal bonds are sold in $5,000 increments but it's difficult to find bonds with good yields in blocks smaller than $10,000–$25,000. And since you always need to diversify, it is difficult to have enough money to buy a balanced portfolio of municipal bonds. You may be thinking that municipal bonds are too difficult to understand and buy for you to invest in them. They may be, as individual issues; that's why bond mutual funds and trusts are so popular.

Tax-Free Unit Investment Trusts

A tax-free unit investment trust, sometimes called a municipal investment trust, is simply a unit investment trust that contains municipal bonds from many issuers. A unit investment trust is an unmanaged portfolio with a fixed maturity. This type of investment trust simply buys municipal bonds and holds them until they mature. When they mature, the principal is paid back to you. Since the portfolio is composed entirely of municipal bonds, the interest receipts are tax free. Interest payments can be received on a monthly, quarterly, or semiannual basis. You can invest in increments as small as $1,000.

Municipal Bond Funds

The difference between a tax-free investment trust and a municipal bond mutual fund is that the fund is managed and the trust is not. The fund manager will buy new bonds when appropriate and sell existing bonds when it's best for the overall safety and total return of the mutual fund.

Municipal bond funds are nothing more than large, diversified, managed groups of municipal bonds. Most municipal bond funds invest in municipal bonds of similar maturity (the number of years before the borrower, in this case the municipality, must pay back the money to the lender).

There are a variety of maturities available. A short-term bond fund concentrates on bonds maturing in the next few years. An intermediate-term fund generally holds bonds that come due within 7–10 years. A long-term municipal bond fund holds bonds maturing in 20 years or so. In contrast to an individual municipal bond that you buy and hold until it matures, a municipal bond fund is always replacing bonds in its portfolio to maintain its average maturity objective.

Municipal bond funds are a convenient way to own municipal bonds when you want to live off dividend income or when you don't want to put all your money in an individual issue.

FEDERALLY TAX-FREE MONEY MARKET FUNDS

These are short-term money market mutual funds comprised of tax-exempt securities that can serve as a substitute to regular money market mutual funds and bank savings accounts if you are in a high tax bracket. Keep in mind, they are not FDIC insured.

Zero Coupon Municipal Bonds

Zero coupon municipal bonds are issued at a deep discount from par, like zero coupon Treasuries. They are for investors seeking capital accumulation and not requiring regular income. You receive only one payment—at maturity—with no interest payments in between. A zero coupon municipal differs from a zero coupon Treasury in that you don't have to pay taxes on the imputed income. Long-range retirement planning and saving for a college nest egg are two possible uses for zero coupon municipal bonds.

The attractive features of municipal bonds. The most attractive feature of municipal bonds is their steady stream of tax-free income, usually arriving every six months, free of federal income tax. In many cases, properly selected bonds issued by your state, municipality, or state agency also provide income free of state and local taxes. Interest on bonds issued by Puerto Rico, the U.S. Virgin Islands, and Guam is exempt from state and local taxes in all 50 states.

Safety. Investment-grade municipal bonds (A-rated or better) have had an excellent history of timely repayment of interest and principal. Even during the Great Depression, more than 98% of all municipalities met their payment obligations; the remainder of those having difficulties eventually met their obligations.

Each bond must be judged on its own merits, but most municipal bonds have demonstrated a historical ability to weather the most difficult economic conditions.

Liquidity. The huge market for municipal bonds means that municipals are highly liquid investments. There is an active secondary market for most issues. The market itself is an over-the-counter network of more than 1,000 broker/dealer and dealer/bank offices throughout the country.

The price you will be offered when you sell a bond is largely determined by market conditions, taking into account the quality of the bond, the source of security, the financial condition of the issuer, the time to maturity, coupon (interest) rates, supply and demand, and other factors affecting the market at that moment.

Flexibility. Municipal bonds are issued in every state, and maturities range from one to 50 years. Generally, the longer the maturity, the higher the interest rate. Thus, they offer virtually limitless choices when buying to meet specific needs and situations.

Capital appreciation. While tax-free income is by far the most common objective of municipal bond buyers, capital gains opportunities are also present. For example, when a discounted bond (one purchased at a price lower than its maturity value) matures, the difference between the initial outlay and the amount of principal returned is considered a capital gain and is taxed accordingly.

A SIMPLE STRATEGY

To keep in line with your basic strategy of diversification, you'll want to spread out your money among different municipal bond funds or trusts, unless you have a substantial amount of money to invest and can diversify sufficiently by creating your own portfolio. Or you'll want to mix a few individual bonds with mutual funds and trusts.

Here's an example of a bank customer who has determined that $100,000 of her assets should be invested in tax-free bonds for income. A simple strategy is to split the investment between an insured tax-free mutual fund ($60,000) that yields 4.00% and four different municipal bonds of $10,000 each ($40,000) that yield 4.50, 5.00, 5.25, and 5.50% because their maturities are staggered over four different years. The mix produces an annual tax-free income of approximately $4,425, or 4.425%, and gives the customer the safety of adequate diversification.

THE BASIC RULE OF PRINCIPAL FLUCTUATION

Individual municipal bonds, municipal bond trusts, and municipal bond funds are long-term investments; if you have to sell before they reach maturity, they may lose some of their underlying value. However, they may also gain value. It depends on where interest rates are at the time you need to sell. If you hold individual bonds and trusts to their maturity, you will receive your principal back in full. Bond mutual funds never mature; therefore, they are most suitable for you if you want current income for a long period and don't care what happens to the principal in the meantime.

SUMMARY

Municipal bonds, commonly called tax-free or tax-exempt bonds, are the only investments whose interest is totally tax free. Tax-deferred investments are also available and have a place in most bank customers' investment plans. Tax-deferred annuities are the subject of the next two chapters.

Chapter Twelve

Understanding Fixed Annuities

An annuity is an investment unlike any other investment. It's a tax-deferred investment issued by an insurance company and distributed by your bank's investment program. Although it is issued by an insurance company, it is not an insurance policy. It's a deposit account with an insurance company, not insurance of any kind.

There are two types of tax-deferred annuities: fixed and variable. A fixed annuity pays a fixed interest rate that generally accrues monthly and compounds yearly. Your principal and interest are guaranteed by the assets of the issuing insurance company. Annuities, even those you get from your bank, are not covered by the FDIC.

A variable annuity is different than a fixed annuity in that the value of your principal, and the interest you earn, can fluctuate. Money you invest in a variable annuity is divided into subaccounts of stocks, bonds, and other investment vehicles. In this respect, a variable annuity is like a tax-deferred mutual fund family. You'll learn more about variable annuities in the next chapter.

A fixed annuity can be further defined by its two phases, the accumulation phase, when the funds are paid in and build on a tax-deferred basis, and the payout phase, when the funds are distributed.

THE ACCUMULATION PHASE

Annuities stand apart from other investments primarily because of their tax-deferral feature. Earnings on an annuity are tax deferred if you leave them in the annuity. When you withdraw the earnings, they are taxed at your current tax rate.

Tax deferral is a powerful way to accumulate assets over a period of time. When you defer your taxes using an annuity, you keep in your control the money that would otherwise be paid in taxes. You earn interest on both the IRS's money and your own money. Having all that money at work for you enables you to accumulate a large nest egg more quickly than if you paid the taxes along the way and only had your money alone working for you.

Exhibit 12–1 illustrates how a $50,000 investment in an annuity grows at 7% compared to 7% in a taxable account. As you can see, your money grows faster using a tax-deferred annuity. The taxes must eventually be paid when you withdraw money from your annuity. However, the great thing about an annuity is that even after paying the taxes upon withdrawal, you have more money than if you would have paid the taxes along the way.

Using the example in Exhibit 12–1, if you had a combined state and federal tax rate of 41% and you took all your money out and paid the taxes all at once (this is the most costly possible way, taxwise, to withdraw from an annuity), you would still have $134,665 left. That's $22,337 more than if you had paid the taxes along the way. In this example, tax deferral added an additional 19% to the after-tax total amount.

THE PAYOUT PHASE

You are probably not going to withdraw all your money at the same time, although you can if you choose. Chances are, you will use your annuity to generate income for your retirement years instead. When you take money out of your annuity, it is called the payout phase or the distribution phase. All withdrawals are taxable (except the portion that is return of your original deposit) and may be subject to a 10% IRS penalty if you are under 59-1/2. This IRS penalty is the reason most fixed-annuity customers tend to be in their 50s or older.

Besides taking your money out all at once, there are two choices for withdrawal. First, you can take out interest or interest and principal in any amount you specify until all your money is

EXHIBIT 12–1
The Power of Tax Deferral

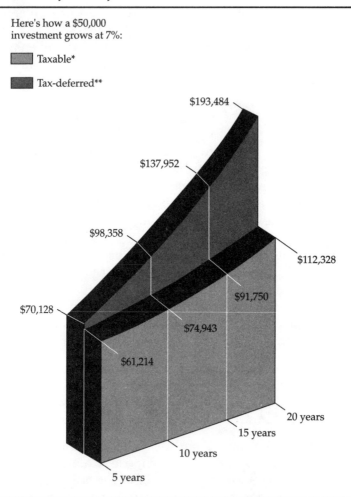

Here's how a $50,000
investment grows at 7%:

☐ Taxable*

■ Tax-deferred**

$193,484

$137,952

$98,358

$112,328

$70,128

$91,750

$74,943

$61,214

20 years

15 years

10 years

5 years

This hypothetical chart is intended only to illustrate the advantage of tax deferral.

*Taxable results assume no withdrawals and a combined 35% federal and 5% state tax rate.

**Tax-deferred results assume no withdrawals and deduction of all applicable fees and charges.

withdrawn. This can be done in a systematic manner using periodic payments you determine or only when you specifically request money be sent.

Second, you can turn your annuity over to the insurance company in exchange for guaranteed periodic payments. This is called annuitization of your annuity contract. Using this method, the insurance company starts making a series of payments consisting of principal and earnings for a defined period of time to you, someone else you choose, or to your designated beneficiary if you are deceased. Among the payout options are the following:

1. *Fixed payment.* These payments are for a fixed period, say 10 years, for example.
2. *Lifetime payment.* These fixed payments are made until you die.
3. *Lifetime with period certain.* These fixed payments continue for a designated period even if you die before the period ends.
4. *Joint and last survivor.* These fixed payments continue until the death of the last survivor. This is a common choice for a married couple.

The amount of the payments is determined by the interest rate at the time of annuitization and the option you choose. These options are best for those people who are concerned that they will not outlive their money. Once you select one of these options you cannot reverse or change your choice.

Although it is important to know the basics of your withdrawal options, you don't need to decide how to withdraw your money now. Wait until you need it. At that time you can work with your bank investment representative to determine the best choice for you. Until that time, use your annuity as a vehicle for accumulating assets. The more you have in it when it's time to take income, the greater your income will be.

This point can be illustrated using the examples in Exhibit 12–1. Suppose at retirement you want to withdraw all your future yearly earnings to supplement your income. Suppose that your money continues to earn 7%, as it had in the past, just to keep this example simple. If you had used a taxable investment, you would have accumulated $112,328 that would generate $7,862 a year in income. Of course, the income will be taxed.

Contrast this to what you would earn if you had used the tax-deferred annuity. The $193,484 you accumulated would now generate, at the same 7%, an annual income of $13,543. That's $5,681 more than the income off the taxable account. Of course, the $13,543 must also be taxed because you took it out of the annuity.

Why the big difference? Because the annuity still contains all those tax-deferred dollars that must eventually be taxed. But, as long as they stay in the annuity, they earn interest and generate income for you. It is possible, if you choose the right annuity, to keep the tax-deferred portion earning income for you and sheltered from taxation until your death. At that time, however, the IRS must be paid the taxes owed on the deferred earnings. There is no 10% IRS penalty at death, even if you die before age 59.

BUYING AND SURRENDERING YOUR ANNUITY

The process of buying the annuity is different from buying a mutual fund or other investment. As the applicant, you fill out an application and write a check to your bank or its brokerage unit, who forwards it to the insurance company. The annuity policy (which looks much like an insurance policy) is delivered to your bank investment representative, normally within two weeks. Your bank investment representative then delivers the policy to you. Upon receipt, you are allowed a "free look," which is at least a 10-day period during which you can reevaluate the annuity and rescind it if you desire. You should keep the annuity policy in a safe place because you must surrender it in order to withdraw your money. (It can be replaced if lost, but only after paying a fee and completing extensive paperwork.)

Many insurance companies that provide annuities offer lobby-issued policies that have the annuity policy attached to the application. The application is completed, a copy is removed, and you leave with the policy in hand. The advantage of a lobby-issued annuity is that it goes into effect immediately. You still have a free-look period, but it also begins immediately. These lobby-issued policies are sometimes referred to as annuity certificates or immediate-issue policies.

A fixed annuity can be either single premium (deposit) or flexible premium. A single-premium annuity requires an initial lump sum deposit (generally a minimum of $5,000) and does not accept any future contributions. Flexible-premium annuities can accept future contributions and often allow a smaller initial deposit.

You pay no front-end commissions (loads) when purchasing an annuity. Your entire investment amount goes into the policy and begins earning interest. Your bank's investment program is paid a commission by the issuing insurance company. Over the life of the annuity, the insurance company will earn enough to recoup the commission as well as make a profit from investing your money at higher rates than you are paid—similar to how you bank earns money on deposits.

Although there is no up-front commission, there are usually back-end surrender charges for early withdrawals from an annuity. In other words, there are penalties for early withdrawal, just as there are penalties for early withdrawal from CDs.

Annuity withdrawal charges and the length of time they apply to the policy vary widely across the industry. An example, however, would be a 7% first-year charge that declines one percentage point per year. After the seventh year, there are no withdrawal charges. In this case, the annuity issuer needs seven years to recoup the commission it paid and make enough money to stay financially sound, hence the seven-year penalty period. One thing that sets annuities apart from CDs is that the insurance company will not dip into your original principal to satisfy your penalty. Your bank can take part of your principal to pay your early withdrawal penalty on a CD.

A newer trend in the industry is to offer annuities with a "market-value adjuster" to replace or offset early surrender penalties. With a market-value adjuster, your principal is adjusted down if current interest rates have risen higher than your annuity is paying. In this case, you're penalized for leaving early. Conversely, your principal it adjusted up if current rates have fallen below what your annuity is paying. In this case, you will get a bonus if you get out of your annuity early.

Most fixed annuities also have a 10% annual free withdrawal provision that gives the you access to 10% of the annuity value annually without paying any surrender charges. Any distributions above 10% annually are subject to the surrender charges. And remember that all distributions in excess of your original deposit are subject to taxes and a 10% IRS penalty if the annuitant (and/or owner) is under 59-1/2 years old.

UNFAMILIAR TERMS

When you complete the annuity application, you will come across some terms you may not be familiar with . Besides the life insurance company, an annuity involves three parties: the contract owner, the annuitant, and the beneficiary. (There are also joint contract owners, contingent annuitants, and beneficiaries.)

The contract owner is the person who invests the money and controls all decisions relative to withdrawals and so on. The annuitant is the person whose life the annuity is based on. In most cases, you would be the contract owner and the annuitant. When the annuitant dies, the money is paid to the beneficiary. This is most often a spouse or another heir.

However, there are many different ways to set up your annuity to provide income and security to yourself and/or others. Your bank investment representative will guide you through the annuity application and help you determine who should be the owner, annuitant, and beneficiary and if anyone should be joint owner or contingent annuitant and contingent beneficiary. You'll be amazed at the number of financial and estate planning needs an annuity can satisfy just by matching the appropriate people to the appropriate spot on the application.

BENEFITS BEYOND TAX DEFERRAL

Fixed annuities are the second most popular investment, behind bond mutual funds, used by bank customers today to expand the power of their money beyond bank accounts. They are popular primarily because they're tax-deferred. There are, however, many other benefits of owning an annuity that should not be overlooked.

Competitive Fixed Interest Rates

The interest rate of a fixed annuity is locked in for at least a year. After the first year, the rate is renewed at a level determined by what the underlying investments (usually bonds) can safely pay. Most annuities offer longer terms to choose from as well. Annuity rates are generally equal to or higher than CD rates of comparable maturity. Ask your bank investment representative to show you a history of renewal rates for any annuity you are considering.

Guaranteed Principal and Interest

Your principal investment doesn't fluctuate in value and is, along with your interest, 100% guaranteed by the issuing insurance company. Even if you surrender your policy and incur penalties, you will never receive less than you invested.

Safety

Insurance companies are regulated by the insurance commissioner in the state they are headquartered. They are held to strict standards when it comes to investing their assets and your premiums (deposits). Because of their past performance as an industry and due to the safeguards enforced by insurance regulations, they are permitted to use the term *guaranteed* when referring to their annuities. Don't get confused, however; they are not FDIC insured. You should review with your bank investment representative the safety rating of every company whose annuity you are considering before you invest. Annuities are rated for safety by several companies including A.M. Best, Moody's, Standard & Poor's, and Duff & Phelps.

Death Benefits/Avoiding Probate

Your annuity contract will pass upon your death directly to the beneficiary you designate on your annuity application. The entire value will avoid the legal delays and expenses of probate and be immediately available to your beneficiary to spend, reinvest, or annuitize for guaranteed income. Your beneficiary is required to pay the deferred taxes when the money is taken out of the annuity. If you annuitize your contract before your death, your beneficiary may or may not receive anything, depending on the income option you selected.

No Fees

As noted earlier, you don't pay any fees or commissions when purchasing an annuity. You are subject to early withdrawal penalties, but it is rare that these last beyond seven years.

Bailout Rate

This feature is offered on some annuities and allows the customer to surrender the annuity with no penalty if the interest rate falls below a certain floor, usually 1– 2% below the initial rate.

Bonus Rate

Many annuities are now offering a bonus of typically 1% for the first year of your contract. This bonus is to entice you to buy the annuity. Remember that a bonus rate is only for the first year. If you invest in a bonus rate annuity, you are virtually guaranteed that your rate will decline at least the amount of the bonus after the first year.

Liquidity

Annuities should only be used if you can commit your money for the long term, at least until the withdrawal penalties expire, because the value of tax deferral isn't fully realized unless given adequate time. There are times, however, when you need to make emergency withdrawals from long-term accounts. Most annuities can accommodate an annual 10% withdrawal without you incurring a penalty. In addition, many annuities now allow penalty-free withdrawals if you are disabled or are confined to a nursing home.

Flexibility

Annuities are flexible and therefore able to fill many special needs not described in this chapter, such as reducing income tax on Social Security income (see Chapter 15), passing assets to individuals not listed in your will, and gifting money to charities, to name a few. They are also exchangeable. If you desire to switch from one insurance company annuity to another, you can do so and continue your tax deferral.

SUMMARY

An annuity is a very safe investment. Industry surveys show that the primary reason investors buy annuities is for their safety, not their rate, and because they want a tax-advantaged investment. The primary purpose for using an annuity in your investment plan is to accumulate assets for future income. Another purpose, if you are already retired, would be to provide income you cannot outlive. However, if you need current income, you are usually better served by using stock and bond mutual funds or individual bonds.

Now that you have an understanding of the basics of fixed annuities, it's time to move on to what many experts consider the near-perfect investment: variable annuities.

Chapter Thirteen

Understanding Variable Annuities

Y ou learned in the last chapter that there are two basic types of tax-deferred annuities: fixed and variable. Fixed and variable annuities have many features in common. Both are tax deferred, have no commission to purchase, and have early withdrawal penalties. In addition, they both have annual penalty-free access to 10% of their value and a 10% IRS penalty for withdrawal of earnings prior to age 59-1/2. They are both issued by life insurance companies, are available at your bank, and are designed primarily for accumulation of assets for future income. However, they can both generate current income.

Other features in common include the avoidance of probate, a wide choice on income options (on demand, life, a specified number of years you choose, etc.), and estate planning capabilities depending on your choice of the annuitant, owner, and beneficiary. Also, most fixed and variable annuities pass directly to the designated beneficiary upon your death without penalty even if you die before your withdrawal charges expire.

These features, which variable annuities have in common with fixed annuities, coupled with the "variable" features that will be discussed beginning on page 123, are what make variable annuities the *near*-perfect investment for many investors.

POPULARITY OF VARIABLE ANNUITIES

Variable annuities are not new. However, they've become more exciting to investors in the last 10 years because they are one of the last tax shelters left. They have surged in popularity since the Tax Reform Act of 1986 eliminated other types of tax shelters, including limited partnerships. In addition, they have benefited from the surge in popularity of mutual funds over the last decade. It stands to reason that if mutual funds, because of their professional management, ease of ownership, diversification, and excellent performance, are popular, a tax-deferred version would be popular as well.

Many investors have a large percentage of their assets earmarked for long-term, retirement-oriented investments. The best way to accumulate for retirement is to use the benefits of tax deferral. Retirement accounts, such as IRAs and 401(k)s are tax deferred and are great vehicles, but they have a limit to the amount you can put in them each year. Tax-deferred fixed and variable annuities do not. Therefore, they are the investment of choice for many people wanting to save all they can for their retirement.

"VARIABLE" FEATURES

Unlike a fixed annuity, where the insurance company guarantees that your money will grow at a specified rate for a specified period of time, a variable annuity's rate of return is not guaranteed. It varies, hence the term *variable annuity.* In a variable annuity, your rate of return is determined by the combined performance of the investments you select from a broad range of mutual fund-like subaccounts offered by the insurance company.

Subaccounts

The subaccounts are, in effect, mutual funds offered by the annuity. These funds can be managed by the insurance company or contracted out to other investment managers, including mutual fund groups. These specific subaccounts, however, are available only to annuity owners, not the general public. The types of subaccounts vary from variable annuity to variable annuity, but typically include at least a common stock fund, a bond fund, and a money market fund. Other types of funds commonly offered include international stock funds, balanced funds, high-yield funds, government bond funds, and managed assets funds. (Most variable annuities also include a fixed account as one of their options, which is not technically a subaccount. It is like a fixed annuity inside a variable annuity. It generally pays a fixed rate that is less than that paid by a fixed annuity.)

One unbeatable feature of a variable annuity is that via the subaccounts you can choose your own investments and have them be tax deferred. You may choose for example to put 50% in stocks, 30% in bonds, and 20% in money markets. With these subaccounts, there is also professional investment management as well as diversification—not only in terms of the types of financial assets you choose as stated above, but in terms of the number of securities in each asset category. For example, 50% of your money may be in the stock subaccount, but the stock subaccount may own 50 to 100 different stocks.

Performance of Variable Annuities

In the last decade, the quality of management and the resulting performance has improved to the point where variable annuities rival mutual funds in total return. Rather than having to choose from a group of often lackluster insurance company funds, as was the case years ago, many variable annuity buyers now find a spectrum of high-performance investment options included in their subaccount choices. This often means top funds run by the brightest money management names around and the ability to switch among funds and management groups. This has significantly contributed to the increased use of variable annuities by those who want to maximize the power of their savings.

Safety of Subaccounts

The principal and interest of a fixed annuity are backed by the assets of the issuing insurance company. With subaccounts, you get whatever the account earns or doesn't earn. In other words, variable annuity subaccounts, like mutual funds, go up and down in value based on the value of their underlying holdings.

However, another important point regarding these subaccounts is that they are not available to the insurance company's creditors should the company run into financial difficulty. The subaccounts are divisions of a separate account that is set apart from the insurance company's general account. The general account, which backs fixed annuities, can be reached by the company's creditors. Subaccounts are kept separate. (The fixed account inside a variable annuity is most often considered part of a company's general account.)

At the same time, however, the financial condition of the insurance company should not be ignored. The insurance aspect of a variable annuity in terms of the death benefit, which is discussed later, is dependent on the insurance company's financial health.

Tax-Free Switching

Not only can you choose to spread out your money among the different subaccounts a variable annuity offers, you can switch your money from one subaccount to another as time goes on without paying taxes on the gain. As long as your money remains under the umbrella of the variable annuity, you can "sell" and "buy" by transferring among subaccounts and not pay current taxes on any gains (see Exhibit 13–1). This tax-deferral capability is a significant advantage of a variable annuity over a mutual fund or individual security.

As your life situation changes, as you get older for example, your needs and objectives change. The different subaccounts allow you to change the allocation of your assets to meet these life changes. Switches among subaccounts can be made with a phone call, and, again, there are no tax consequences for switches inside an annuity unlike switching among mutual fund accounts, which is taxable. However, some variable annuities charge a fee for "excessive" switching and restrict the amount that can be switched out of the fixed account as well as how often the fixed account can be accessed.

Tax-Deferred Stocks

A major reason for owning a variable annuity rather than a fixed annuity is to take advantage of the bond subaccounts and particularly the common stock subaccounts. Historically, common stocks have kept well ahead of inflation and have outperformed fixed-income securities as well. For the period 1926 through 1994, common stocks had a compound, annual total return of 10.2%;

EXHIBIT 13–1
Under the Variable Annuity's Tax-Deferred Umbrella

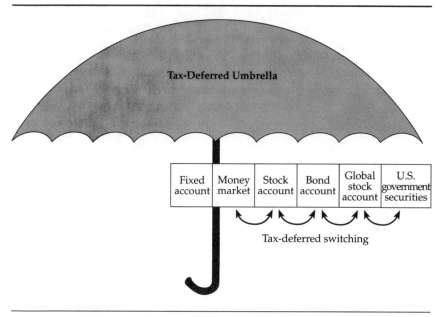

long-term corporate bonds returned 4.8%; Treasury bills returned 3.7%; and inflation was 3.5%. For additional perspective, for the 10-year period of 1985 through 1994, those figures were 14.4%, 11.6%, 5.8%, and 6.2%, respectively. Clearly, common stocks stayed well ahead of inflation and were superior to bonds and Treasury bills in total return. The price for this superiority is, of course, volatility of principal.

Flexible Deposits

Variable annuities offer you flexibility in terms of the payments into them. A single premium (deposit) involves one lump sum payment into the annuity. The flexible premium plan opens the annuity with a low minimum such as $5,000 or $10,000. You may make additional contributions into the variable annuity as you wish. Sums deposited all at once, or over time, purchase "accumulation units" in the subaccount(s) you designate, which are comparable to mutual fund shares.

People who want to invest a lump sum in a common stock subaccount but are afraid the stock market is too high, can instead place the money into the money market subaccount, for example, and then have it transferred systematically into the stock subaccount at regular intervals. This is called dollar cost averaging (see page 50, Chapter 6). For example, you could put $25,000 into a money market subaccount, which has a stable principal, and dollar cost average it over time into the common stock subaccount. That way, you can gradually get into stocks without worrying that you're getting in at the top of the market. Or, if you choose, you can just add more premium (make a deposit) each month from your checking account until you reach the desired amount in the stock subaccount. The advantage of using the dollar cost averaging within the variable annuity between subaccounts is that while you're waiting, all the money is tax deferred. The portion you leave in your checking or other bank account is not tax deferred until it is added to the variable annuity.

Death Benefit

During the accumulation period, variable annuities offer a death benefit, which guarantees that if the value of the annuity at the time of the annuitant's death is less than the amount invested, the life insurance company will pay the beneficiary the amount invested. Some companies also pay additional interest, and some will increase the death benefit periodically. For example, if you buy an annuity for $100,000, which seven years later is worth $150,000, the company might increase the death benefit from $100,000 to $150,000 at that time.

This death benefit feature is especially valuable if you are in your later years and have money you want to pass on to your heirs that you don't need in order to support yourself. You can invest in variable annuity stock subaccounts to earn the maximum possible for your heirs, but at the same time be guaranteed by the issuing insurance company that your heirs will get what you invested or what it has grown to, whichever is greater. A stock account with no risk to your heirs is one of the features that make variable annuities excellent investments for older Americans who have more than enough for their needs.

Withdrawal Options

As with fixed annuities, you can withdraw your money from a variable annuity all at once or a little at a time. When it comes time to start periodic withdrawals (annuitization) from a variable annuity, accumulation units are converted to "annuity units." Typically, a certain number of annuity units are sold each period to provide the checks to the annuitant. The checks, however, are based on the value of the units. For example, if 10 annuity units are sold for each periodic payment, but the value per unit changes due to the underlying investment such as a subaccount in stocks, the payment amount will change. If the annuity unit is worth $10 one month and $11 the next month, the monthly payments will be $100 and $110, respectively. Of course, like mutual fund shares, the annuity units can also decrease in value, resulting in a lower payment than in the previous period.

Each annuity payment consists of an investment return (which is fully taxable) and a return of original capital (which is not taxable, assuming the contributions into the annuity were made with after-tax dollars). The percentage of each payment that is taxable income is determined by an "exclusion ratio." This ratio is calculated by the insurance company and is the ratio of the investment in the contract to the expected return under the contract. Once the annuitant has received a return of capital equal to the investment in the contract, subsequent payments are fully taxable (annuities purchased before August 14, 1982, receive different tax treatment).

One of the biggest concerns of retirees is outliving their income. This concern can be alleviated by selecting a "life annuity" option. With a variable annuity, the fixed number of annuity units will be sold for each payment as long as the annuitant lives. This provides the largest annuity payment of all the annuitization options. When the annuitant dies, there is nothing left for heirs, which is the major reason many people do not select this option. However, it does satisfy the initial concern regarding outliving your income.

A more popular withdrawal option is a joint and survivor life annuity. It makes annuity payments for as long as one of two people is alive. For a couple in retirement, if one dies, payments continue for as long as the surviving spouse lives, although sometimes the amount of each payment decreases in this situation.

The following are other withdrawal options available through variable annuities:

1. *Life and period certain.* Should the annuitant die before the end of the period selected by the owner, say a period of 10 or 20 years for example, the beneficiary continues to receive the annuity payments until that period is reached.

2. *Life and refund certain.* At the time of the annuitant's death the beneficiary is refunded any amount of the investment in the annuity not previously paid to the annuitant.

3. *Joint and survivor life annuity with period certain.* The beneficiary continues to receive payments up to the period selected by the owner if both annuitants die before that period.

4. *Joint and survivor life annuity with refund certain.* The beneficiary is refunded any amount of the investment not received by the annuitants at the time of the last one's death.

Again, variable annuities have great flexibility in meeting your needs or the needs or your loved ones during annuitization.

It is important to remember, however, that once the annuity payments begin, the annuity option usually cannot be changed. For this reason, it may be appropriate for you not to lock into an annuitization plan, but to withdraw funds on an as-wanted basis. In some rare cases, a lump sum withdrawal may be appropriate and is possible if a contract has not been annuitized. But, as with fixed annuities, withdrawal decisions should be made in consultation with your bank investment representative when you need income. Now is the time to focus on tax-deferred accumulation.

Costs

There is no front-end sales commission when you buy fixed or variable annuities. All of your money goes to work at once. However, there normally will be a sliding scale of surrender charges, such as 7% the first year, 6% the second year, and so on until the charges vanish. Since only long-term assets should be invested in annuities, you should never have to incur a surrender charge except in an emergency situation.

With variable annuities, there are some internal expenses you need to be aware of. There is an annual contract maintenance fee of $25–$40 and a mortality and expense-risk charge that can range from 0.5%–1.75% of the average account value. These last two charges provide for the guaranteed death benefit and the assurance that contract expenses will not be increased over the life of the annuity. The subaccounts also have operating expenses similar to regular mutual funds. The size of these fees has a direct bearing on how long it takes for the tax-deferred advantage to offset these expenses. The higher the investment returns, of course, the more quickly the expenses will be offset. As a result, a strong case can be made that a purchaser of a variable annuity should intend to put at least some, and perhaps all, of the money into a common stock subaccount.

In addition to these internal fees, don't forget that the federal government will impose a 10% penalty on any withdrawal of the earnings, other than those due to death and disability, made before the age of 59-1/2. Regular income tax must be paid on earnings taken out, and it is assumed that earnings are withdrawn first and then principal.

NEAR PERFECT, BUT NOT PERFECT FOR EVERYONE

Variable annuities aren't for every investor. The variable annuity makes excellent sense when you have tapped out the rest of your retirement account options, such IRAs and 401(k)s. Variable annuities, like few other tools, can also be used to pass on assets to beneficiaries without going through probate. That can save on the publicity and expense of probate. Variable annuities are excellent long-term investment vehicles when you want to combine the benefits of tax deferral and investing in the stock and bond markets. But they are clearly not for you if you need immediate income that can't fluctuate or if your investment time horizon is short term.

Most bank customers suited to variable annuities are in their 50s and 60s, planning for retirement. These are people who have minimized their obligations, have money coming in, and are looking for something to maximize the power of their retirement savings.

The tax benefits are clearly most valuable for you if you are in the higher tax brackets, but variable annuities are suitable for investors of all income levels. Many contracts have initial investment requirements of $5,000 and accept additional amounts of $100. But, don't get caught up in the idea of beating the IRS at all cost. If you are in a low tax bracket and expect your tax bracket to increase in the future, you may be better off investing in taxable mutual funds or other investments and paying the taxes now rather than deferring.

Some investors use variable annuities to fund nonretirement expenses, such as children's college costs or saving for a house. There is one pitfall, however, that you have to be careful of, namely that withdrawal of earnings before age 59 1/2 creates a 10% tax penalty. Annuities of all types are designed primarily for accumulation of assets in preparation for retirement and income generation during retirement. That's why the IRS penalty is imposed for early withdrawal. Given this, other uses are possible, but need to be examined carefully.

SUMMARY

In summary, there are advantages offered through variable annuities that you can get in other investments, but there is no other investment that combines so many important features into one vehicle. The following are the most significant advantages offered by variable annuities:

- *Tax-deferred compounding.* This is the most important feature. The higher your combined federal-plus-state bracket, the greater your benefit. Also, the sooner you start, the greater the advantage. In addition, annuities can help reduce the taxes retirees pay on their Social Security income. (See Chapter 15.)

- *Growth potential.* By choosing well-managed stock-oriented funds, you can get long-term growth as you would with regular mutual funds.
- *Variety of choices.* Many variable annuities offer a half dozen or more subaccounts. The selection may include several specialized products, such as index funds, real estate funds, and international funds.
- *Diversification.* Each subaccount contains a significant number of individual securities to maximize return and reduce risk.
- *Professional money management.* Subaccounts are managed by some of the world's leading money managers, and their total returns are often impressive.
- *No investment ceiling.* Unlike tax-qualified retirement plans, you face no maximum on what you can invest during the accumulation period.
- *Switch privileges.* You can move money among different types of asset categories under the tax-deferral umbrella of a variable annuity. You pay no taxes until you take the money out of the annuity.
- *Guaranteed death benefit.* You are guaranteed that on the annuitant's (usually your) death, the beneficiary will get at least what you originally invested, even if you invest in subaccounts that can go down in value.
- *No commissions.* All of your money goes to work for you immediately.
- *Flexible deposits.* You can deposit large or small amounts, and you can add to your variable annuity at any time.
- *Frequent statements.* You receive frequent statements detailing the activity in your subaccounts. The statements are often monthly but at least quarterly.

IV

STRATEGIES FOR SENIORS

Chapter Fourteen

Preparing for Retirement

I f you are not yet retired, retirement plans (accounts) are your most important tax-advantaged investment vehicles. These retirement plans, such as pension and profit-sharing plans, individual retirement accounts (IRAs), 401(k)s, SEP-IRAs, and Keoghs, should be used to their maximum before you use annuities, tax-free bonds, or taxable investments to save for retirement.

Once money is in a retirement account, any interest, dividends, and appreciation adds to your account without being taxed. These accounts don't allow for permanent avoidance of taxes. You pay taxes when you withdraw the money, generally anytime after the age of 59 1/2. (Prior withdrawals are penalized 10%, plus taxed at your then-current rate.) You must also begin taking the money out at age 70 1/2. However, while the money is invested you are, in effect, compounding interest and earnings on the government's money as well as your own, resulting in a faster-growing nest egg.

Retirement accounts not only provide the unbeatable benefit of tax deferral, they provide a tax deduction as well. For example, if your contribute $1,000 to a retirement account such as an IRA or 401(k), you can deduct it from your earned income, thus reducing your taxable income. If your combined federal and state income tax bracket is 35%, for example, you will pay $350 less in income taxes because of a $1,000 contribution to your retirement account. This, in effect, means the government contributes $350 to your retirement for every $1,000 you contribute. Where else, but in a retirement account, can you get an instant 35% return?

Nowhere! So, always put into your retirement accounts the maximum amount you are allowed to invest before investing after-tax dollars for retirement. Remember, to invest $1,000 in after-tax dollars you have to earn $1,350.

Of course, although maximizing your retirement plan contributions is a must, it's only the first step, because the maximum you are allowed to contribute probably isn't enough to result in your having enough money to retire.

TIME TO GET SERIOUS

Before you know it, your retirement day will be here. If ever there is an event that needs advanced planning, retirement is it. Whatever your age, the best time to start planning is now. Sure, it is better to start planning when you're young, so you have time for your investments to grow. But, chances are, if you're like most people, you haven't given it much thought unless you are over the age of 55.

If you're approaching retirement age in the next 10 years and you haven't done much planning or saving, you are at a serious disadvantage. The situation isn't hopeless if you take immediate action. Regardless of your age, but especially if you are over age 50 and just now getting started or if you have done only a little saving and planning, it's best to begin your serious preparations by asking yourself four questions:

1. How much income will I need each year after I retire?
2. How much money is currently working for me that will be used to generate my income when I retire?
3. How much money will I need by the time I retire to generate the income I need?
4. How much more money must I invest each month/year to have enough at retirement?

Enough Is All You Need

The answers to these questions are best reached with the help of your bank investment representative, but you can determine accurate answers yourself using the information that follows.

The answer to the first question depends on many factors, some of which you can control and some of which you cannot control. Most people aren't expecting to continue their current lifestyle during retirement. They just want "enough," to not be wanting for the necessities and a few luxuries. They also want to remain self-sufficient, to not outlive their money.

Two recent studies[1] reveal that most Americans feel an adequate retirement, having enough, would be to have an income of about 60% of their current income. Both studies also indicate that a majority of preretirees are confident they can achieve this level of income after retirement. However, the studies also clearly show that most Americans are mostly talk when it comes to planning and saving for the dream of having enough when retired. Those who don't take action by planning and investing will have no more than a dream when the time comes.

The 60% level is a good benchmark, but it is important to gauge your personal expectations by evaluating your own lifestyle and determining how much *your* financial needs and wants will change at retirement. The best way to do this is to examine your current annual expenses and compare them to what you think they will be during retirement. Use Exhibit 14–1 to assist you.

You now have an idea of the amount of income you will need during retirement. It might be more or less than the 60% others estimate. Now that you have your personal estimate, plan on inflation increasing it. Inflation is one of the things you have no control over, but need to plan for because the chances are it will eat into your lifestyle during retirement. Even with today's modest inflation rates, you will need almost $140,000 in 20 years to maintain a $50,000 lifestyle. And the average 55-year old today will be alive in 20 years. Many people age 65 will be alive as well.

So, to answer the question of how much income you will need each year, estimate it using Exhibit 14–1, then add up to 5% more each year to account for the impact of inflation.

[1] *Promises to Keep: How Leaders and the Public Respond to Saving and Retirement,* report from the Public Agenda and the Employee Benefit Research Institute, 1994: the Oppenheimer Funds/*Money Magazine* Retirement Survey, 1994.

EXHIBIT 14–1
Your Expenses after Retirement

For each item, write your current annual expenditure and then estimate the annual expenditure upon retirement.		
Expenses That Usually Decrease	*$ Now*	*$ Retirement*
Mortgage Payments (eventually eliminated)		
Food		
Clothing		
Taxes (income and Social Security)		
Debt repayment (hopefully eliminated)		
Transportation		
Disability income insurance (probably eliminated)		
Life insurance		
Household furnishings		
Personal care		
Medical insurance (often reduces at age 65, but increases later)		
Savings and investments		
Total expenses that decrease		
Expenses That Usually Increase		
Rent		
Property tax		
House upkeep (repairs and maintenance)		
Utilities and telephone		
Auto, home, and liability insurance		
Long-term-care insurance		
Vacation and travel		
Recreation and entertainment		
Contributions and gifts		
Total expenses that increase		
Total expenses (decrease + increase)		

Reprinted from: *The Financial Monitor*, American Society of CLU & ChFC.

TAKE INVENTORY

You have an estimate of what you will need; now complete an inventory of the assets you currently have working for you. This will later help you determine if you are going to fall short of what you need. There are three components to your future retirement income: Social Security, employer-sponsored pensions, and personal savings.

Inventory each of these three areas so you know where you currently stand.

Social Security

The amount of your Social Security income will be based on what you contribute in the years prior to retirement. Therefore, it is important that the Social Security Administration has accurate records of your contributions. You can request a record of your earnings, Form SSA-7004, by calling 800-772-1213. You should check this record for accuracy every three–five years. The report you receive will also estimate your income if you were to retire or if you became disabled.

When you examine this report, you will be in for a shock if you're like 39% of Americans who plan on Social Security as their sole source of income during retirement. A single person, age 65, who earned over $61,200 in 1995, can get a maximum annual benefit of only $14,388. A retiree, with a spouse who didn't work, can receive a maximum of $21,582. If both spouses worked, a married couple can receive up to $28,776 if each earned $61,200 a year or more prior to retirement. There will be slight increases over the years due to cost-of-living adjustments. It is plain to see that these amounts are considerably less than 60% of a $61,200 income.

Also, note that half your Social Security income will be subject to federal income tax if you have additional income each year while retired that results in you earning, including your Social Security income, over $44,000 per couple or $34,000 per individual. Depending on how much more you earn above these levels, up to 85% of your Social Security income could be subject to federal income tax. (See Chapter 15 for details and a strategy for reducing this tax.) The bottom line is that Social Security income alone is not enough to retire on.

But, it's more than most people 20, 30, and 40 years old say they believe they will get. It is impossible to tell at this point what the future will bring, but there are valid reasons for their concerns. According to the Social Security Administration, at the end of World War II there were 42 workers paying into Social Security for each person receiving benefits. Today, three people contribute for each recipient. Projections are that by 2030—when most Baby Boomers will have retired—just two working people will contribute for each person receiving benefits. It just won't be possible to provide adequate benefits with so few people contributing.

Employer-Sponsored Pension Plans

The second component to your retirement income comes from pension plans. In years past, company pension plans promised, and generally delivered, a certain guaranteed retirement benefit based on an employee's salary and length of employment. These plans are called defined-benefit plans. The company contributes whatever amount over the years is necessary to provide this benefit. These plans are most commonly found at large corporations or governments. If you have this type of plan with your employer, ask the personnel department for an estimate of what your benefit will be when you retire based on what you are currently earning.

However, it is very possible you don't have a pension plan of this type where you work because they are becoming less common. Company pension plans today are often defined-contribution plans instead of defined-benefit plans. This type of plan doesn't guarantee what it will pay you when you retire; it only guarantees what will be contributed to the plan in your behalf, based on your salary and length of employment. If you belong to this type of plan, your employer can currently contribute each year up to 25% of your salary or $30,000, whichever is less.

What you get when you retire depends on what the investments in the plan earn over the years. And you are responsible for choosing the investments from a list of approved choices. The result of employers switching from defined-benefit to defined-contribution plans is that *you* are now responsible for making investment choices, not your employer.

A profit-sharing plan is a kind of defined-contribution plan. If your employer makes money, some of it is put in your retirement account. A 401(k) plan is also a defined-contribution plan. It not only removes the burden from your employer of guaranteeing a certain defined benefit, but can also shift some of the burden of contributions on to you. It allows you to put up to $9,240 a year in your account. Most employers match all or part of your contribution.

Similar plans for employees of universities, schools, and nonprofit organizations are called 403(b) plans. Small businesses often use simplified employee pensions (SEPs), which provide contributions of up to 15% or $30,000, whichever is less. SEPs and Keoghs are pension plans used by self-employed individuals. Your bank investment representative can help you establish a retirement plan for yourself if you're self-employed or for your company if you are a business owner.

As mentioned previously, all contributions, yours and your employer's, to pension plans are pretax dollars and therefore reduce your taxable income or that of your employer. The earnings in all company pension plans are tax deferred until you take the money out.

If you have an employee-sponsored, defined-contribution plan, contact your employer to obtain an estimate of the amount of money you will have at retirement to generate the income you need. If you are self-employed, you should contact the financial advisor you used to establish your plan and obtain an estimate of what you will have at retirement.

Personal Savings

The third component of your retirement income comes from your personal savings and investments. This is your long-term retirement savings, not short-term money. Take some time to inventory your personal assets earmarked for retirement to determine where you currently stand. This includes any IRAs you many have in addition to all other savings accounts, investment securities, insurance policies with cash value, investment real estate (not your residence), and all other holdings you consider investments for retirement.

Every person with earned income can contribute 100% of that income up to $2,000 into an individual retirement account (IRA) each year until age 70. Married couples, where one of them is a nonworking spouse and has no earned income, can contribute a total of $2,250 each year into an IRA. However, no more than $2,000 can be contributed in any one name. (Legislation is now pending in Congress to change this rule and allow a $2,000 annual contribution for a nonworking spouse.)

Although every working American is eligible to contribute to an IRA and enjoy its tax-deferred advantage, not everyone can claim a tax deduction for their contribution. You can deduct your annual contribution from your taxable income if neither you or your spouse have a retirement plan available through your employer. However, if either you or your spouse have a retirement plan available at work, you are restricted, based on your level of income, on the amount of your annual contribution you can deduct. If adjusted gross income for joint filers exceeds $50,000 ($35,000 for singles), none of the IRA contributions can be deducted. You can still make them and enjoy the tax-deferred advantages, but you cannot deduct the contribution from your taxes. If joint adjusted gross income is less than $40,000 ($25,000 for singles), the entire contribution is deductible. Those couples with adjusted gross incomes between $40,000 and $50,000 ($25,000 to $35,000 for singles) can claim a prorated deduction. For example, a $45,000 joint adjusted gross income results in a $1,000 deduction. There is generally a 10% early withdrawal penalty before age 59-1/2, and you must start making minimum withdrawals before age 70-1/2. Minimum withdrawals are based on IRS life expectancy tables.

The tax deductions and the tax-deferred feature on an IRA make it an extremely valuable investment tool. If you qualify for an IRA and don't yet have one, you should open one and contribute to it each year before your make other investments for your retirement.

As mentioned earlier, it would be a mistake to rely solely on Social Security for retirement income. You also read earlier that you should maximize the use of all the pension accounts available to you. But even after all that, it is your personal savings that is going to make the difference in how well you can retire. Enhancing your personal savings now will enable you to achieve the necessary level of income when you retire.

Once you have added up the current value of all personal investments earmarked for retirement, estimate what they will be worth when you retire. Do this by assigning to it a hypothetical annual rate of return you think is achievable based on the investments you have. Be conservative so as not to be unrealistic and eventually disappointed. Your bank investment representative can help you make this calculation. (You may discover during the process that several investments are earning less than you need. Consult with your bank investment representative about alternatives.)

You may feel, for example, that 7% is an achievable annual rate of return. If so, increase the value of your total personal retirement investments ($100,000, for example) by 7% for each year you have until you retire (see Exhibit 14–2).

To keep it simple, you may want to use the Rule of 72 to estimate what your investments will be worth. The rule is to divide the number 72 by the compound interest rate you have chosen. The result is the number of years it takes your money to double in value. Using the example above, divide 72 by 7 and you get 10.28 years to double your money. Similarly, if you have 10 years until retirement, divide 72 by 10 and you see that your need to earn 7.2% a year to double your money by the time you retire.

Put It All Together

Once you have estimated how much you'll have at retirement from both pension assets and personal assets, you need to determine the amount of income they will generate each year until you die. This is not easy because you don't know how long you will live. Your bank investment representative can give you some estimated projections based on average life expectancy to help you plan, however.

Income Shortfall

You have an idea of the income you'll need when you retire. You have taken an inventory of the three components of retirement income: Social Security, employee-sponsored pensions, and

EXHIBIT 14–2
Growth of $100,000 at 7% a Year

End of Year	Amount
1	107,000
2	114,490
3	122,504
4	131,079
5	140,255
6	150,073
7	160,578
8	171,818
9	183,845
10	196,715

EXHIBIT 14–3
Projected Monthly Income from $100,000

	Annual Rate of Return Earned			
	4%	*6%*	*8%*	*10%*
5 years (60 months)	$1,842	$1,933	$2,028	$2,125
10 years (120 months)	1,012	1,110	1,213	1,322
15 years (180 months)	740	844	956	1,075
20 years (240 months)	606	716	836	965

The $100,000 is used up by the end of the time period.

personal investments. Apply your estimated Social Security income to what you think you'll need. Then apply the amount of income you think your pension and personal retirement investments will safely generate each year of your life. This will help you determine if you have a shortfall. Consider the example in Exhibit 14–4.

EXHIBIT 14–4
Retirement Income Shortfall

Annual income needed	$45,000
Social Security income	− 14,000
Pension income	− 16,000
Personal investment income	− 10,000
Income shortfall	5,000

EXHIBIT 14–5
Amount You Need to Invest Monthly

	Retirement Savings Target for Age 65		
Age	$300,000	$500,000	$1,000,000
25	$ 114	$ 190	$ 380
35	$ 246	$ 410	$ 820
45	$ 576	$ 960	$1,920
55	$1,733	$2,889	$5,778

Assumes a 7% tax-deferred return.

Using this example, you would need to save and invest enough additional money to generate $5,000 a year in income. Also, it is very important to keep in mind that you need to account for how inflation will erode your purchasing power. Therefore, you need some of your retirement assets, even after you are retired, not producing income, but invested for growth.

As you've learned from previous chapters, you will probably need to invest all of the after-tax earnings you can (10–15% minimum, more if you're over age 55) to have enough money to retire. To help determine the dollar amount you need to invest over the years to make up your estimated shortfall, consider Exhibit 14–5.

A secure retirement is your responsibility. It is something you need to focus on immediately. It is the single most important financial need you should discuss with your bank investment representative, who can help you determine how much you will need, how much to invest, and what investments are best for your retirement assets. And if you started planning and saving for retirement relatively late in life, you won't get much help from the most powerful asset accumulation tool: time. You're playing catch-up, therefore, proper investment selection is of the utmost importance.

TIPS FOR RETIREMENT AND RETIREMENT PREPARATION

If you are approaching retirement in the next 10–15 years, the following dozen tips will be of value to you. They include reminders, strategies, and investments. The investments are those that are most likely going be recommended to you by your investment advisor. Many of these same investments are also appropriate after you're retired, especially for those assets that you want to continue to grow to offset the impact of inflation. The next chapter will discuss many of the important investments and strategies that apply exclusively to those who are already retired.

Tip 1: Don't Retire Too Early

For most people, the dream of retiring prior to age 65 should be nothing more than a dream. The reality is that Americans are living longer. They need to be realistic about how many years they can be retired without earned income. The normal retirement age will be approaching age 70 within the next 25 years, according to many experts. One of the biggest threats to retirees is outliving their income. It stands to reason that working longer will decrease the chance of this happening. Also, be careful not to retire too early because your last years of employment are often high-earning years that count toward increasing your pension and Social Security income.

Tip 2: Delay Taking Social Security Income

You can start taking Social Security income at age 62 if you have stopped working, but your income will be permanently reduced by 20% compared to receiving income beginning at age 65. Also, note that current regulations call for the eligibility age for full Social Security benefits to increase gradually from 65 today to 66 in 2005 and 67 in 2022. Most experts say that eligibility will need to be delayed even further for the government to cut its deficit spending and approach a balanced budget.

Tip 3: Spend Much Less Than You Make

This means save more. This applies not only if you are preparing for retirement, but also if you have already retired. It is absolutely necessary to save and invest wisely before and after retirement to lessen the impact of inflation on your purchasing power in the future.

Tip 4: Maximize the Use of Your Pension and Retirement Accounts

Taxes have a big impact on how fast and how much you can accumulate money for retirement. You should take full advantage of retirement plans at work as well as IRAs, if you are eligible so that more of your assets can grow tax deferred. Even more important is the tax deduction you receive by being allowed to invest pretax dollars. Consider it an unbreakable rule: If you are investing for retirement, always use qualified retirement accounts first before other investments.

Tip 5: Keep Your Home on Sacred Ground

You may be tempted to consider equity in your home as part of your retirement savings. This may be the case if upon retirement you can sell your home and purchase another for a lesser amount, thus keeping the difference to supplement your retirement. Chance are, considering the spiraling cost of residential real estate, you will not be able to realize much profit from the sale and subsequent repurchase, unless of course you have a very large, expensive home and are reducing your lifestyle considerably. Most retirees should consider their current home, or the one they trade for at retirement, as a sacred asset that is used only as a last resort. Bottom line: Keep your home out of your calculations for retirement.

Tip 6: Use Tax-Advantaged Investments

The key to having a secure retirement is to accumulate as much money as possible to later use to generate income. You learned in Chapter 12 about the power of tax-deferred compound interest. Besides retirement accounts, annuities are the best investments to grow your assets in a tax-deferred manner. Remember, when you defer taxes, you keep the money you would have paid to the IRS under your control. Then, at retirement, you generate income off of both your money and the IRS's money, giving you a higher income. Tax-free municipal bonds (individual bonds, mutual funds, and UITs) are the investments of choice if you need *current* income and are in a high tax bracket.

Tip 7: Focus on Investments That Beat Inflation

Besides taxes, inflation is the most dangerous thief of a secure retirement. Over just 10 years, even a modest 4% annual inflation rate can whittle down the value of $100,000 to $67,556. To have an adequate retirement in today's demanding economic environment, a portion of your money must be in growth-oriented investments (stocks, stock mutual funds, or stock subaccounts in variable annuities). Stocks are the only financial investments that have consistently beat inflation over time. The amount of money you put in stocks should be determined by consulting with your bank investment representative. However, one rule of thumb used by many financial planners is to subtract your age from 100 to get the appropriate percentage of growth-oriented investments you should have.

Tip 8: Put Only Short-Term Money in Short-Term Accounts

To take full advantage of the power of time, you need to put money that is for retirement in long-term investments such as mutual funds, annuities, UITs, stocks, and bonds. Putting retirement money in CDs, money market accounts, and short-term bonds will rob you of higher total returns. Keep short-term money out of long-term investments and long-term money out of short-term investments.

Tip 9: Spread Your Money out among Various Asset Categories

When one type of investment does poorly, another is doing well. By spreading you retirement money among guaranteed accounts, domestic stocks, foreign bonds, and government bonds, for example, you can reduce your overall risk and increase your overall return. Bottom line: Don't put all your eggs in one or similar baskets.

Tip 10: Don't Rely on Medicare for Nursing Home or Long-Term Health Care Expenses

Chances are that the government is not going to provide the financial assistance you need when faced with the cost of nursing home care. Therefore, you need to invest now to have a lump sum available in your later years to pay for your physical care. This is beyond what you'll need to generate income. Health care costs are rising faster than other costs, so inflation-beating stock mutual funds and variable annuities are excellent choices. Annuities are particularly good because they often have a provision that allows for early withdrawal if you are confined to a nursing home or are disabled.

Tip 11: Roll Over Your Pension Assets when You Retire

If you have a defined contribution pension plan, chances are you can take control of your money and remove it from your employer's plan when you retire by transferring it into an IRA rollover. Most often, this is preferable because it gives you control over your own money while keeping it tax deferred as it was in your employer-sponsored pension plan. Putting it in a IRA rollover provides a large number of choices to invest your money and generate income compared to the choices offered by your employer's plan. However, this is not always the best thing to do. Consult with your tax advisor and bank investment representative when you retire to determine what choice is best for you. If you do roll it over, make sure you roll your money directly into an IRA so you don't have to pay 20% of it to the IRS, as is the case if you personally take possession of the assets before rein-vesting in an IRA. There are very few cases where you are better off taking all your money out of your retirement plan when you retire, paying all the taxes at once, and then reinvesting the money outside of an IRA. However, it is permitted in many cases. Be very careful to get expert advice before choosing this or any other option.

Tip 12: Have Annual Investment Checkups

Things change. Markets change, interest rates change, tax laws change, your estimate of what you will need at retirement will change. Therefore, it is important to meet with your bank investment representative annually to reevaluate your plans and investments. The next worst thing to not planning and invest-ing for retirement is to neglect your plans by failing to follow through, monitor, and reassess your progress.

Chapter Fifteen

Beyond Retirement
Your Later Years

I f you are already retired, you have some special needs and goals that other bank customers don't have. You also have a set of skills and a level of experience that should be used to your advantage.

Paramount among your needs and goals is the safety of your money. It's simple. You are beyond your earning years, you have a finite amount of money to last you the rest of your life, therefore, you don't want to lose it. That's why you have relied on your bank for so many years. You can trust it to keep your money safe.

However, this need for safety must be balanced somewhat with the second most important need for most seniors—to keep your independence, to remain self-sufficient, to not outlive your money. And looming in the distance is the probability that you will be a resident of a nursing home in the future. To remain independent and meet all your needs without running out of money, you need to maximize the return you can safely earn on your savings and investments.

SAFETY FIRST

In the late 1970s and early 1980s when interest rates on FDIC-insured CDs ranged between 12 and 16%, seniors found it relatively simple to maximize the performance of their money while satisfying their need for feeling safe. That was a very unusual time, however, one that has never occurred before and should not be counted on to return. The reality is that high returns and safety don't come together. Unfortunately, many retirees who became

accustomed to those high, safe rates of return have had a difficult time adjusting their expectations over the last decade as interest rates have declined.

Today, like most times in the past with this one notable excep-
tion, high returns and complete safety of principal are on opposite ends of the spectrum. Consequently, they cannot be achieved
with the simple use of a bank deposit account or any other investment. But, with some effort, the rethinking of old habits, the implementation of some proven investment strategies, and the
all-important help of a professional investment advisor, an
acceptable balance between the two can be reached. You can meet
many of your needs and sleep well in the process.

Since the use of investment products that are not FDIC insured,
together with your bank accounts, is relatively new to you, it's
normal to be apprehensive. This is where your bank and your
bank investment representative can assist you. The importance
of using a trusted investment advisor to help strike a comfortable balance between safety and return cannot be overstated.
Your licensed bank investment representative, available to you
whenever you visit your bank or via the telephone, can guide
you, educate you, answer your questions, and help you monitor your progress.

In addition to using a trusted financial advisor, another way
to help ensure that your safety needs are met is for you to move
slowly. The old adage, "haste makes waste" surely applies. Investing versus simply saving is relatively new to you, and you need
time to evaluate your choices. Not that you should delay simply
because you fear trying something new. Just get the facts, obtain
advice from a trusted advisor, and then rely on your experience
as a seasoned consumer to make prudent decisions. You may
not have a lot of specific experience purchasing investments, but
you have spent a lifetime developing keen "buying" skills, which
you should use to your advantage. You'll know when something is right for you and when it's not.

EARNING ALL YOU CAN SAFELY EARN

There are investment strategies, methods of constructing an investment portfolio, and particular investments that can help you

balance your need for safety with your desire to remain independent and not outlive your money. Let's review some of the main strategies, methods, and investments so you can choose what might be best for you. Your bank investment representative will recommend these and possibly others that specifically apply to your unique situation.

"I'm Not Going to Be Around That Long"

One simple, effective, and safe way to increase the amount of your income or rate of return is to lengthen your time horizon. The longer the holding term of an investment, the higher the potential return. Selecting longer maturities on CDs and bonds, for example, increases your current return. Selecting bond funds with average maturities of 7–10 years will increase your current income over bond funds with shorter maturities. Long-term stock mutual funds have superior track records compared to investing elsewhere in short-term investments.

It's not uncommon to resist lengthening your time horizons. There are two reasons cited by most seniors for remaining short-term with their money. First, is the fear of losing out if interest rates go up after making a commitment to a long-term investment. Second, is the tendency to make investment decisions based on your anticipated life expectancy. A very common response to the recommendation that a longer-term investment be chosen is, "I won't be around that long." Both of these reasons need to be reexamined.

Fear of losing out on other opportunities, such as higher interest rates, is an understandable reason for not investing *all* of your money for the long term, but it should not keep you from investing *some* of your money in longer-term, higher-paying investments. After all, interest rates may also go down. Then you will have missed out on higher rates, all right. Many retirees make the mistake of being so consumed with getting rates as high as those available in the late 70s and early 80s, for example, that they remain in short-term, low-paying accounts for years. In effect, they have imposed a penalty on their money: lower interest rates than they could have been earning.

The most prudent strategy, since nobody knows for sure what the future will bring, is to ladder the time horizons of your various investments. Have some money in short-term investments, some in medium-term, and some in long-term. As they mature, you climb up the ladder with the new investments you buy. This means that when the short-term investments mature, you invest the proceeds in long-term investments—you move them up to the top of the ladder. Over time, those investments that were originally medium-term are now your short-term investments. Original long-term investments are now medium-term, and so on. Once again, you have investments in each time horizon. The advantage of this laddering strategy is that after the initial investments are made, all subsequent investments are long term and, since long-term rates are the highest, you get the highest available current rate. And if rates go up after you invest, you are not panicked because you know you have some short-term money maturing soon that can be locked in at the higher, long-term rates when you reinvest it. This is a much superior strategy to keeping all of your money in short-term accounts, where you can't possibly earn enough to meet your future income and health care needs.

As stated above, the other reason cited by many seniors for not lengthening their investment time horizon is because the feel they "won't be around that long." You may be very surprised how long you will be around. The average life expectancy of older Americans is rising each year. Find your age on Exhibit 15–1 to determine your average life expectancy.

Notice that if you live as long as the averages predict, you have a good chance of living even longer. For example, a male currently age 70 has an average life expectancy of nearly 11 years, to age 81. However, if you are a male who lives to age 81, you have a life expectancy of 5.8 more years. Again, you may be surprised how long you live. Let's hope you have good health and the income you need to make it not just a surprise, but a pleasant surprise. Whatever the future brings, it's best to plan financially for a long life, rather than a short one.

So, to say, "I won't be around that long," may or may not be true, but it isn't a reason to invest in short-term accounts and shun long-term accounts. In fact, it's a reason to do just the opposite.

EXHIBIT 15–1
Average Life Expectancy

Age	Male Expectancy, Years	Female Expectancy, Years	Age	Male Expectancy, Years	Female Expectancy, Years
0	70.83	75.83	34	39.54	43.91
1	70.13	75.04	35	38.61	42.98
2	69.20	74.11	36	37.69	42.05
3	68.27	73.17	37	36.78	41.12
4	67.34	72.23	38	35.87	40.20
5	66.40	71.28	39	34.96	39.28
6	65.46	70.34	40	34.05	38.36
7	64.52	69.39	41	33.16	37.46
8	63.57	68.44	42	32.26	36.55
9	62.62	67.48	43	31.38	35.66
10	61.66	66.53	44	30.50	34.77
11	60.71	65.58	45	29.62	33.88
12	59.75	64.62	46	28.76	33.00
13	58.80	63.67	47	27.90	32.12
14	57.86	62.71	48	27.04	31.25
15	56.93	61.76	49	26.20	30.39
16	56.00	60.82	50	25.36	29.53
17	55.09	59.87	51	24.52	28.67
18	54.18	58.93	52	23.70	27.82
19	53.27	57.98	53	22.89	26.98
20	52.37	57.04	54	22.08	26.14
21	51.47	56.10	55	21.29	25.31
22	50.57	55.16	56	20.51	24.49
23	49.66	54.22	57	19.74	23.67
24	48.75	53.28	58	18.99	22.86
25	47.84	52.34	59	18.24	22.05
26	46.93	51.40	60	17.51	21.25
27	46.01	50.46	61	16.79	20.44
28	45.09	49.52	62	16.08	19.65
29	44.16	48.59	63	15.38	18.86
30	43.24	47.65	64	14.70	18.08
31	42.31	46.71	65	14.04	17.32
32	41.38	45.78	66	13.39	16.57
33	40.46	44.84	67	12.76	15.83

(continued)

EXHIBIT 15–1
Average Life Expectancy   (concluded)

Age	Male Expectancy, Years	Female Expectancy, Years	Age	Male Expectancy, Years	Female Expectancy, Years
68	12.14	15.10	84	4.77	5.59
69	11.54	14.38	85	4.46	5.18
70	10.96	13.67	86	4.18	4.80
71	10.39	12.97	87	3.91	4.43
72	9.84	12.28	88	3.66	4.09
73	9.30	11.60	89	3.41	3.77
74	8.79	10.95	90	3.18	3.45
75	8.31	10.32	91	2.94	3.15
76	7.84	9.71	92	2.70	2.85
77	7.40	9.12	93	2.44	2.55
78	6.97	8.55	94	2.17	2.24
79	6.57	8.01	95	1.87	1.91
80	6.18	7.48	96	1.54	1.56
81	5.80	6.98	97	1.20	1.21
82	5.44	6.49	98	0.84	0.84
83	5.09	6.03	99	0.50	0.50

Source: Derived from the mortality tables in the "Report of the Special Committee to Recommend New Mortality Table for Valuation," *Transactions of the Society of Actuaries*, Vol. XXXIII (1981), p. 617.

There is a natural tendency to structure investment maturity dates to coincide with your expected date of death. Granted, you need some money available as you get older to pay for possible nursing home and extended health care costs, but not all your money is going to be needed at once.

You are much better served, even if you are trying to generate current income, to chose long-term accounts or investments with some of your money. While you're living, *you* can benefit from higher returns; and when you die, your heirs will benefit. After all, the more you make, the less of your principal you will have to spend. It's true that in some rare cases your heirs may have to pay a penalty to have instant access to your money after you die, but chances are the penalty will be less than the "self-imposed penalty" you pay when you keep too much of your money in lower-yielding, short-term accounts. Bottom line: Safely maximize the earning power of your money while you are still living. Both you and your heirs will benefit.

Use a Variety of Appropriate Investments

Bank accounts have their appropriate place in the investment plan of every American and especially retired investors who are concerned about their principal fluctuating in value. However, as mentioned above, it is absolutely essential for retirees to invest some of their assets in investment products that fluctuate in value in order to stay ahead of inflation and meet the future or current demands for more income. These products are not FDIC insured even though they are sold at your bank, but they have their appropriate place in your overall investment plan.

The importance of having some money in stocks cannot be overemphasized. Even retirees should have a conservative component of stocks, usually stock mutual funds or variable annuities, in order to stay ahead of inflation because there is no other category of financial assets that have consistently outpaced inflation. These are the investments that will help make it possible for you to meet the rising costs of nursing home care. Consult with your bank investment representative to determine which stock-based investments are most appropriate for you and the amount that you should invest.

One tendency common to retirees investing for the first time that should be avoided is investing exclusively or primarily in bank account look-alike investment products such as government bonds and government bond funds. These investments have their place in moderation, but don't be tempted to put too much of your money in these investments just because they contain bonds backed by the full faith and credit of the federal government. This is a common mistake because many people equate such a backing to the coverage provided by the FDIC, an agency of the federal government. Many people reason that if they need investments, they'd better get the safest ones. Because these accounts look, smell, and taste kind of like a bank account, these people move a lot of their money over, assuming they can safely earn a higher rate of return.

These investments are paying higher rates than FDIC-insured bank accounts because they are taking more risk. Even though the federal government is backing the credit risk of their bonds, the principal value of the bonds can go up and down in response to the change in current interest rates. (See Chapter 9, Understanding Bonds, and Chapter 10, Understanding Mutual Funds.) In short, there are no investments you should buy because they appear to be like bank accounts. If you need bank accounts, use bank accounts. Use every investment for the purpose it was designed.

Of course, this leads to the next important point for investors who are already retired: diversify. For safety reasons, never put your money in one investment or one type of investment. Also, have your bank investment representative develop an asset allocation plan for you that goes beyond diversification. It will take into consideration all your goals and needs and determine how much money should be in various investments that act dissimilar to each other. This way you have increased safety. If one investment is going down because of forces in the economy and financial markets, you have another investment that was specifically selected because it will be going up under the same conditions.

Ways to Take Income from Your Investments

Most of this book has concentrated on accumulating assets, but when you're in your later years, your primary need is usually current income. So how can you maximize the amount of income your money can generate, and how can you generate income and hedge against rising costs at the same time?

First, let's review ways to maximize your income. One way is to reduce the amount of taxes you pay on the income and interest you earn. What you really need is to concentrate on the amount of income you get to keep and spend: after-tax income. Reducing taxes will be covered in the next section of this chapter.

Another way to increase your income is to buy investments that pay a higher yield. This may seem obvious, but there are some important strategies to consider since higher yields are accompanied by higher risks. The safest way to increase your yield on interest-bearing accounts and bond-based investments

EXHIBIT 15–2
Reducing Overall Risk while Increasing Overall Return

	Annual Return			
Amount Invested	No Risk 5%	Low Risk 8%	Medium Risk 10%	High Risk 15%
$100,000	$5,000	$8,000	$10,000	$15,000
$ 50,000	$2,500	$4,000	$ 5,000	$ 7,500
$ 25,000	$1,250	$2,000	$ 2,500	$ 3,750

is to lengthen your time horizon using the laddering strategy described earlier in this chapter. But, in addition, use a laddering technique for levels of risk as well and lengths of maturity. For example, have investments with short, medium, and long maturities and investments with no risk, low risk, and medium risk. The result is that you have money that is earning higher rates overall and maturing frequently to fill your emergency needs due to your laddering of maturity dates. In addition, using the risk-laddering technique, you have the potential to achieve higher returns overall because your medium-risk investments are earning more than your no-risk and low-risk investments.

Using Exhibit 15–2, assume you have $100,000 to invest. Investing $50,000 in the no-risk category will earn you $2,500, $25,000 in the low-risk category will yield $2,000, and $25,000 in the medium-risk category will result in $2,500 for a combined earnings of $7,000. That's $2,000 more than if you left the entire amount in the no-risk category. To earn the additional amount, half of your money was exposed to low and medium risk. Exhibit 15–3 shows some of the investments that fall into the no-risk, low-risk, medium-risk, and high-risk categories.

It's important that the investments you choose, using the investment pyramid as a guide, can pay current income. Most investments can, including stock funds.

Stock funds are excellent investments for producing income and hedging against inflation. Stock funds can generate an income you designate while the principal continues to grow. For example, a stock fund may be averaging a 12% annual rate of return.

EXHIBIT 15–3
Investment Pyramid

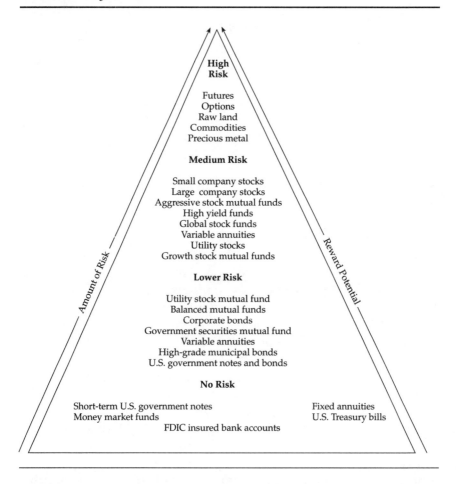

You can opt to have some of it sent to you on a regular basis, say 8% a year but paid monthly. The remaining 4% remains in the fund and grows for your future. Of course, if the fund doesn't earn 12% in a given year and you still elect to take an income of 8%, you will eat into your principal. But, if it earns more than 12%, you will accumulate more than 4%. The key is to take out a conservative amount so there is a reasonable chance the principal will grow.

A similar technique can be used with bond funds, fixed annuities, and variable annuities. You can elect to have some of your earnings or interest paid to you while keeping the rest in the investment. This is simply spending less than you earn, a rule that should always be followed.

However, the older you get and the less money you have, the more difficult it is to live off interest without dipping into your principal. Your optimal guideline should be that in the first third of the time you're retired you should live on less income than your retirement plans, Social Security, and personal investments will generate. During the second third, if necessary, you could spend all the income that your personal investments, Social Security, and pension can provide. And not until you reach the last third of your estimated years of retirement should you start dipping into your principal.

One investment that is worth considering, whenever you are ready to dip into your principal to generate income, is an annuity. Both fixed and variable annuities can provide income you cannot outlive and are appropriate for investors in their later years. (See Chapters 12 and 13 for details.)

Reducing Taxes

Taxes are a problem for all investors in the higher tax brackets, but they are particularly harmful to retirees who generally have a fixed amount of money to generate income for the rest of their lives. Determine if you fall into a high tax bracket by examining Exhibit 15–4.

To get a more accurate picture of your tax situation, add the percentage you pay in federal taxes to the appropriate percentage of your state income tax, if you have one (generally 5% to 9%). Subtract the percentage of your tax from the return on your taxable investments to see what you are really keeping for your own needs.

For retirees, like other investors, the rule of thumb if you are in a combined federal and state tax bracket over 20% is to use some tax-free bonds and tax-free bond funds for income and defer whatever interest or earnings you are not spending.

EXHIBIT 15–4
1995 Federal Income Tax Brackets and Rates

Singles Taxable Income	Married, Filing Jointly	Federal Tax Rate
Less than $23,350	Less than $39,000	15.0%
$ 23,350–$ 56,549	$ 39,000–$ 94,249	25.0%
$ 56,550–$117,949	$ 94,250–$143,599	31.0%
$117,949–$256,499	$143,600–$256,500	36.0%
Over $256,500	Over $256,500	39.6%

Note: Taxable income levels adjust annually based on the Consumer Price Index. To determine your taxable income, find the "Taxable Income" line (line 37) on your last year's 1040 form. Other categories may apply (i.e. head of household, corporate, trust.)

Deferring taxes increases the size of the nest egg under your control that can later be used to generate an increased level of income when needed. It just doesn't make sense to put the majority of your savings in low-yielding savings accounts that are taxable and result in you keeping substantially less after taxes, especially if you don't need the income to support yourself. If you don't need it, earn more and defer it, using fixed and variable annuities or stock mutual funds that have small dividends and capital gains, but concentrate on appreciation. If you are not paying over 20% in income taxes, it is most often better to invest in taxable accounts, pay the taxes, and keep what's left over. There are many exceptions to this 20% rule of thumb, so consult with your tax advisor and bank investment representative on your unique situation.

One tax you may find especially troubling is the income tax on your Social Security income. Current tax law requires you to pay income tax on up to 85% of your Social Security income if you have a total taxable income (including 1/2 your Social Security income) of up to $34,000 if you are single and $44,000 if you are married, filing jointly. Please note that tax-free interest from tax-free municipal bonds and funds must be added to your income for purposes of determining if, or what portion of, your Social Security income is taxable. You don't pay taxes on the income directly from these bonds, but they must be included in the calculation as though they were taxable for the purpose of determining the taxability of Social Security income.

The way to limit or avoid this taxation of your Social Security income is to shift money earning taxable or tax-free interest over to tax-deferred annuities. Tax-deferred interest generated by annuities, if kept inside the annuity, is not required to be included in the calculation for determining how much of your Social Security income is taxable.

Your bank investment representative can help you determine how much of your money that you are not using to generate current income should be moved to annuities if you want to reduce or eliminate this tax. Depending on your individual tax situation, the shifting of a modest amount of money to annuities can result in a significant tax reduction.

The other tax that often affects seniors is the gift tax. Just remember, to avoid paying a gift tax, you can only give to any individual $10,000 or less in a calendar year. You and your spouse can give $10,000 each, if you wish, effectively making it possible to give an individual $20,000 a year.

OTHER IMPORTANT REMINDERS

Don't Rely on Your Will Alone

Chances are, if you are like most people today, a last will and testament isn't all you need to ensure your assets will safely pass on to your heirs. A will is a good way of communicating many of your feelings and wishes to your heirs, appointing a guardian for your minor children; and expressing your wishes regarding your financial estate; but it won't protect your assets from costly probate or estate taxes.

To avoid having your estate settled or probated by the courts, which can be costly and time-consuming, consider having your attorney establish today a living trust for a significant portion of your assets. Such a trust enables your assets to skip over probate and pass directly to your heirs with minimal expense or delay. In addition, consider placing some of your assets in an annuity and/or life insurance so that a portion of your estate can pass to your heirs automatically without passing through probate. Also, you may want to title many of your accounts as joint accounts with rights of survivorship. This enables your heir (joint account holder) to have immediate access to the account. However, be careful with this option because once another name is put on your account, the other person *owns* half of the account.

Don't Give It All Away

You don't know for sure how much money you are going to need to last you until your death. And one of your goals throughout retirement is to remain self-sufficient. Therefore, be careful about giving too much away to your children, relatives, and charities. Many retirees are tempted to give money away as a method of reducing taxes. (Less money = less interest income = less taxes.) This is the worst possible tax-reduction method. The key to remaining financially independent for the rest of your life is to keep your money under your control until your death, then give it away. It is absolutely essential, for your own safety, that you review all major gifts with your tax advisor and financial advisor before you give.

Reducing taxes is not the only potentially unwise reason some seniors are tempted to prematurely give money to their children. Fear of losing it all to nursing home expenses is another. Be careful about shifting assets out of your name to your children for the sole purpose of keeping it in the family while qualifying for governmental assistance. Remember that the government can go back three years and recoup any assets you have given away to relatives. Therefore, any money gifted to children needs to be done years before you apply for assistance. It is also not unheard of for children to succumb to temptation and spend money that they have been given to "hide" instead of keeping it to generate income for you or serve as your safety net. It is best to keep your assets under your control as long as you can.

Keep Close to Home

It is amazing how many conservative investors, both old and young, agonize more than necessary over taking the absolutely essential step of broadening their investment choices beyond bank accounts, only to quickly fall prey to a get-rich-quick scheme pitched by a smooth-talking salesman calling on the telephone or passing through town.

You do need to maximize the earning power of your money, but do so close to home, using an advisor you trust who sells only registered, regulated securities, annuities, or bank accounts. There are risks associated with the non-FDIC-backed investments you will get from your bank investment representative, but you won't be defrauded by a con artist.

Bottom line: Never, never, buy any investment over the phone or through the mail from someone or some company you don't know and can't go and visit. Your money is too important. Remember, if it's too good to be true, it's not true. Deal only with organizations and people that you know from past experience you can trust. That's why your bank is a great place to start.

It's not only important that you can trust the honesty and integrity of the individual and company you are dealing with, you must also feel confident they know what they are doing. Rely on a professional, licensed investment advisor with whom you feel comfortable. (See Chapter 3, Advice and Advisors.)

THE PROCESS
OF INVESTING

Chapter Sixteen

How to Read a Prospectus

Just the word *prospectus* causes most peoples' minds to shut down and their eyes to glaze over. Unless you know beforehand what to look for, reading a prospectus can be a long, tedious, and confusing process. It's no secret that most prospectuses go unread.

A prospectus should be viewed as nothing more than a not-so-handy reference guide for investors. The law requires investments classified as securities (e.g., stocks, bonds, mutual funds, UITs, and variable annuities) have a document disclosing organizational, management, performance, expense, and potential risk details to potential investors. Such a document is called a prospectus.

Unfortunately, any prospectus you're likely to see will be unbearably long, dense, and dull. Most of the blame for this must fall on the Securities and Exchange Commission. The SEC demands that companies transmit certain detailed information to potential investors. However, much of this information is useless to the investor. In fact, the information can be misleading at times to the average reader because of all the legal requirements placed on the writers.

The SEC requires every conceivable datum about the company in question to be included in the prospectus. The problem is that they add additional requirements from time to time, but the additions and revisions don't eliminate the obsolete requirements. So, the tangled mass of requirements grows ever thicker. The average prospectus now contains about 50 pages of fine print. This may cause the potential investor to miss seeing the "forest" (the investment) for the "trees" (all of the dense, fine print of the prospectus).

Federal regulators, investor advocate groups, and industry associations are now working on plans to ensure the prospectus will be shortened to about 10 pages of plain, readable English. Current regulations allow a sales brochure written in plain language to accompany a prospectus. These four-color glossy publications are useful sources of information but are promotional, emphasizing the investment's potential, and must be read with some skepticism.

Until the shorter, more understandable prospectuses are allowed, knowing how to pick through the important parts of these dense documents will save you time and put your mind at ease.

WHERE TO GET A PROSPECTUS

Your bank investment representative can give you a prospectus for an investment you are considering. In fact, regulations require that you be given a mutual fund or variable annuity prospectus prior to investing or at the very least within three days following the day you invest.

Although a prospectus is created for every investment security, stock and bond prospectuses are available only when the stock or bond is being offered for the first time. Since most stocks and bonds are purchased on an exchange or over the counter from other individuals and not from the companies themselves, prospectuses are not provided. Information about a company's stocks or bonds can be found in their quarterly and annual reports. These are available by contacting a company directly.

As a bank customer, it is the prospectuses of mutual funds and variable annuities and other managed investment products that you will most often want to examine. These are available directly from the investment and insurance companies, but it is easier to get them from your bank investment representative.

Ask your investment representative to go through the prospectus with you and point out the areas you will want to examine.

IMPORTANT HIGHLIGHTS OF A PROSPECTUS

Following are important things to look for when reading a mutual fund prospectus. First, on the cover of every prospectus, in large letters, is the following disclaimer:

These securities have not not been approved or disapproved by the Securities and Exchange Commission nor has the Commission passed upon the accuracy of this prospectus. Any representation to the contrary is a criminal offense.

This intimidating caption shouldn't scare you away. It's designed to inform you that the government isn't *recommending* anything.

There is another disclaimer on the first page of a prospectus that you receive at your bank. It is a notice that investments are not FDIC insured. Read both disclaimers, but keep in mind that they are there at the behest of regulators and lawyers and are, for the most part, just a boilerplate defense against lawsuits. Don't let them scare you off. They do not contain the information you need to make a sensible judgment about an offering's merits. That's in the text of the prospectus itself.

Let's move into that dense forest of text. Look for the following information.

Management experience. Look in the table of contents on the back of the cover. Have the people managing the mutual fund company been doing so a long time, or are they newcomers? Management's background and experience are one of the most important aspects of a mutual fund. You should pay particular attention to it because in their business, experience counts for a lot.

Track record. This too, can be located via the table of contents. The SEC requires that only the most recent 3 years of a mutual fund's history be shown here. What about the last 5 or 10 years? The sales brochure usually shows a longer track record. Your bank investment representative can give you the fund's complete historical performance record sliced and diced anyway you want it (e.g., 5-year, 10-year, previous-year's, etc.). But what if you're looking at a new mutual fund that hasn't yet established a track record? The best thing to do is not look at one. Why start out with a new one when you can choose from thousands of funds already doing business? If you choose to consider one, however, dig deep into the other parts of the prospectus outlined below.

Investment objectives.   Here's where you find out if the fund's objectives match your investment needs (e.g., growth, income, appreciation, etc.)

Investment risks.   Here you can find out if investing in this fund exceeds your risk tolerance.

Investment policies.   Examples include the types of securities that may be purchased, how the fund's asset allocation may be changed, and the degree (if any) to which the manager might use risky investments such as options and futures.

How to purchase and redeem shares.   Here you find out how to buy and sell the fund, including a description of commissions and sales charges you must pay to invest.

Shareholder transaction costs and ongoing expenses.   All funds have ongoing expenses. They are spelled out here so you can compare them to other mutual funds.

Fund advisor.   These are the people who actually make the investment decisions. This information will give you insight into their capabilities.

Fund custodian, transfer agent, and dividend-disbursing agent.   Their names and addresses are listed here. These are the companies that keep the books and handle the money.

Rights and privileges.   Telephone exchange privilege, automatic share purchase plans, withdrawal plans, and tax-sheltered retirement programs are explained. You'll want to use these and can rely on your bank investment representative to interpret them for you.

List of distributions.   Dividend and capital gains distributions and a discussion of tax consequences for the investor are in this section.

Moving to the sections of a prospectus listed above and skimming the rest will make the reading of a prospectus more of a valuable experience and less of a drudgery. If you have questions concerning any part of the prospectus, talk to your bank investment representative.

BEYOND THE PROSPECTUS

Annual and quarterly reports are great sources of information on a mutual fund or variable annuity. These professionally produced booklets are sent to you regularly once you are a shareholder, but your bank investment representative may be able to make one available to you prior to investing. (They are also available on individual companies that issue stocks and bonds.)

They recount the activity of the mutual fund or variable annuity accounts for the given period and list all of the securities owned. Unlike reading a prospectus, reading these can actually be fun.

These reports should be examined periodically and discussed with your bank investment representative if you have any questions or concerns.

Chapter Seventeen

The Real Costs
of Investing

There are costs associated with all investments. Sometimes investors are aware of the costs; other times they are not because the costs are hidden.

Even CDs have a cost. Your bank doesn't lend out your money and pay you interest for free. Your bank doesn't provide you with FDIC insurance for free. It couldn't because it has to pay an insurance premium to the FDIC in order to extend the coverage to you.

When you place money in a CD, you give your bank the use of your money. You allow the bank to lend it out to borrowers at a higher rate of interest than the bank pays you. The cost of a CD, what you pay your bank to loan out your money, is the difference between what the bank earns on it and what it pays you.

If you bypassed the bank and loaned your money directly to a borrower, you could keep all the interest it earned. Of course, you would have to do your own credit check on the borrower, create your own legally binding loan agreement, keep your own records, follow up on late payments, and pursue the borrower if the money wasn't repaid. In addition, you'd be running naked without FDIC insurance to guarantee the safety of your money.

Chances are, you are comfortable "paying" your bank—letting it have part of the interest your money is earning—because it provides valuable services that you can't easily duplicate. Herein lies the key to paying for every product and service you buy, including investments. If you get real value for your fee, commission, sales charge, or sales load, you are comfortable paying. The cost of paying your bank's brokerage unit, and consequently your bank investment representative for investments and professional advice, is more than fair considering the fact that they are providing something you need and can't easily duplicate.

THE VALUE OF A PROFESSIONAL'S ADVICE

When it comes to your health, you rely on medical professionals to advise you and provide valuable services, medications, and treatments. However, you don't rely on them for everything related to health and illness. For example, you probably handle the flu and common cold without their help in most cases. It's true you may seek advice when a health problem first surfaces, but then you often diagnosis and treat the problem yourself when it surfaces again, perhaps with the use of over-the-counter medication. This is possible because your medical advisor has educated you about the illness. Even individuals with persistent illnesses or diseases, such as diabetics, can do much for themselves under the direction of their physician.

However, when complex medical problems arise, when a serious illness needs diagnosis and treatment, when there is medical matter of great importance, the services of a trusted medical professional are vital.

Maintaining your financial health is similar to maintaining your physical health. You can handle your day-to-day financial matters and deal with your short-term financial needs. You can choose appropriate savings accounts and identify some investments that may be appropriate. But, when it comes to your long-term investment strategy, it's best to rely on a licensed investment representative to help you determine your needs and goals, select investments that match your needs, and allocate your assets among the appropriate asset categories based on your age and life situation. And, equally important, you need your bank investment representative to keep track of the complex financial markets and your investments so they remain appropriate investments over time. You also need your bank investment representative to keep you informed and educated about your investments. Briefly stated, you need the value a professional advisor provides. (See Chapter 3, Advice and Advisors.)

WAYS YOU ARE CHARGED

When you buy an investment you pay a cost that is either fully disclosed to you or hidden in the structure of the investment, as is the case with CDs. Before you can feel comfortable about the cost of an investment, you need to know what the costs are and weigh them against the value you are receiving. Let's review some examples of the costs of investing in the most popular investments you'll encounter, so you can get an idea for future reference. However, rest assured that unlike some investment providers, your bank will make sure you know the exact costs of every investment you buy. You will even be asked to sign a disclosure form for your protection, verifying that your bank investment representative remembered to tell you the costs of an investment.

Certificate of Deposit (CD)

There are no direct fees, charges, commissions, or sales loads. Your bank is simply making more money than it is paying you. You will pay a penalty if you withdraw your money before a CD matures.

Fixed Annuities

You pay no fees, charges, sales loads, or commissions on single-premium fixed annuities. The insurance company pays your bank a commission from its own funds, then recoups the commission and makes a profit from investing your deposit at a rate higher than you receive. Flexible-premium fixed annuities may have an annual $25 to $50 service fee to pay for the costs of administering your annuity. Nearly all fixed annuities have surrender charges (typically declining 1% each year and expiring within 5–7 years) if you withdraw your money earlier than the specified term.

Variable Annuities

Variable annuities are the same as flexible-premium fixed annuities with the following additions: There is an annual mortality and expense-risk charge that can range from 0.5% to 1.75% of the average value of the subaccounts. It is to pay for the guaranteed death benefit and assurance that the expenses will not increase over the life of the investment. There are also annual subaccount operating expenses similar to those charged by mutual funds: 0.5% to 1% of subaccount values.

Unit Investment Trusts

You pay a commission of between 1.5% and 4%, depending on the type of trust. Trusts containing bonds are usually more expensive than those containing stocks. Generally, long-term trusts cost more than short-term trusts. When you buy an existing trust from another investor through your bank or when you buy a new trust, you pay a commission. However, depending on the confirmation system your bank uses, it may appear that you are not. Hidden or not, some of the money you invest is going to the bank. Have your bank investment representative explain how your bank shows the commission.

Bonds

You pay between $10 and $50 for $10,000 in corporate bonds that are listed on bond exchanges. Government bonds, tax-free bonds, and corporate bonds, held in your bank broker/dealer's inventory and then sold to you, generally cost from $50–$200 per $10,000 invested. You may not always see the commission on your confirmation ticket because the charge is figured into the price of the bond, thus increasing your price and slightly reducing your yield. The only bonds that have no cost to buy are new issues. These are bonds being offered (via your bank) to the public by the issuer for the first time.

Stocks

You pay a commission to buy individual stocks. The commission is a function of the number of shares you buy and the total dollar amount you invest. For example, under the current commission schedule at many brokerages, if you buy 100 shares of IBM selling at 73-1/4 ($73.25) per share, you will pay a commission of $1.07 per share for a total of $107. That's a 1.46% commission. However, if you buy 1,000 shares, you would be charged only $0.81 per share, a 1.1% commission. As a general rule, the more you invest in a single transaction, the lower is the commission percentage on the amount invested.

Shares of stocks that are being offered to the public for the first time are free of a commission, just like newly offered bonds. The issuing company, or municipality in the case of municipal bonds, pays your bank's brokerage for placing their security with you.

Mutual Funds

The cost of investing in mutual funds depends on the class of shares you buy. There are class A, class B, and class C shares. A and B are the classes sold by most investment providers, including banks.

Class A shares have an up-front sales charge called a *load*. You may pay up to 5.75% of what you invest. The larger the dollar amount you invest, the lower the load goes (see Exhibit 17–1). The amount you invest is reduced by the amount of the load as shares are purchased. The mutual fund company and your bank divide the load, and the remainder is used to buy your shares. A loaded mutual fund also charges you annual internal fees that you don't see of between 0.50% and 1.5%. These fees are used to pay the management, operation, and transaction fees each year. A small portion is passed on to your bank to pay the cost of servicing your mutual fund account each year.

Class B shares cost nothing to buy, but you pay a contingent deferred sales charge if you sell the funds within a specified number of years. These are called *back-end loaded* mutual funds. An example of a contingent deferred sales charge is 5% if you sell in the first year, 4% if you sell in the second year, and so on, declining 1% a year over five years. Upon your purchase, the mutual fund, from its own assets, advances your bank a commission that is comparable to what the bank would have earned if you had bought class A shares.

While your money is in the fund, you pay annual internal fees as much as 1% higher than the fees inside a loaded fund. A small portion of these fees is passed on to your bank to pay the cost of servicing your mutual fund account each year. These fees drop down to a level equal to the fees of class A shares after enough years have passed for the fund to recoup the commission paid to your bank.

In the final analysis, you pay approximately the same amount regardless of the class of shares you buy. Back-end loaded funds are more popular with investors than front-end loaded funds, but this is due more to perception than reality. It is human nature to delay the cost of something, but in reality you pay approximately the same either way.

There is one good argument for buying class A (loaded) over class B (back-end loaded) funds. You are better off paying up front than along the way or on the back end if your fund is doing what it is supposed to do: going up in value each year. This is because when you pay a percentage of what you invest up front, you are most likely paying on a lesser amount than if you pay along the way.

There are also the new class C shares being offered, but they are rare. They allow you to invest with no initial fee and pay no contingent deferred sales charge for selling after a specified period, usually no longer than 18 months. However, there are annual internal fees high enough for the mutual fund company to make money, cover its expenses, and pay your bank up to 1% of the value of your account each year you remain in the fund. Again, there is always a cost to investing.

The last "class" of mutual funds you need to know about when examining the costs of investing is no-load funds. These are the type of fund you see advertised extensively in the back of magazines and financial newspapers. There is no commission to purchase these funds. They are not generally offered by your bank's brokerage unit or traditional stock brokerage firms because they do not compensate your advisor when you invest. Like other mutual funds, they have internal management and service fees, but they also have other fees. For example, one fee you're charged pays for the no-load fund's advertising campaign to attract new investors. Loaded funds rely on professional investment advisors to sell their shares. No-load funds rely primarily on advertising, and advertising can be expensive. On average, the internal fees of no-load funds are substantially more than those of loaded funds.

The Cost of No Advice

It is possible to pay less initially using a no-load than a loaded fund, but chances are over the long-term it will cost you in other ways—both financially and emotionally. Investing without the insights of a professional advisor can mean that you select an investment that may have been good for other investors but is not currently appropriate for you. It may take more risk than you can handle, for example.

You could reason that you are better off in a no-load fund than a loaded fund since you don't have to pay a commission and therefore more of your money is invested. But, *not* paying a load costs you something: the advice of a licensed professional investment advisor. You not only lose help in selecting the right fund, but in analyzing your investment objectives, establishing an appropriate asset mix, monitoring your mutual funds and other investments, and evaluating your investments on an ongoing basis. Advice, or the absence of advice, can have a greater impact on your investment results than anything else.

Consider which of the following statements is true. "No-load funds outperform load funds" or "No-load investors outperform investors who purchase load funds." There are times when the first statement is true. There are few times, however, when the second statement is true.

The two fundamental differences between load and no-load funds are the way they're marketed and the length of time they're held by shareholders. Often, the no-load mutual funds with the most recent, hottest records get the big advertising push, attracting new shareholders after their shares have had a big increase in price. Never will a no-load mutual fund advertisement even suggest it is underperforming the market or has risen too high given current conditions, or give advice as to whether or not it is a good time to sell.

Left on their own, no-load mutual fund shareholders run the risk of getting in at the wrong time and getting out too soon, as was the case during the 1987 stock market crash. Many mutual fund shareholders, primarily of no-load funds, bailed out of their funds after the market declined sharply, only to see the market rise sharply over following months and years. Investors who received good advice stayed in their funds and earned record returns. In the long run, good advice pays off. It's what enables load-fund investors to outperform no-load investors.

WAYS TO REDUCE THE COST OF INVESTING

It's important to note that the commissions charged on mutual funds, annuities, and unit investment trusts are subject to securities regulations that currently prohibit one brokerage firm or bank from offering the same investment for more or less of a cost than another brokerage firm or bank. Knowing this enables you to concentrate on deciding who gives the best advice and who you feel most comfortable working with, rather than wondering if you can get a better deal elsewhere.

There are three things you can do to reduce the cost of investing. First, take advantage of commission breakpoints on mutual funds. If you place enough money with one mutual fund family, you are entitled to a "break" on your commission. The typical breakpoints are listed in Exhibit 17–1. However, some mutual fund families have lower breakpoints than those illustrated.

You will pay the percentage listed until you cross over the next breakpoint. For example, if you invest up to $49,999, you will pay a 5% commission, but if you invest $50,000 you will only be charged 4%. Here's another example: If you invested $40,000 a year ago and paid a 5% commission and now you want to invest another $10,000 you will be charged 4% on the $10,000. If your original $40,000 had grown to $44,000, for example, by the time you wanted to invest more, you would only have to invest $6,000 to reach the $50,000 breakpoint. You would be charged 4% on the $6,000.

There is a way to qualify for a lower commission even before you reach a breakpoint. If you sign a "letter of intent," stating that you intend to invest enough over the following 13 months to reach a breakpoint, you will be charged the lower commission from the beginning. If you change your mind or for any reason fail to invest enough to reach a breakpoint, you will be charged the appropriate amount based on whatever breakpoint you did reach, if any.

Although cost savings is important, it is not as important as diversification. Work with your bank investment representative to help you qualify for lower mutual fund commissions, while making sure you have sufficient diversification among types of mutual funds and among several mutual fund families.

EXHIBIT 17–1
Commission Schedule for Typical Stock Mutual Fund

| | Sales Commission as a Percentage of: | |
Purchase Amount	Public Offering	Net Amount Invested
Less than $50,000	5.75%	6.10%
$50,000 but less than $100,000	4.50%	4.71%
$100,000 but less than $250,000	3.50%	3.63%
$250,000 but less than $500,000	2.50%	2.56%
$500,000 but less than $1,000,000	2.00%	2.04%
$1,000,000 or more	0.00%	0.00%

Note: Bond mutual funds usually have a lower commission.

The second way to reduce the costs of investing is to consolidate your accounts. Many brokerage accounts charge an annual maintenance fee on each account you have. This fee, usually $50, can be avoided by making a purchase or sale in your account once a year. Evaluate if you need more than one account. For example, do you need a single account as well as a joint account, a gift to minors account, a revocable trust account, and so on?

Individual retirement accounts (IRA) are the most common accounts to be duplicated because people have a tendancy to open a new acount each year at the institution offering the highest rate that year, rather than adding to an existing IRA. You only need one account when dealing with your bank's brokerage. You can pay just one annual fee and have many mutual funds, stocks, and bonds in the same account.

The third way to reduce the costs of investing is to use your bank's discount brokerage when selling or buying individual stocks. Most banks have a discount brokerage as part of their brokerage operation. However, this should only be done if you know what and when you want to buy or sell since a discount brokerage does not give advice on individual stocks. It just executes your trade. In the unlikely event you want to include individual stocks in your investment strategy, you will need investment advice and therefore will pay full commission prices rather than discounted prices. Of course, you will want to make sure your bank can offer such advice.

Most banks don't offer buy and sell recommendations on individual stocks because there is little demand for it. Bank customers don't want to pay the higher fees when they feel more comfortable in managed investments anyway.

Chapter Eighteen

The Mechanics of Investing at Your Bank

I nvesting at your bank requires you to follow the same policies and procedures required at any brokerage firm, with a few minor differences. There are new account and tax forms to complete and sign, methods of payment that must be met, and disclosure and arbitration agreements that must be examined.

These policies and procedures are designed to inform you and protect you as well as the bank and its brokerage unit. You'll find that with the help of your bank investment representative, the mechanics of investing are easily understood.

Following is a review of the basic procedures involved and the forms you must sign and complete.

NEW ACCOUNT APPLICATIONS

Your bank investment representative is required by securities regulations to know enough about you to make appropriate investment recommendations. This is called the Know Your Customer Rule. This is accomplished through a joint discovery process that helps identify your needs, wants, risk tolerance, and investment experience. (See Chapters 4, 5, and 6.) This process also includes completing the new account application.

New account applications require slightly more personal and financial information than the average bank account application with which you are familiar. They vary in their design from one bank to the next, but they all ask for the same basic information outlined below.

- *Account Registration.* Name, social security or tax ID number, date of birth.

- *Residence.* Legal residence, mailing address, home and work telephone numbers, country of citizenship.
- *Employment Status.* Name of your employer, position/title, length of employment, business address. If not employed: homemaker, student, retired, or unemployed.
- *Corporate Affiliations.* Applicants must disclose if they are affiliated or a co-account holder with an insurance or trust company, a securities firm, or a bank and if they are a director, major stockholder, or officer of a publicly traded company. (If so, they are restricted in their dealings in investments related to the companies they are affiliated with.)
- *Account Type.* Most accounts are regular cash accounts or margin accounts (where you borrow money against your investments); option accounts and precious metals accounts involve substantial risk and require additional paperwork.
- *Account Ownership.* Choose from individual, joint tenants with rights of survivorship, tenants in common, custodial, or sole proprietorship. Trust, partnership, corporation, investment club, estate, and retirement accounts are available but require the completion of additional forms.
- *Account Servicing.* Here you list the banks you use and how you want to pay for your investments, which is called the settlement option. You can choose from cash, check, transfer from a bank account, or opening a money market account as part of the investment account. You also choose if you want your investments held in this account and periodic statements sent to you or if you want to take physical possession of the certificates. (The latter is not recommended. Ask your bank investment representative for the details.)
- *Current Status.* Information on marital status, number of dependents, total assets, approximate household net worth (excluding home), tax bracket, salary, household annual income, funds available for investment, estimated number and size of investment transactions per year, and listing of other brokerage accounts are required. (Some information requested may not always be required to open an account. Discuss the exceptions with your bank investment representative.)

- *Investment Objectives, Experience, and Knowledge.* Here
  you allocate investment objectives among tax reduction,
  income, principal safety, growth, and speculation; verify
  the types of investments you own or have owned and
  how long you have owned them; and declare how you
  view your investment experience: none, limited, moderate,
  or extensive.
- *Customer Agreement.* This section outlines the policies
  and procedures of the investment account, including the
  method for payment of your legal responsibilities and
  those of your bank's brokerage unit. This section contains
  the legal "fine print." It includes a predispute arbitration
  agreement for the settlement of disputes that could arise.
  It is standard throughout the financial services industry.
  Read it carefully and discuss it with your bank investment
  representative.
- *Signatures.* All parties with an interest in the account
  must sign. By signing you agree to the customer
  agreement and declare the information on the application
  correct. Your bank investment representative also signs
  the new account form.

You will receive a copy of the application upon completion.
One will be retained by your bank investment representative, and
one will be sent to the bank brokerage's main office.

OTHER APPLICATIONS

Some banks don't offer a consolidated investment account for
making all investment product purchases. Therefore, in some
cases, you will be asked to complete a separate application for
each investment. These applications are not as detailed as the new
account application described above.

W-9 Form

This form is most often included within the new account application but in some cases may be a separate form. It is required
by the IRS. On it, you simply list your Social Security or tax ID

number and sign it to verify that the number is correct. Failure to complete the W-9 form will result in the IRS withholding 31% of any interest you earn and any proceeds generated from the sale of an investment.

Disclosure Forms

The use of disclosure forms is where the bank brokerage differs from other investment providers. Your bank and government regulators want you to know that investments are not obligations of the bank and therefore are not covered by the FDIC; only traditional bank accounts are so covered. You will be asked to sign a form declaring that this was disclosed to you by your bank investment representative.

In addition, your bank goes the extra mile to educate you on other aspects of investing by including them on the disclosure form. What other providers of investments gloss over or downplay, your bank clearly communicates to you, first orally and then in writing on disclosure forms. These disclosures include, but are not limited to, the fees and commissions you pay, the fact that commissions on mutual funds can be reduced after certain amounts are invested or by using a letter of intent, the fact that values on investments fluctuate up and down, and the fact that you should receive a prospectus before investing in mutual funds and variable annuities.

Disclosure forms also explain who you are buying the investments from. This could be your bank itself, a subsidiary, an affiliated company, or a broker/dealer that has contracted with your bank to offer this service. (See Appendix E.)

Disclosure forms are for your benefit. They provide clear statements about investing that help you make decisions. Your bank sets itself apart from other providers of investments by its commitment to helping you understand investments before you invest.

Annuities Applications

Annuities are issued by insurance companies and require an additional application when they are purchased. The applications are short and require name, address, amount invested, and most important, the person whose life the annuity is based on and a declaration of the beneficiary. In addition, since annuities are substantially different from mutual funds and other securities, an additional disclosure form accompanies the application. This disclosure form reminds you that annuities are not obligations of the bank and are not FDIC insured. It also reminds you of any penalties and tax consequences upon withdrawal.

PAYING FOR YOUR INVESTMENTS

Just for illustration purposes, let's assume you invest $10,000. The money is usually paid when the investment is ordered if it is the first investment you have made with your bank investment representative. Subsequent investments don't require the money be paid until the settlement date, which is three business days after the investment is ordered. The day it is ordered on your instructions by your bank investment representative is called the trade date. So if you order $10,000 in mutual fund shares be purchased in your account on Monday, your bank investment representative sends in the order, and the trade occurs at the close of that day. Three days later, Thursday, the $10,000 must be paid.

When you are selling an investment such as a mutual fund, you have three days to deliver or have your account deliver the shares. It takes the same three days after the trade date to receive your money.

During the three days between the trade date and the settlement date, the necessary work is being done to transfer ownership and register the investments in a new owner's name.

Payment when due can be in the form of a check or transferred funds from a money market or bank account. Cash is also acceptable.

STATEMENTS

Confirmation Statements

On or before settlement date, you will receive in the mail a confirmation statement that details what action your bank investment representative took in your behalf. It simply confirms your order. It will list the amount due you in the case of a sale or the amount you owe in the case of a buy. It describes the investment involved and, in many cases, lists any commission you paid. If your name is spelled incorrectly, the investment involved is incorrect, or you have questions about amounts owed or due, contact your bank investment representative.

If you do not receive a confirmation statement, something has gone wrong. Contact your bank investment representative about the delay. Please note that a confirmation statement is for informational purposes; it's not a receipt or an invoice. Whether or not you receive a confirmation statement, the trade settles on settlement date, and your money is due.

Periodic Account Statements

Your bank brokerage account statement will come monthly if any transactions take place that month. Otherwise, it will come quarterly. Some banks don't offer consolidated statements that list all of your holdings and transactions on one statement. In such a case, you may receive statements directly from each of your investments.

Have your bank investment representative list what statements you will receive and when. When you receive them, read them and then keep them until you have a portfolio review with your bank investment representative. At that time, he or she can review them with you and show you which ones to keep.

CUSTOMER COMPLAINTS AND ARBITRATION

If you have a concern or complaint, discuss it with your bank investment representative. Most problems are misunderstandings that can be easily resolved. However, if this doesn't satisfy you, put your concerns or complaints in letter form and ask to speak with a supervisor.

Bank brokerage management will be responsive to your concerns. The law requires them to respond to written complaints and to keep records of such complaints and how they were resolved for regulators to examine.

In the unlikely event that you and your bank's brokerage program fail to resolve your differences, your disagreement is handled by an independent arbitration panel. This is the standard procedure for handling disputes that arise in the financial securities industry. For details on how this works, carefully reread the predispute arbitration agreement you signed when you opened the account and then discuss it with your bank's investment program managers.

For more information and assistance, contact your state government's securities division or the National Association of Securities Dealers (NASD); Compliance Department; 1735 K Street, N.W.; Washington, D.C.; or call 1-800-289-9999.

Chapter Nineteen

Tips for Getting Started

Y ou've come a long way since the first chapter. By now you should clearly see the necessity of combining investments with your bank accounts to reach your financial goals. You should also have a clearer understanding of your personal financial goals. And finally, chances are you feel that successful investing is within your reach.

Relying on financial direction, advice, and guidance from a trusted professional advisor is vital to your success. But, ultimately, it is you, after you have determined your needs and specified your goals with the assistance of a bank investment representative, who must choose to implement a recommended investment strategy or financial plan. And it is you who must make the final decisions on the investments that are recommended to you.

This book has provided the information you need to understand investing and communicate knowledgeably with your bank investment representative. Now it is time to start your own safe and smart investing. Here are 14 simple tips that review much of what you've learned and will help you to take action.

TIP 1: ACT NOW

Act now; don't wait for the perfect time to invest because no one has perfect timing. Suppose, however, you did have perfect timing—perfectly awful timing. Suppose you were one of the unfortunate few whose timing is always off, and over

EXHIBIT 19–1
Investing at the Worst Possible Time

Year	Date Share Price Was Highest	Cumulative Investment	Value of Account at Year-end
1	12/20/79	$ 5,000	$ 4,993
2	11/20/80	10,000	11,480
3	01/15/81	15,000	14,150
4	12/30/82	20,000	23,341
5	01/13/83	25,000	28,413
6	01/05/84	30,000	28,650
7	07/18/85	35,000	41,865
8	09/04/86	40,000	54,639
9	08/13/87	45,000	60,938
10	11/03/88	50,000	74,704
11	10/05/89	55,000	98,729
12	06/07/90	60,000	96,128
13	11/07/91	65,000	137,054
14	12/10/92	70,000	166,683
15	09/30/93	75,000	200,642

XYZ fund represents an actual fund. Each $5,000 investment was reduced by 5% to account for the sales commission.

Source: Lipper Analytical Securities Corporation.

the last 15 years since you began investing in a stock mutual fund you always invested at the worst possible time, when the market was the highest.

If you invested for your retirement by putting a lump sum of $5,000 a year for 15 years in XYZ stock mutual fund, but did so on the day the stock share price of the fund was the highest, how would have you done? (Remember, you're supposed to buy low and sell high, not buy high like you did.)

You would now have $200,642, and you only invested $75,000 total during the 15 years. Not bad! Fortunately for you, the XYZ mutual fund you chose earned on average 15.2 percent a year (see Exhibit 19–1).

This illustrates that any day, even the worst possible day, is a good day to invest if you leave your money invested for the long term. Investing on the worst days is still better than keeping your money in a savings account where you would be worth $139,282 at the end of the 15-year period.

Imagine how well you would have done if you had chosen to invest each year on the best possible day when the XYZ stock fund share price was at its yearly low. You would have a total of $311,701.

When it comes to investing, any time is better than never, and now is better than waiting around until the time feels right. There is no more perfect time to start investing than now. Get started!

TIP 2: SELECT AN ADVISOR TO GUIDE AND ASSIST YOU

Choose as your financial advisor a bank investment representative you feel confident about and can communicate with. Don't settle for the first person you come across. Look around; ask questions. Your advisor should be someone who clearly puts your needs first and treats your money with the same respect you do.

TIP 3: COMPLETE THE FINANCIAL NEEDS DISCOVERY WORKSHEET

The worksheet in Chapter 5 will help you determine your personal financial needs and place your financial goals in realistic time frames. An investment plan must be matched to your own personality, fears, needs, and wants. Defining them in writing will help you get a clear picture of your situation and prepare you to consult with your bank investment representative.

TIP 4: DETERMINE YOUR RISK TOLERANCE

You should determine the level of risk you are comfortable with. For example, a 3% annual loss might be tolerable, while an 8% decline in a single year might be too aggressive for you. Don't set yourself up for failure. Recognize that there could be down years in all investments except fixed annuities and bank accounts and you need to be ready to ride through those years. You must accept some degree of risk, or you will never stay ahead of inflation and enjoy financial security. It's a matter of trying to decide in advance how much risk you can handle.

Remember that even keeping all of your long-term money in FDIC-insured bank accounts carries some risk: the risk that you will not maintain your purchasing power.

TIP 5: SET TARGET RATES OF RETURN

Setting realistic targets with the help of your bank investment representative will allow you to match your expectations with the appropriate investments. Ask to see different mixes of investment products that have the highest probability of meeting your target rates of return and the various amounts needed to invest at those rates. Comparing different mixes will help you anchor your expectations in reality.

TIP 6: KNOW YOUR PRODUCTS

Understand what a stock and bond are since they are the basic instruments of all financial investment products. Know the basics of the various types of investments and how they can work with your bank accounts. Remember, every bank account and investment has inappropriate as well as appropriate uses.

TIP 7: USE MANAGED PRODUCTS

Managed products such as mutual funds and variable annuities are preferable over buying individual stocks and bonds separately. You and your investment representative have enough to do developing, implementing, monitoring, and adjusting your investment plan and strategy without worrying about what's happening with thousands of stocks on any given day. Professional money managers, who spend all day evaluating, tracking, and trading individual stocks and bonds on your behalf can serve you better.

TIP 8: ESTABLISH TIME HORIZONS

Set time horizons that match the investment and the eventual use of the money. If your money needs to be available in less than two years, use certificates of deposit, savings accounts, and money market accounts. For three- to-five year time horizons, look first to bank accounts, then to short-term bonds and bond funds. For five years and longer, there are many possibilities, including stock mutual funds, bonds, and fixed and variable annuities. Rely on your bank investment representative for help.

Stocks, whether in a mutual fund or variable annuity, should only be considered for this long-term horizon because the stock market goes down one year in every four, on average, and no one has ever been able to predict accurately which year it will decline. If you have short-term money in stocks and you need to withdraw it during a down year, you will take a loss.

TIP 9: AVOID OVEREXPOSURE TO BONDS

Because bonds are look-alike products to CDs, there is a tendency by bank customers to look at them as just another bank product with higher yields. They are not. Bonds are another way of earning interest, but they do not build your long-term growth, their principal fluctuates in value, and they are not FDIC insured. Your bank representative can help you find the appropriate mix of bonds and other investment products.

TIP 10: AVOID UNDEREXPOSURE TO STOCKS

Stocks are the only financial assets that have exceeded inflation over long periods of time. Every investor should have some component of stocks in his or her portfolio, but the tendency is to be underexposed or not have enough stocks in a portfolio to create meaningful growth.

TIP 11: ASK FOR A PLAN AND INVESTMENT RECOMMENDATIONS

By now you should have a pretty good understanding of investments and your own needs, so let your bank investment representative go to work for you. All you have learned has been leading up to the point where you're ready to make decisions. Now it's time to ask the professional for advice about a plan. Ask you bank investment representative for investment recommendations so that you can compare these against what you know and see if they seem to fit your needs.

TIP 12: START SLOW, BUT START NOW

The idea is not to jump in and invest in everything at once. Get your plan completed, then take one or two components of your plan and start investing. Build on your plan as time goes on and as you feel more confident.

TIP 13: WORRY ABOUT TAXES LAST

If you are in a high tax bracket, using investments that reduce or defer taxes is wise. But avoid allowing your desire to pay fewer taxes weigh too heavily in your investment selection process. An investment should be evaluated first for its ability to increase in value or generate income. If you are satisfied it is an investment with value irrespective of its tax advantages, tax advantages are a welcomed bonus.

TIP 14: MAXIMIZE THE VALUE OF YOUR RETIREMENT ACCOUNTS

If you are investing for the long term, first use the retirement accounts offered through your employment (401(k), pension, and profit-sharing plans, SEPs) and your personal individual retirement accounts. Put as much money as you can afford into these types of accounts because of their tax-deferral features and because you can deduct from your taxes your portion of the contributions to these accounts. For example, if you are in the 28% tax bracket and are eligible for an IRA, you can invest $2,000 and receive a tax deduction. This deduction is equivalent to the government putting $560 (28% of $2,000) into your account. Where else can you get an instant 28% return?

REMIND YOURSELF

There is often a period of uncertainty and adjustment after the implementation of an investment plan is underway. You may need to remind yourself now and then of your goals and objectives in order to stay the course and keep your emotions from interfering with the plan.

Congratulations, you've almost done it! You've almost made it through the book and hopefully started your investment program. Take a little more time and read Chapter 20. It will give you seven investment tips that should help you stay on course.

Chapter Twenty

Staying the Course

M any investors need to be reminded now and then of their goals and objectives in order to stay on course after implementation of their investment plan is underway. Emotions can interfere with any carefully devised plan if the long-term strategy is not kept in view. The following seven tips are designed to help you stay on course and ensure your success.

TIP 1: EXPECT YOUR INVESTMENTS TO FLUCTUATE IN VALUE

Having investments is a lot like having a thermostat: You have the frequent urge to fiddle. When you see long-term bonds go from 6% to more than 8%, for example, you'll want to make a change. You'll hate the heat and want to cool off. When the stock market goes up or down, you'll want to fiddle some more. And when you really start to shiver, you'll have the urge to warm up in a savings account.

According to a University of Michigan study, if you missed just 20 of the biggest days of the 1982–87 bull market (20 days represents 1% of this time period), your compounded annual return was cut in half, from 26% to 13%. If you missed the 40 days with the biggest gains, your annualized return dropped to 4.3%.

The secret to controlling the investments thermostat is to stop running around. Sit still, and you'll cool off. The thermostat works just fine. Don't let sudden drops or rises in the stock market cause you to react in panic or to get greedy. Don't be jumping in and out of your investments because you might lose out on the up days. Just keep a long-term perspective, expect your investments to fluctuate in value, and don't adjust your investment portfolio at every turn.

TIP 2: NEVER ACT HASTILY—TIME IS ON YOUR SIDE

No sensible investor should knowingly invest in stock-based investments only for one day or one month, or even for one year. Such brief time periods are clearly too short for investment in stocks because the expected variation in returns is too large in comparison to the average expected return. Such short-term holdings in stocks are not investments, they are rank speculations. Also, don't act hastily when your long-term investments appear to be underperforming your expectations in the short term. Give them enough time to be investments, not instruments of speculation.

Most investors remember the 30% drop in the stock market in 1987. Many mutual fund investors panicked and sold out, taking a loss. Those who didn't react hastily and stayed the course went on to receive record returns in the following years.

If you can get past the emotional reactions of short-term swings, you will discover that the longer investments are held, the closer the actual returns in a portfolio will come to the expected average.

This understanding will enable you to increase your tolerance for short-term market fluctuations. This makes it easier to concentrate on the long-term purpose of a success-driven portfolio and takes advantage of the one variable you can always count on: time.

A commitment to long-term investing is the investor's principal responsibility and main opportunity. Commit to the strategy. By combining investment products with bank accounts and adding the ingredient of time, you can almost be ensured of success.

What's long term and what's short term? Conventional wisdom measures rates of returns through one-year periods. While this is a conventional and thus a widely used method, this 12-month time frame is misleading.

The longer the stocks are held, the more the ups and downs tend to straighten out. Wars and threats of wars, political unrest, and economic setbacks become blips on the chart. Events are put in their proper perspective.

Exhibit 20–1 shows how time affects risk. It presents a chart of the correlation of risk over time. Notice the one-year-at-a-time rates of return on common stocks over the years show both large gains and losses. Shifting to five-year periods, the losses are not as great, and the gains appear more consistently. Shifting to 10-year periods increases the consistency of returns significantly. Only one loss is experienced, and most periods show positive average annual gains. Compounding over a decade overwhelms the single-year differences. Twenty-year periods bring even more consistency. **There are no losses, only gains.** The gains cluster more and more closely together around the long-term expected average rate of return.

Even with the obvious substantial differences in the range or distribution of returns in each time frame, there is one central constant: The average actual rate of return is almost the same in all cases. Patterns that seem random or confusing when viewed or experienced day-by-day, month-by month, or year-by-year take on a predictable average through longer periods of time. Analysis shows again and again the trade-off between risk and reward is driven by one key factor: time.

TIP 3: FOLLOW THROUGH AND INVEST REGULARLY

Once you start your investing plan, stick with it by making the appropriate investments when money comes available. Some adjustment will have to be made as your needs change and economic and political cycles run their course. When you have money to invest, check with your bank investment representative to see if any changes to your plan should be made; then follow through with your original or adjusted plan.

If you are like most investors, you can find a few extra dollars each month that you want to save. Rather than always accumulating it in a savings account or just spending it, invest it

EXHIBIT 20–1
Correlation of Risk Over Time (1926–1994 Compound Annual Rates of Return)

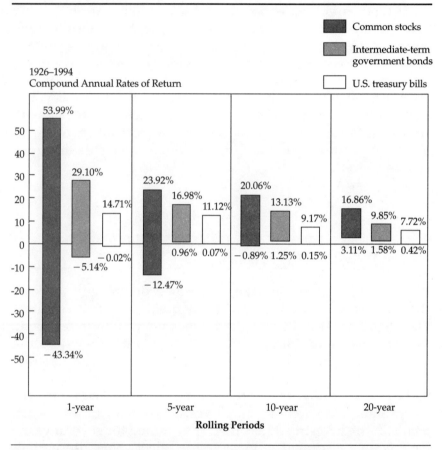

1926–1994
Compound Annual Rates of Return

Legend:
- Common stocks
- Intermediate-term government bonds
- U.S. treasury bills

Rolling Periods

systematically. This simple strategy will add significantly to your worth and is one of the safest ways to invest.

The mechanics of regularly adding to your mutual fund or variable annuity are simple. You can send a check whenever you want, or you can have a specified amount automatically withdrawn from your checking account on a monthly or quarterly basis.

TIP 4: NEVER CHASE THE "HOT" TIP

Financial publications are filled with rankings of the top perform-ing investments. Chances are, your investments are not going to be among them. High performers take high risks, something you want to avoid. In addition, when comparing your invest-ments to last year's top performers, remember that past perfor-mance is no guarantee of the future. In fact, try an experiment. Compare last year's top performing mutual fund with this year's and you'll see a whole new group for the most part. Stick with your well-thought-out plan. Chasing the next hot investment can set you up for an emotional roller-coaster ride and lead you nowhere.

TIP 5: NEVER FALL IN LOVE WITH YOUR OWN INVESTMENTS

When you life situation changes or the economy and tax laws change, you will want to consider adjusting your investment plan. Separate from this is the replacement of an investment, not because your needs have changed, but because the investment is underperforming other investments of its kind. Review your investments once a year with the help of your bank investment representative. At that time, compare the performance of each of your investments with other invest-ments. If the investment has underperformed for several years, have your investment representative select some alternatives for you to consider.

Keep investments for the right reasons, and replace them for the right reasons. Change is difficult for many people, but investments should always be considered on their own merit. Avoid keeping investments for invalid reasons such as your parents bought them for you, your deceased spouse told you to *never* sell them, or because they have become part of your comfort zone. You owe it to yourself and your future to maxi-mize the power of your money by unemotionally moving it when prudent.

TIP 6: KEEP ACCURATE RECORDS AS YOU MEASURE, NOT TRACK, YOUR INVESTMENTS

You need to keep records, but you don't need to keep track of every last little fluctuation in the stock market. Doing so will wear on your nerves. When you receive your investment statements, read them so you feel confident that your money is still there and to see if you are still meeting your targets. Tracking the day-to-day movement of your money is the job of the professional money manager directing your mutual fund, for example. Leave the stressful part of investing to him or her.

When keeping records, concentrate on keeping your year-end statements and your purchase/sales confirmations and receipts so you can satisfy the IRS.

TIP 7: HAVE AN ANNUAL CHECKUP

Just as you see your doctor regularly, ask for an annual appointment with your bank investment representative to review your investment program and ensure that you are on course. Take this time to set new investment goals and rebalance if need be. Rebalancing is nothing more than bringing your investments into balance with your current needs and with trends in the economy. As the values of some investment categories change disproportionately to others, a portfolio needs to be realigned to the efficient frontier (the highest expected rate of return for the chosen risk level of that portfolio).

CONCLUSION

Maximizing the power of your savings by moving beyond FDIC-insured bank accounts is essential to achieving the personal financial independence you need in an increasingly complex world. You now have, at the very minimum, the knowledge you need to determine your needs and formulate a plan of action to move from being exclusively a saver toward being a successful investor. This knowledge, coupled with the assistance of a bank investment representative you trust, will put the power in your savings.

APPENDIXES:
QUICK REFERENCES

Mutual Funds Distributed through Banks

Mutual funds are the most common investments used by investors to meet their financial goals. The American consumer can choose from among thousands of mutual funds bundled into hundreds of mutual fund groups, often called families. The leading mutual fund families listed below are the most prominent families distributed by bank investment programs. Included is the name and address, the telephone number of the shareholder services department, total assets under management, and the year the fund was founded.

AETNA Series Funds
151 Farmington Avenue
Hartford, CT 06156-8962
800-367-7732
$907 million
Year founded: 1990

AIM Management Group
PO Box 4739
Houston, TX 77210-4739
1-800-959-4246
$16 billion
Year founded: 1976

Alliance Capital Management LP
1345 Avenue of Americas
New York, NY 10105
800-221-5672
$35 billion
Year founded: 1971

American Express Financial
 Advisors Inc.
PO Box 157
Minneapolis, MN 55440-0157
612-671-3733
$36.7 billion
Year founded: 1894

American Funds
135 South Station College Boulevard
Brea, CA 92622
800-421-0180
$102 billion
Year founded: 1934

Calvert Group
4550 Montgomery Avenue,
 Suite 1000
Bethesda, MD 20814
800-368-2745
$4.1 billion
Year founded: 1976

Colonial Funds
One Financial Center
Boston, MA 02111
800-345-6611
$13.4 billion
Year founded: 1931

Columbia Funds
PO Box 1350
Portland, OR 97207
800-547-1707
$3.3 billion
Year founded: 1967

Delaware Group
1818 Market Street
Philadelphia, PA 19103
800-523-4640
$10 billion
Year founded: 1929

Dreyfus
PO Box 9671
Providence, RI 02940
800-645-6561
$60 billion
Year founded: 1951

Eaton Vance
53 State Street
Boston, MA 02109
800-262-1122
$15 billion
Year founded: 1924

Evergreen Funds
2500 Westchester Avenue
Purchase, NY 10577
800-235-0064
$2.8 billion
Year founded: 1971

Federated Investors
Liberty and Fortress Groups
Federated Investors Tower
Pittsburgh, PA 15222-3779
800-245-4770
$72 billion
Year founded: 1955

Fidelity Investments
PO Box 2269
Boston, MA 02107-2269
800-544-6666
$398 billion
Year founded: 1930

Flagship Funds
c/o BFDS
PO Box 8509
Boston, MA 02266
800-225-8530
$4.5 billion
Year founded: 1984

Fortis Mutual Funds
500 Bielenburg Drive
Woodburg, MN 55125
800-800-3016
$3.3 billion
Year founded: 1940

Franklin/Templeton Group
777 Mariners Island Boulevard
San Mateo, CA 94404
800-393-3001
$114 billion
Year founded: 1947

GE Investments
c/o BFDS
PO Box 8309
Boston, MA 02266-8309
800-242-0134
$146.5 million
Year founded: 1993

GT Global
50 California Street, 27th Floor
San Francisco, CA 94111
800-223-2138
$9.3 billion
Year founded: 1969

Heartland Funds
790 North Milwaukee Street
Milwaukee, WI 53202
800-432-7856
$565 million
Year founded: 1984

IDEX Funds
201 Highland Avenue
Largo, FL 34640
800-851-9777, x-6521
$994 million
Year founded: 1984

Investors Trust Mutual Funds
PO Box 490
Seattle, WA 98111
800-656-6626
$1.2 billion
Year founded: 1987

Janus Funds
PO Box 173375
Denver, CO 80217
800-525-3713
$17 million
Year founded: 1970

John Hancock Mutual Funds
PO Box 9116
Boston, MA 02205-9116
800-225-5291
$14 billion
Year founded: 1968

Kemper Mutual Funds
811 Main Street
PO Box 419557
Kansas City, MO 64105
800-621-1048
$38 billion
Year founded: 1948

Keystone Mutual Funds
PO Box 2121
Boston, MA 02106-2121
800-343-2898
$10.5 billion
Year founded: 1932

Lord Abbett & Co.
767 5th Avenue
New York, NY 10153
800-821-5129
$16 billion
Year founded: 1929

Met Life/State Street
1 Financial Center, 30th floor
Boston, MA 02111
800-882-0052
$4.4 billion
Year founded: 1924

MFS (Massachussetts Financial
    Services)
500 Boylston Street
Boston, MA 02116
800-225-2606
$36 billion
Year founded: 1924

Nicholas Applegate Mutual
    Funds
600 West Broadway, 29th Floor
San Diego, CA 92101
800-551-8043
$977 million
Year founded: 1993

North American Funds
116 Huntington Avenue
Boston, MA 02116
800-872-8037
$555 million
Year founded: 1989

Nuveen
333 West Wacker Drive
Chicago, IL 60606
800-621-7227
$50 billion
Year founded: 1976

Oppenheimer Funds
PO Box 5270
3410 S. Galina
Denver, CO 80231
800-525-7048
$20.6 billion
Year founded: 1947

Overland Express Funds
PO Box 63084
San Francisco, CA 94163
800-572-7797
$3.4 billion
Year founded: 1988

Pasadena Group
5690 DTC Boulevard, Suite 400
Englewood, CO 80111
800-648-8050
$577 million
Year founded: 1986

Phoenix Funds
100 Bright Meadow Boulevard
Enfield, CT 06082
800-243-4361
$8.1 billion
Year founded: 1969

Pilgrim Group
10100 Santa Monica Boulevard,
    21st Floor
Los Angeles, CA 90067
800-331-1080
$1.7 billion
Year founded: 1969

PIMCO Advisor Funds
PO Box 5866
Denver, CO 80217-5866
800-426-0107
$4.4 billion
Year founded: 1984

Pioneer
60 State Street
Boston, MA 02109
800-225-6292
$11.1 billion
Year founded: 1928

PRINCOR
711 High Street
Des Moines, IA 50309
800-451-5447
$2.0 billion
Year founded: 1969

Putnam Investments
PO Box 41203
Providence, RI 02940-1203
800-225-1581
$101 billion
Year founded: 1937

Quest for Value
2 World Financial Center,
    16th Floor
225 Liberty Street
New York, NY 10281
800-232-3863
$1.1 billion
Year founded: 1980

Rochester Funds
350 Linden Oaks
Rochester, NY 14625
716-383-1300
$2.5 billion
Year founded: 1980

Scudder Funds
PO Box 2291
Boston, MA 02017-2291
800-225-5163
$20 billion
Year founded: 1928

Security Funds
700 SW Harrison
Topeka, KS 66636
800-888-2461
$2 billion
Year founded: 1944

Seligman Funds
100 Park Avenue
New York, NY 10017
800-221-2450
$6.5 billion
Year founded: 1929

Sierra Trust Funds
9301 Corbin Avenue, Suite 333
Northridge, CA 91328
800-222-5852
$2.9 billion
Year founded: 1989

Sogen Funds
PO Box 9123
Boston, MA 02209-9123
800-443-7046
$2.3 billion
Year founded: 1969

Stein Roe Mutual Funds
PO Box 804058
Chicago, IL 60680-4058
800-338-2550
$4.5 billion
Year founded: 1932

SunAmerica
733 3rd Avenue, 3rd floor
New York, NY 10017
800-858-8850
$2.0 billion
Year founded: 1985

Thornburg Funds
119 East Marcy Street, Suite 202
Santa Fe, NM 87501
800-847-0200
$1.5 billion
Year founded: 1984

Vanguard Group
PO Box 2600
Valley Forge, PA 19482-2600
800-662-2739
$131.5 billion
Year founded: 1929

Van Kampen American Capital
PO Box 419001
Kansas City, MO 64141-6001
800-341-2911
$27.9 billion
Year founded: 1946

Vista Mutual Funds
PO Box 419392
Kansas City, MO 64141
800-648-4782
$6.6 billion
Year founded: 1987

Wright Investors
1000 Lafayette Boulevard
Bridgeport, CT 06604
800-232-0013
$1.0 billion
Year founded: 1983

ZWEIG Series Trust
5 Hanover Square, 17th floor
New York, NY 10004
800-272-2700
$2.3 billion
Year founded: 1989

Source: *1994 National Census of Bank Investment Services,* American Brokerage Data
Services, Inc., and the companies listed.

Appendix B

Bank Proprietary Mutual Funds

More than 100 of the largest banks in the country have founded their own mutual funds exclusively for their customers. These bank proprietary mutual funds, as they are called, are generally offered to customers as just another option along with other nationally known independent mutual funds. However, some banks emphasize the purchase of their own mutual funds over others, and a few banks offer only their own mutual funds to customers.

Below is a list of banks that sponsor their own mutual funds, the name, address and phone number of the fund group, total assets and the year of inception.

AMCORE Bank
Rockford, IL
  AMCORE Vintage Funds
  1900 East Dublin-Granville Road
  Columbus, OH 43229
  800-438-6375
  $357 million
  Year founded: 1992

AmSouth Bank
Birmingham, AL
  AmSouth Mutual Funds
  1900 East Dublin-Granville Road
  Columbus, OH 43230
  800-451-8379
  $1,595 million
  Year founded: 1988

Bank of America
San Francisco, CA
  Pacific Horizon Funds
  7863 Girard Avenue, Suite 306
  La Jolla, CA 92037
  800-332-3863
  Seafirst Retirement Funds
  PO Box 84248
  Seattle, WA 98124
  800-323-9919
  $3,735 million
  Year founded:1973

Bank of California
San Francixco, CA
  HighMark Group
  PO Box 7591
  San Francisco, CA 94120
  800-433-6884
  $236 million
  Year founded: 1991

Bank of Hawaii
Honolulu, HI
   Hawaiian Tax-Free
     Trust/Pacific Capital Funds
   Administrative Data Mgmt.
   Attn: Pacific Capital Funds
   10 Woodbridge Center Drive
   Woodbridge, NJ 07095
   800-258-9232
   $1,294 million
   Year founded:1984

Bank of New York
New York, NY
   BNY Hamilton Funds
   7863 Girard Avenue, Suite 306
   La Jolla, CA 92037
   800-426-9363
   $237 million
   Year founded: 1992

Bank of Oklahoma,
Tulsa, OK
   American Performance Funds
   1900 East Dublin-Grandville
    Road
   Columbus, OH 43229
   800-762-7085
   $622 million
   Year founded: 1990

Bank One, N.A.
Columbus, OH
   The One Group/Tax-Free Trust
    of Arizona
   PO Box 176
   Westerville, OH 43086-9801
   800-480-4111
   $714 million
   Year founded: 1986

Bank South N.A.
Atlanta, GA
   Peachtree Funds
   PO Box 4387, MC 683
   Atlanta, GA 30302
   800-282-6680
   $353 million
   Year founded: 1994

Bankers Trust Co.
New York, NY
   BT Investment Funds/BT
    Pyramid Funds
   BT Mutual Funds
   210 West 10th Street, 8th Floor
   Kansas City, MO 64105
   800-422-6577
   $2,477 million
   Year founded: 1987

Barnett Banks Trust Co.
Jacksonville, FL
   Emerald Funds
   Barnett Securities
   Attn: Emerald Funds
   9000 Southside Boulevard,
    Building 100, 9th Floor
   Jacksonville, FL 32256
   800-637-6336
   $428 million
   Year founded: 1991

BayBanks, Inc.
Boston, MA
   Bay Funds
   PO Box 665
   Waltham, MA 02154
   800-229-3863
   $267 million
   Year founded: 1993

Bessemer Trust Co.
New York, NY
  Old Westbury International Fund
  6 St. James Avenue
  Boston, MA 02116
  800-545-1074
  $89 million
  Year founded: 1993

Boatmen's Trust Co.
St. Louis, MO
  Pilot Funds
  7863 Girard Avenue, Suite 306
  La Jolla, CA 92037
  800-844-1235
  $32 million
  Year founded: 1968

Branch Banking & Trust Co., N.C.
Wilson, NC
  BB&T Mutual Funds
  1900 East Dublin-Granville Road
  Columbus, OH 43229
  800-228-1872
  $41 million
  Year founded: 1993

Brenton Bank, N.A.
Des Moines, IA
  The Brenton Funds
  Dept. L-1413
  Columbus, OH 43260-1413
  800-706-3863
  $58 million
  Year founded: 1994

Brown Brothers Harriman & Co.
New York, NY
  59 Wall Street Funds
  6 St. James Avenue
  Boston, MA 02116
  212-493-8100
  $926 million
  Year founded: 1983

Canandaigua National Bank
  & Trust
Canandaigua, NY
  Canandaigua National
    Collective Investment Fund
    for Qualified Trusts
  72 South Main Street
  Canandaigua, NY 14424
  800-724-2621 ext. 216
  $6 million
  Year founded: 1992

Central Carolina Bank
Durham, NC
  111 Corcoran Funds
  PO Box 2006
  Durham, NC 27702
  800-422-2080
  $121 million
  Year founded: 1992

Central Fidelity Banks
Richmond, VA
  MarketWatch Funds
  Preferred Accounts Service
    Center
  6800 Paragon Place,
    Suite 526
  Richmond, VA 23230
  800-232-9091
  $223 million
  Year founded:1993

Centura Bank
Rocky Point, NC
  Centura Funds
  237 Park Avenue, 9th Floor
  New York, NY 10017
  800-442-3688
  $2 million
  Year founded: 1994

Chase Manhattan Bank, N.A.
New York, NY
  Vista Funds/Growth Fund of
    Washington
  Vista Service Center
  PO Box 419392
  Kansas City, MO 64141
  800-348-4782 800-348-4782
  $3,934 million
  Year founded: 1983

Chemical Bank, N.A.
New York, NY
  Hanover Funds
  237 Park Avenue, 9th Floor
  New York, NY 10017
  800-821-2371
  $5,288 million
  Year founded: 1989

Citibank, N.A.
New York, NY
  Landmark Funds
  6 St. James Avenue
  Boston, MA 02116
  800-331-1792
  $2,853 million
  Year founded: 1984

Citizens Commercial and Savings
  Bank
Flint, MI
  The Golden Oak Funds
  c/o SSC
  PO Box 419947
  Kansas City, MO 64141
  800-331-1792
  $0.4 million
  Year founded: 1993

Citizens Trust Co.
Providence, RI
  Narranganset Insured Tax-Free
    Income Fund
  10 Woodbridge Center
    Drive
  Woodbridge, NJ 07095-1198
  800-637-4633
  $30 million
  Year founded: 1992

Comerica Bank-Detroit
Detroit, MI
  Ambassador Funds
  Funds Distributor
  Attn: Ambassador Funds
  One Exchange Place,
    Mail Zone 025-010A
  Boston, MA 02109
  800-892-4366
  $70 million
  Year founded: 1992

Compass Bank
Birmingham, AL
  Starburst Funds
  Compass Bank
  Attn: Starburst Funds
  701 South 32nd Street
  Birmingham, AL 35232
  800-239-1930
  $118 million
  Year founded:1991

CoreStates Bank, N.A.
Philadelphia, PA
  CoreFunds
  PO Box 470
  Wayne, PA 19087
  800-252-1784
  $48 million
  Year founded: 1993

Crestar Bank
Richmond, VA
   CrestFunds, Inc.
   PO Box 2798
   Boston, MA 02208-9915
   800-451-5435 (press #3)
   $38 million
   Year founded: 1993

Deposit Guaranty National Bank
Jackson, MS
   DG Investor Series
   Deposit Guaranty Trust Division
   Attn: Mutual Funds
   PO Box 23100
   Jackson, MS 39225-3100
   800-432-6106
   $732 million
   Year founded: 1992

Fifth Third Bank
Cincinnati, OH
   Fountain Square Funds
   Federated Investors Tower
   Pittsburgh, PA 15222-3779
   513-579-4358
   $720 million
   Year founded: 1988

First Alabama Bank
Birmingham, AL
   First Priority Funds
   417 North 20th Street, 9th Floor
   Birmingham, AL 35203
   800-433-2829
   $82 million
   Year founded: 1992

First American National Bank
Nashville, TN
   ValueStar Funds
   Ameristar Capital Markets
   Attn: ValueStar Funds
   First American Center,
      4th Floor
   Nashville, TN 37237
   800-824-3741
   $400 million
   Year founded: 1994

First Bank, N.A.
St. Paul, MN
   First American Funds/First
      American Investment Funds/
      First American Mutual Funds
   680 East Swedeford Road
   Wayne, PA 19087
   800-637-2548
   $131 million
   Year founded: 1982

First Fidelity Bank
Newark, NJ
   FFB Lexicon Funds
   c/o SEI Corporation
   680 East Swedesford Rd.
   Wayne, PA 19087
   800-833-8974
   $1,480 million
   Year founded: 1986

First Interstate Bank
Los Angeles, CA
   Westcore Funds
   370 17th Street, Suite 2700
   Denver, CO 80202
   800-392-2673

Pacifica Funds
PO Box 4490
Grand Central Station
New York, NY 10163
800-662-8417
$2,532 million
Year founded: 1985

First Michigan Bank Corporation
Holland, MI
   FMB Funds
   237 Park Avenue
   New York, NY 10017
   800-453-4234
   $3 million
   Year founded: 1991

First National Bank of Boston
Boston, MA
   1784 Funds
   PO Box 1784
   Wayne, PA 19087
   800-355-2673
   $1,173 million
   Year founded: 1993

First National Bank of Chicago
Chicago, IL
   First Prairie Funds
   First Chicago Investment
     Services
   Mail Suite 0291, 2nd Floor
   First Chicago National Plaza
   Chicago, IL 60670
   800-370-9446
   $481 million
   Year founded: 1986

First National Bank of Ohio
Akron, OH
   Portage Funds
   FBOH Investor Services, Inc.
   4100 Embassy Parkway
   Akron, OH 44333
   800-626-1110
   $68 million
   Year founded: 1991

First National Bank of Omaha
Omaha, NE
   First Omaha Funds
   PO Box 419002
   Kansas City, MO 64141-6022
   800-662-4203
   $307 million
   Year founded: 1991

First of America Bank—Michigan
Kalamazoo, MI
   Parkstone Funds
   Shareholder Services
   157 South Kalamazoo Mall
   Kalamazoo, MI 49007
   800-451-8377
   $792 million
   Year founded: 1993

First Security Bank
Salt Lake City, UT
   Tax Free Fund for Utah
   Administrative Data Mgmt. Corp.
   10 Woodbridge Center
   Woodbridge, NJ 07095-1198
   800-446-8824
   $24 million
   Year founded: 1992

First Tennessee Bank, N.A.
Memphis, TN
   First Funds
   National Financial Services Corp.
   82 Devonshire Street,
     Mail Zone L12C
   Boston, MA 02109
   800-442-1941
   $10 million
   Year founded: 1993

First Union National
Bank of North Carolina
Charlotte, NC
   First Union Funds
   One First Union Center,
     NCL1173
   301 South College
   Charlotte, NC 28288
   800-347-1246
   $2,379 million
   Year founded: 1985

Firstar Trust Co.
Milwaukee, WI
   Portico Funds
   PO Box 3011
   Milwaukee, WI 53201-3011
   800-982-8909
   $1,835 million
   Year founded: 1988

Fleet National Bank
Providence, RI
   Galaxy Funds
   Box 7
   440 Lincoln Street
   Worcester, MA 01653-0007
   800-628-0413
   $2,160 million
   Year founded: 1986

FNB of Commerce in New Orleans
New Orleans, LA
   Marquis Funds
   First Commerce Investment
     Services
   210 Baronne Street
   PO Box 61239
   New Orleans, LA 70161
   800-814-3396
   $362 million
   Year founded: 1993

Great Western Savings Bank
Los Angeles, CA
   Sierra Trust Funds
   9301 Corbin Avenue, Suite 333
   PO Box 1160
   Northridge, CA 91328-1160
   800-222-5852
   $2,574 million
   Year founded: 1989

Harris Trust & Savings Bank
Chicago, IL
   Harris Insight Funds
   Funds Distributor
   One Exchange, 10th Floor
   Boston, MA 02109
   800-441-7762
   $1,245 million
   Year founded: 1988

Hibernia National Bank
New Orleans, LA
   Tower Mutual Funds
   PO Box 61540
   New Orleans, LA 70131
   504-533-2180
   $592 million
   Year founded: 1988

Home Savings and Savings of
    America
Santa Fe Springs, CA
    Griffin Funds
    PO Box 419245
    Kansas City, MO 64141
    800-676-4450
    $118 million
    Year founded: 1993

Huntington Trust Co., N.A.
Columbus, OH
    Monitor Funds
    c/o Huntington Trust Company
    41 South High Street,
        11th Floor
    Columbus, OH 43287
    800-253-0412
    $110 million
    Year founded: 1991

Integra Trust Co.
Pittsburgh, PA
    Inventor Funds
    680 East Swedesford
    Wayne, PA 19087
    800-646-8363
    $496 million
    Year founded: 1994

Key Trust Company
Cleveland, OH
    Victory Funds/Victory
        Portfolios
    Primary Fund Service
    PO Box 9741
    Providence, RI 02940-9741
    800-362-5365
    $4,432 million
    Year founded: 1983

LaSalle National Trust
Chicago, IL
    Rembrandt Funds
    680 East Swedesford
    Wayne, PA 19087
    800-443-4725
    $20 million
    Year founded: 1993

Manufacturers and Traders Trust
    Company
Horsham, PA
    Vision Funds
    PO Box 4556
    Buffalo, NY 14240-4556
    800-836-2211
    $720 million
    Year founded: 1988

Marine Midland Bank, N.A.
New York, NY
    Mariner Mutual Funds Trust
    370 17th Street, Suite 2700
    Denver, CO 80202
    800-634-2536
    $825 million
    Year founded: 1982

Mark Twain Bank
Ladue, MO
    Arrow Funds
    Mark Twain Brokerage
    1630 South Lindberg Boulevard
    St. Louis, MO 63131
    800-688-9246
    $481 million
    Year founded: 1993

Marshall & Ilsley Corp.
Milwaukee, WI
  Marshall Funds
  Marshall & Ilsley Trust Company
  1000 North Water Street
  Milwaukee, WI 53202
  800-236-8554
  $1,206 million
  Year founded: 1992

Mellon Bank
Pittsburgh, PA
  Dreyfus-Laurel Funds
    /Dreyfus-Laurel Investment
    Series/Dreyfus-Laurel
    Tax-Free Municipal Funds
  200 Park Avenue
  New York, NY 10166
  800-548-2868
  $946 million
  Year founded: 1947

Mercantile Bank of St. Louis, N.A.
St. Louis, MO
  Arch Funds/Arch Tax-Exempt
    Trust
  Attn: Shareholder Services
  1900 East Dublin-Granville Rd.
  Columbus, OH 43229
  800-452-2724
  $4,134 million
  Year founded: 1983

Mercantile-Safe Deposit &
  Trust Co.
Baltimore, MD
  MSD&T Funds
  c/o Mercantile Safe Deposit &
    Trust Co.
  2 Hopkins Plaza
  PO Box 1477
  Baltimore, MD 21203
  800-551-2145
  N/A
  Year founded: 1989

Meridian Bancorp, Inc.
Malvern, PA
  Conestoga Family of Funds
  1900 East Dublin-Granville Rd.
  Columbus, OH 43229
  800-344-2716
  $668 million
  Year founded: 1989

Michigan National Bank
Farmington Hills, MI
  Independence One Mutual
    Funds
  Federated Investors Tower
  Pittsburgh, PA 15222-3779
  800-934-3883
  $594 million
  Year founded: 1989

Midlantic National Bank
Edison, NJ
  Compass Capital Group
  680 East Swedesford
  Wayne, PA 19087
  800-451-8371
  $1,986 million
  Year founded: 1988

Morgan Guaranty Trust Company
of New York
New York, NY
  Pierpont Funds
  J.P. Morgan Funds Services
  9 West 57th Street,
    11th Floor
  New York, NY 10019
  800-521-5411
  $4,190 million
  Year founded: 1982

National Bank of Commerce
Memphis, TN
  Riverside Capital Funds
  Attn: Shareholder Services
  1900 East Dublin-Granville Rd
  Columbus, OH 43229
  800-874-8376
  $311 million
  Year founded: 1988

National City Bank,
Cleveland, OH
National City Columbus,
National City Kentucky,
(National City Corp.)
  ARMADA Funds
  c/o 440 Financial Distributors
  440 Lincoln Street
  Worcester, MA 01653
  800-622-3863
  $227 million
  Year founded: 1991

NationsBank
Charlotte, NC
  Nations Fund Trust/Nations
    Funds
  One Nations Bank Plaza
  Charlotte, NC 28255
  800-321-7854
  $1,871 million
  Year founded: 1989

NBD Bank, N.A.
Detroit, MI
  Woodward Funds
  Attn: Shareholder Services
  c/o NBD Bank
  PO Box 7058
  Detroit, MI 48007-7058
  800-688-3350
  $3,121 million
  Year founded: 1987

Northern Trust Co.
Chicago, IL
  Northern Funds
  50 South LaSalle Street, C45
  Chicago, IL 60675
  800-595-9111
  $2,149 million
  Year founded: 1994

Norwest Bank Minnesota, N.A.
Minneapolis, MN
  Norwest Funds
  Norwest Bank Minnesota, N.A.
  Transfer Agent
  733 Marquette Avenue
  Minneapolis, MN 55479-0040
  800-338-1348
  $3,576 million
  Year founded: 1988

Old Kent Bank & Trust Company
Grand Rapids, MI
  The Kent Funds
  c/o 440 Financial Distributors
  440 Lincoln Street
  Worcester, MA 01653
  800-633-5368
  $45 million
  Year founded: 1992

One Valley Bank, N.A.
Charleston, WV
   The Arbor OVB Funds
   c/o Supervised Service
     Company
   PO Box 419947
   Kansas City, MO 64141-6947
   800-545-6331
   $3.7 million
   Year founded: 1993

PNC Bank Kentucky
Louisville, KY
   Churchill Funds
   380 Madison Avenue,
     Suite 2300
   New York, NY 10017
   212-697-6666
   $408 million
   Year founded: 1985

PNC Bank, N.A.
Pittsburgh, PA
   PNC Funds
   PFPC
   PO Box 8907
   Wilmington, DE 19899-8908
   800-422-6538
   $199 million
   Year founded: 1989

Premier Bank, N.A.
Baton Rouge, LA
   Paragon Portfolios
   c/o NFDS
   PO Box 419711
   Kansas City, MO 64141
   800-525-7907
   $1,228 million
   Year founded: 1989

Provident Bank—Cincinnati
Cincinnati, OH
   Riverfront Funds
   PO Box 14967
   Cincinnati, OH 45250-0967
   800-424-2295
   $217 million
   Year founded: 1992

Republic National Bank of
  New York
New York, NY
   Fund Trust
   c/o Investors Bank &
     Trust Co.
   PO Box 1537, MFD23
   Boston, MA 02205-1537
   800-638-1896
   $327 million
   Year founded: 1984

Riggs National Bank of
  Washington, DC
Washington, DC
   RIMCO Monument
     Funds
   PO Box 96656
   Washington, DC 20090-6656
   800-934-3883
   $569 million
   Year founded: 1991

Shawmut Bank N.A.
Boston, MA
   Shawmut Funds
   PO Box 1365
   Framingham, MA 01701
   800-333-7384
   $371 million
   Year founded: 1993

Signet Bank
Richmond, VA
  Medalist Funds
  c/o Signet Financial
    Services
  PO Box 26301
  Richmond, VA 23286-8192
  800-333-7384
  $312 million
  Year founded: 1990

SouthTrust Bank of Alabama, N.A.
Birmingham, AL
  SouthTrust Vulcan Funds
  PO Box 2554
  Birmingham, AL 39290
  800-239-7470
  $417 million
  Year founded: 1992

Star Bank, N.A.
Cincinnati, OH
  Star Funds
  Federated Investors Tower
  Pittsburgh, PA 15222-3779
  800-677-3863
  $788 million
  Year founded: 1989

State Street Bank & Trust
Boston, MA
  Star Funds
  Seven Seas Series Fund
  Boston Financial
  Attn: Seven Seas Funds
  PO Box 8317
  Boston, MA 02266-8317
  800-647-7327
  $4,910 million
  Year founded: 1988

Sunburst Bank, MS
Grenada, MS
  Starburst Funds
  PO Box 23053
  Jackson, MS 39225-3053
  800-467-2506
  $11 million
  Year founded: 1993

SunTrust Banks
Orlando, FL
  STI Class Funds
  SunBank, N.A.
  200 South Orange Avenue,
    Tower 10
  Orlando, FL 32801
  800-428-6970
  $549 million
  Year founded: 1992

Swiss Bank Corp.
New York, NY
  SwissKey Funds
  6 St. James Avenue
  Boston, MA 02116
  800-524-9984
  $64 million
  Year founded: 1992

Trustmark National Bank
Jackson, MS
  Performance Funds Trust
  PO Box 4490
  Grand Central Station
  New York, NY 10163
  800-737-3676
  $8 million
  Year founded: 1992

Union Bank
San Diego, CA
    Stepstone Funds
    Union Capital Advisors
    445 South Figueroa Street,
        5th Floor
    Los Angeles, CA 90071
    800-634-1100
    $273 million
    Year founded: 1991

Union Bank & Trust Company
Lincoln, NE
    Stratus Funds
    500 Centre Terrace
    1225 L Street
    Lincoln, NE 68508
    800-279-7437
    N/A
    Year founded:1991

Union Planters National Bank
Memphis, TN
    The Planters Funds
    Union Planters National Bank
    PO Box 387
    Memphis, TN 38147
    800-618-8573
    $37 million
    Year founded: 1993

United Jersey Bank
Hackensack, NJ
    The Pillar Funds
    PO Box 239
    Wayne, PA 19087
    800-932-7782
    $56 million
    Year founded: 1992

United Missouri Bank
Kansas City, MO
    UMB Funds
    2440 Pershing Road, Suite G-15
    Kansas City, MO 64108
    800-422-2766
    $729 million
    Year founded: 1982

United States Trust Company of
New York
New York, NY
    UST Master Funds
    7863 Girard Avenue, Suite 306
    La Jolla, CA 92037
    800-233-1136
    $3,476 million
    Year founded: 1985

U.S. National Bank of Oregon
Portland, OR
    The Cascades Trust/Qualivest
        Funds
    1900 East Dublin-Granville Road
    Columbus, OH 43229
    800-743-8637
    $427 million
    Year founded: 1986

Wachovia Trust Co.
Winston-Salem, NC
    Biltmore Funds
    Wachovia Investment Services
    PO Box 110
    Winston-Salem, NC 27102
    800-462-7538
    $1,085 million
    Year founded: 1991

Washington Mutual Savings Bank
Seattle, WA
  Composite Funds
  601 West Main Avenue,
    Suite 801
  Spokane, WA 99201-0613
  800-543-8072
  $1,095 million
  Year founded: 1949

Wells Fargo Bank
San Francisco, CA
  Overland Express Funds
  Shareholder Services
  PO Box 63084
  San Francisco, CA 94163
  800-572-7797

  Stagecoach Funds
  PO Box 7066
  San Francisco, CA 94120
  800-222-8222
  $7,935 million
  Year founded: 1984

Wilmington Trust Co.
Wilmington, DE
  Rodney Square Funds
  c/o Rodney Square Mgmt
    (RSMC)
  PO Box 8987
  Wilmington, DE 19899
  800-336-9970
  $1,436 million
  Year founded: 1982

World Savings & Loan Association
Oakland, CA
  Atlas Assets, Inc.
  1901 Harrison Street
  Oakland, CA 94612
  800-933-2852
  $686 million
  Year founded: 1990

Source: Lipper Analytical Services, Inc., January 1994, to obtain more information call Lipper at 303-534-3472.

Appendix C

Annuity Providers to Bank Customers

There is an excellent chance that an annuity will be an appropriate part of your investment portfolio in the near future. Tax-deferred annuities are popular products with bank customers.

Since 1991, banks placed with their customers more than 30% of all fixed annuities sold by all insurance companies. In 1994 alone, this amounted to an estimated $1.3 billion invested through banks into fixed annuities. Sales of variable annuities are currently the fastest growing of any investment product sold through banks. An estimated 13% of all variable annuities were sold through banks in 1994.

Below is a list of insurance companies that are the most prominent providers of annuities through banks. Each company's address and telephone number are included.

AIG Life Insurance Co.
One Alico Plaza
Wilmington, DE 19801
302-594-2000

Alexander Hamilton Life
    Insurance Co. of America
33045 Hamilton Court
Farmington Hills, MI 48334
810-553-2000

All American Life Insurance Co.
8501 West Higgins Road
Chicago, IL 60631
312-399-6500

Allied Life Insurance Co.
701 Fifth Avenue
Des Moines, IA 50391-2000
515-280-4211

American Benefit Life
    Insurance Co.
421 New Karner Road
Albany, NY 12205
518-456-8164

American Enterprise Life
    Insurance Co.
80 South A Street
Minneapolis, MN 55440
800-333-3437

American General Life
    Insurance Co.
2727-A Allen Parkway
Houston, TX 77019
713-522-1111

American International Life
   Assurance Company of NY
(AILife)
80 Pine Street
New York, NY 10005
212-478-7000

American Investor's Life
   Insurance Co.
415 Southwest 8th Avenue
Topeka, KS 66603
913-232-6945

American Life and Casualty
   Insurance Co.
405 6th Avenue, Des Moines
   Building
Des Moines, IA 50309
515-284-7500

American Mutual Life Assurance
   Co.
611 Fifth Avenue
Des Moines, IA 50309
515-283-2371

American National Insurance Co.
One Moody Plaza
Galveston, TX 77550
409-763-4661

American Skandia Life Assurance
   Corporation
One Corporate Drive, 10th Floor
Shelton, CT 06484
203-926-1888

Anchor National Life Insurance Co.
1 SunAmerica Center
Los Angeles, CA 90067
800-871-2000

Banker's Security Life Insurance
   Society
146 EAB Plaza
Uniondale, NY 11556
703-875-3500

Banker's United Life Assurance Co.
4333 Edgewood Road N.E.
Cedar Rapids, IA 52499
319-398-8511

CU Life Insurance Co. of New York
100 Corporate Parkway, Suite 300
Buffalo, NY 14226
716-862-5600

Central National Life
400 Beneficial Center
Peapack, NJ 07977
908-781-4000

Century Life Insurance Co.
2000 Heritage Way
Waverly, IA 50677
319-352-4090

Charter National Life
8301 Maryland Avenue
St. Louis, MO 63105
314-725-7575

Commercial Union Life Insurance
   Co. of America
108 Myrtle Street
PO Box 9174
Boston, MA 02205-9174
800-343-5660

Constitution Life Insurance Co.
4211 Norbourne Boulevard
Louisville, KY 40207
502-897-1861

Federal Home Life Insurance Co.
300 North Meridian Street
Indianapolis, IN 46204
407-345-2600

Fidelity Standard Life
  Insurance Co.
11365 West Olympic Boulevard
Los Angeles, CA 90064
310-312-6100

Financial Horizons Life
  Insurance Co.
Two Nationwide Plaza, 5th Floor
Columbus, OH 43215
800-882-2822

First Colony Life Insurance Co.
700 Main Street
Lynchburg, VA 24504
804-845-0911

Ford Life Insurance Co.
One American Road
PO Box 1799
Dearborn, MI 48121
800-765-5433

Fortis Benefits Insurance Co.
Fortis Financial Group
PO Box 64271
St. Paul, MN 55164-0271
612-738-4000

Franklin Life Insurance Co.
One Franklin Square
Springfield, IL 62713
217-528-2011

Great Northern Insured Annuity
  Corporation
5600 Two Union Square
Seattle, WA 98101
206-625-1755

Great-West Life & Annuity
  Insurance Co.
8515 East Orchard Road
Englewood, CO 80111
303-689-3000

Guarantee Mutual Life Co.
8801 Indian Hills Drive
Omaha, NE 68114
402-390-7300

Hartford Life Insurance Co.
200 Hopmeadow Street
Simsbury, CT 06089
203-843-8216

IDS Life Insurance Co.
IDS Tower 10
Minneapolis, MN 55440
612-671-3131

Integon Life Insurance
  Corporation
500 West Fifth Street
Winston-Salem, NC 27152
910-770-2000

International Life Investors
  Insurance Co.
666 Fifth Avenue, 25th Floor
New York, NY 10103
212-621-9590

Inter-State Assurance
  Company
1206 Mulberry Street
Des Moines, IA 50309
515-283-2501

ITT Hartford Life and Annuity
  Insurance Co.
505 No. Highway 169
Plymouth, MN 55441
612-545-2100

Jackson National Life
  Insurance Co.
5901 Executive Drive
Lansing, MI 48911
517-394-3400

Jefferson National Life
Insurance Co.
11815 N. Pennsylvania Street
Carmel, IN 46032
317-817-3500

Jefferson-Pilot Life
Insurance Co.
100 North Greene Street
PO Box 21008
Greensboro, NC 27420
910-691-3000

John Alden Life Insurance Co.
5100 Gamble Drive
St. Louis Park, MN 55416
305-715-2000

John Hancock Mutual Life
Insurance Co.
John Hancock Place, PO Box 111
Boston, MA 02117
617-572-6000

Kansas City Life Insurance Co.
PO Box 419139
Kansas City, MO 64141-6139
816-753-7000

Kemper Investors Life
Insurance Co.
One Kemper Drive, T-1
Long Grove, IL 60049
708-320-4500

Keyport Life Insurance Co.
125 High Street
Boston, MA 02110-2712
617-526-1400

Life Insurance Co. of the
Southwest
1300 West Mockingbird Lane
Dallas, TX 75247
214-638-7100

Life Insurance Co. of Virginia
6610 West Broad Street
Richmond, VA 23230
804-281-6000

Life Investors Insurance Co. of
America
4333 Edgewood Road, N.E.
Cedar Rapids, IA 52499
319-398-8511

Lincoln Benefit Life Company
134 South 13th Street
Lincoln, NE 68508
402-475-4061

Lincoln Mutual Life Insurance Co.
5601 South 27th Street
Lincoln, NE 68512
402-423-7191

Lincoln National Life Insurance Co.
1300 South Clinton Street
Fort Wayne, IN 46801
219-455-2000

Lincoln Security Life Insurance Co.
Rt. 312 Southeast Executive Park
Brewster, NY 10509
914-278-2860

Minnesota Mutual Life
Insurance Co.
Minnesota Mutual Center 400
Robert Street N.
St. Paul, MN 55101
612-298-3500

Monumental Life Insurance Co.
1111 North Charles Street
Baltimore, MD 21201
410-685-2900

Mutual of Omaha Insurance Co.
Mutual of Omaha Plaza
Omaha, NE 68175
402-342-7600

National Fidelity Life
   Insurance Co.
11815 North Pennsylvania
Carmel, IN 46032
317-817-2890

National Home Life Assurance Co.
237 East High Street
Jefferson City, MO 65102
610-648-5000

National Integrity Life
   Insurance Co.
200 Park Avenue, 20th Floor
New York, NY 10166
212-973-2230

Nationwide Life Insurance Co.
Two Nationwide Plaza
Columbus, OH 43215
800-882-2822

North American Company for
   Life & Health Insurance
222 South Riverside Plaza
Chicago, IL 60606
800-882-2822

North American Security Life
1455 East Putnam Avenue
Old Greenwich, CT 06870
800-931-BANK (2265)

The Paul Revere Life Insurance Co.
18 Chestnut Street
Worcester, MA 01608
508-799-4441

Pacific Mutual Life Insurance
   Company
700 Newport Center Drive
Newport Beach, CA 92660
800-800-7646

Penn Mutual Life Insurance Co.
Independence Square
Philadelphia, PA 19172
215-956-8000

PFL Life Insurance Co.
4333 Edgewood Road, N.E.
Cedar Rapids, IA 52499
319-398-8511

Phoenix Home Life Mutual
   Insurance Co.
99 Troy Road
East Greenbush, NY 12061
518-479-8000

Principal Mutual Life
   Insurance Co.
711 High Street
Des Moines, IA 50392
515-247-5111

Protective Life Insurance Co.
2801 Highway 280 S
Burmingham, AL 35223-2448
205-879-9230

Provident Life & Accident
   Insurance Co.
One Fountain Square
Chattanooga, TN 37402
615-755-1011

Provident Mutual Life Insurance
   Co. of Philadelphia
1600 Market Street
Philadelphia, PA 19103
215-636-5000

Royal Life Insurance Co. of America
500 Winding Brook Drive
Glastonbury, CT 06033
810-357-4800

SAFECO Life Insurance Co.
15411 N.E. 51st Street
Redmond, WA 98052
206-867-8000

Seaboard Life Insurance Co.
2165 West Broadway
Vancouver, B.C. Canada V6K 4N5
604-734-1667

Security Benefit Life Insurance Co.
700 Harrison Street
Topeka, KS 66636
913-295-3000

Security-Connecticut Life
  Insurance Co.
20 Security Drive
Avon, CT 06001
203-677-8621

Security First Life Insurance Co.
11365 West Olympic Boulevard
Los Angeles, CA 90064
800-933-4536

Standard Insurance Co.
PO Box 711
Portland, OR 97207
503-321-7000

State Bond and Mortgage Life
  Insurance Co.
8400 Normandale Lake
  Boulevard, Suite 1150
Minneapolis, MN 55437
612-835-0097

Sun Life Assurance Company
  of Canada
150 King Street West
Toronto, Canada M5H 1J9
416-979-9966

TMG Life Insurance Co.
PO Box 2907
Fargo, ND 58108
701-237-5700
$980 million

Transamerica Life Insurance and
  Annuity Co.
1150 South Olive Street
Los Angeles, CA 90015
213-742-3111

United Companies Life
  Insurance Co.
One United Plaza, 4041 Essen Lane
Baton Rouge, LA 70809
504-924-6007

United Life Insurance Co.
118 Second Avenue S.E.
Cedar Rapids, IA 52401
319-399-5700

United of Omaha Life
  Insurance Co.
Mutual of Omaha Plaza
Omaha, NE 68175
402-342-7600

United Presidential Life
  Insurance Co.
One Presidential Parkway
Kokomo, IN 46904
317-453-0602

United Services Life Insurance Co.
4601 N. Fairfax Drive
Arlington, VA 22203
703-875-3400

USG Annuity & Life Co.
604 Locust Street
Des Moines, IA 50309
515-282-3230

Western National Life
   Insurance Co.
5555 San Felipe, Suite 900
Houston, TX 77056
713-888-7800

Western Reserve Life Assurance
   Co. of Ohio
PO Box 5048
Clearwater, FL 34618
813-587-1800

Western-Southern Life
   Assurance Co.
418 Broadway
Cincinnati, OH 45202
513-629-1800

William Penn Life Insurance Co.
   of New York
100 Quentin Roosevelt Boulevard
Garden City, NY 11530
516-794-3700

Xerox Financial Services Life
   Insurance Co.
237 East High Street
Jefferson City, MO 65101
708-368-6215

Sources: *1994 National Census of Bank Investment Services*; American Brokerage Data Services, Inc.; and *The Annuity Review*, Paragon Publications, Fraser, Michigan.

Appendix D

Bank-Related
Variable Annuities

With the popularity of variable annuities soaring, a small but growing number of the nation's larger banks are sponsoring their own variable annuities. To provide the tax-deferred and death-benefit features of its variable annuity, a bank must have an insurance company as a partner. Banks, along with other organizations, manage the investment accounts.

Below is a list of those variable annuities currently available that are proprietary to a bank. Included is the name and headquarters of the bank, the name of the variable annuity product, the insurance company, the address and phone number for the variable annuity, total assets as of December 1994, and the year founded.

Banc One, N.A.
Columbus, OH
    One Investors Annuity
    Financial Horizons Life
       Insurance Co.
    PO Box 182008
    Columbus, OH 43218-2008
    800-533-5622
    Year founded: 1994

First of American Bank-Michigan
Kalamazoo, MI
    Parkstone Variable Annuity
    Security Benefit Life Insurance
       Co.
    700 Harrison Street
    Topeka, KS 66636
    800-888-2461
    Year founded: 1993

Fleet National Bank
Providence, RI
    Galaxy Variable Annuity
    American Skandia Life
       Assurance Corp.
    Tower One, Corporate Drive
    Shelton, CT 06484
    800-541-3087
    Year founded: 1992

Great Western Savings Bank
Los Angeles, CA
    Sierra Advantage
    American General Life
       Insurance Co.
    PO Box 1401
    Houston, TX 77251
    800-231-3655
    Year founded: 1993

Norwest Bank Minn. NA
Minneapolis, MN
   Fortis Benefits Life Insurance Co.
   PO Box 64271
   St. Paul, MN 55164
   612-738-4000
   Year founded: 1994

Premier Bank, N.A.
Baton Rouge, LA
   Paragon Power Variable Annuity
   Great Northern Insured
     Annuity Co.
   Two Union Square, PO Box 490
   Seattle, WA 98111-0490
   206-625-1755
   Year founded: 1995

Signet Bank
Richmond, VA
   Signet Select Variable Annuity
   Security first Life Insurance Co.
   11365 West Olympic Blvd.
   Los Angeles, CA 90064
   800-284-4536
   Year founded: 1993

Wells Fargo Bank
San Francisco, CA
   Stagecoach
   American Skandia Life
     Assurance Corp.
   Tower One, Corporate Drive
   Shelton, CT 06484
   800-541-3087
   Year founded: 1994

Source: Lipper Analytical Services, Inc. To obtain more information call Lipper at 303-534-3472.

Appendix E

Marketers and Broker/ Dealers Active in Banks

More than 80% of the nation's banks, S&Ls, and credit unions that have investment programs contract with specialized marketing companies and broker/dealers to help provide their banking customers with investment products and services. These companies make it possible for banks of any size to provide their customers with services and benefits equal to those provided by major brokerage firms. You'll notice on your bank investment representative's business card, new account forms, and your bank's investment literature the name of the company your bank is using. More than 200 such companies are active in the bank brokerage industry, but the industry is dominated by 20 companies that have up to 200 banks as clients. Below is a list of 78 of the most prominent marketers and broker/dealers active in banks.

AEGON USA Securities, Inc.
4333 Edgewood Road, N. E.
Cedar Rapids, IA 52499
800-551-4042

Affiliated Financial Services, Inc.
7840 East Berry Place, Suite 200
Englewood, CO 80111
303-770-4429

Affiliated Financial Services, Inc.
303 North 52nd, Suite 225
Lincoln, NE 68504
402-466-6761
800-242-1237

AMCORP
801 Nicollet Mall, Suite 1410
Minneapolis, MN 55402
612-341-4550
800-229-8455

Ameritrade/Amerivest
4211 South 102nd Street
Omaha, NE 68127-1031
800-237-8692
402-331-2740

AON Financial Institution Services
230 West Monroe, 12th Floor
Chicago, IL 60606
312-456-1337

ARAGON Financial Marketing, Inc.
3755 Capital of Texas Hwy.,
    South, Suite 190
Austin, TX 78704
800-451-6094

Bancsource Insurance Services, Inc.
7400 Metro Boulevard, Suite 417
Edina, MN 55436
800-347-7901
612-347-7917

Bankers Financial Partners, Inc.
7 East Redwood Street
Baltimore, MD 21202
800-790-6247
410-830-9082

Bankmark
301 Gibralter Drive, Suite 2A
Morris Plains, NJ 07950
800-227-4389

BHC Securities, Inc.
2005 Market Street, 12th Floor
Philadelphia, PA 19103-3212
215-636-3000

Brynwood Financial Services
6072 Brynwood Drive, Suite 100
Rockford, IL 61144
815-636-0150

Capital Funding Corporation
122 West Jackson Street
Sullivan, IN 47882
812-268-3777

CFS Brokerage Corp.
9800 Bren Road East
Minnetonka, MN 55343
800-388-7009
612-938-7009

Community Financial
   Services, Inc.
1700 Lincoln Street, Suite 2200
Denver, CO 80203
800-306-3739

Compass Securities
1 Gateway Center
Newton, MA 02158
617-969-8636

Compulife, Inc.
2820 Waterford Lake Drive,
   Suite 103
Midlothian, VA 23112
800-726-9000

Corelink Resources, Inc.
1855 Gateway Boulevard, Suite 750
Concord, CA 94520
510-602-9300

Cozad Asset Management, Inc.
2500 Galen Drive
Champaign, IL 61821
800-437-1686
217-356-8363

Cross Marketing, Inc.
87 Main Street
Peapack, NJ 07977
908-781-2006

Equity Bancing Services, Inc.
14707 California Street, Suite 5
Omaha, NE 68154-1900
402-492-8300

Essex Corporation
825 3rd Avenue, 30th floor
New York, NY 10022
214-691-0063 Southern U.S.
412-934-4311 Northern U.S.
800-621-2233 Community Banking

F & G Investment Services
(Sterne, Agee & Leach, Inc.)
1901 Sixth Avenue North,
   Suite 2100
Brimingham, AL 35203
800-633-4638

FIMARK
21700 Oxnard Street, Suite 1550
Woodland Hills, CA 91367
818-710-7700
800-232-5229

FIMCO
111 East Kilbourn Avenue,
    Suite 1850
Milwaukee, WI 53202
414-289-3100
800-331-8872

FIMI (First Institutional
    Marketing, Inc.)
5555 San Felipe, Fifth fl.
Houston, TX 77056
713-961-5967
800-935-3464

Financial Horizons Distributors
    Agency
Two Nationwide Plaza, 5th Floor
Columbus, OH 43215
614-249-4538

Financial Network Investment Corp.
2780 Skypark Drive, Suite 300
Torrance, CA 90505
800-879-8100
310-326-3100

Financial Protection Life & Annuity
    Corp./Signal Securities Inc.
PO Box 795008
Dallas, TX 75379
800-892-0127

Fixed Income Securities, Inc.
7220 Trade Street, Suite 315
San Diego, CA 92121
800-697-7220

GNA Corporation
Two Union Square, Suite 5600
Seattle, WA 98101
800-426-5520
206-625-1755

The Holden Group
11365 West Olympic Boulevard
Los Angeles, CA 90064
800-888-8486
310-312-6431

Independent Financial Marketing
    Group, Inc.
244 Westchester Avenue
White Plains, NY 10604
914-997-5600
800-873-4374

INVEST Financial Corp.
5404 Cypress Center Drive
Tampa, FL 33609
813-289-0722
800-242-4732

Investment Centers of America, Inc.
First Dakota Building
212 North 4th Street
Bismarck, ND 58501
800-544-7113

Investment Professionals, Inc.
10100 Reunion Place,
    Suite 100
San Antonio, TX 78216
210-308-8800
800-593-8800

Investors Capital Corporation
230 Broadway
Lynnfield, MA 01940-2320
617-593-8565
800-949-1422

Kevlin Financial Resources
14665 Midway Road
Dallas, TX 75244
800-442-6575

Kingland Capital Corp
9 North Federal Avenue
Mason City, IA 50401
515-424-0844

Laughlin Group
8305 Southwest Creekside Place
Beaverton, OR 97005
503-643-7032
800-929-4427

LCL Investments, Inc.
1440 West North Avenue,
    Suite 400
Melrose Park, IL 60160
708-343-4450
800-343-4415

Richard Leahy Corporation
12900 White Water Drive,
    Suite 290
Minnetonka, MN 55343
612-935-0996
800-617-4548

Liberty Financial Bank Group
600 Atlantic Avenue
Boston, MA 02210
617-722-6000
800-253-4108

Linsco/Private Ledger Corp.
155 Federal Street, 14th Floor
Boston, MA 02110
800-877-7210

The Lloyd Financial Group
220 Park Boulevard, Suite 113
Grapevine, TX 76051
817-329-2191

Main Street Financial Services
329 North Main Street
St. Charles, MO 63301
314-949-0999
800-755-0998

Marketing One, Inc.
851 Southwest 6th Avenue
Portland, OR 97204
800-632-5678

Market Street Securities, Inc,
800 Market Street, LBP 3113
St. Louis, MO 63101
800-754-8540
314-466-8540

Mericorp, A Division of Meridian
    Associates
1819 Main Street, Suite 1000
Sarasota, FL 34238
813-365-1329
800-777-1819

Mid-America Partners
9020 North May Avenue
Oklahoma City, OK 73120
800-776-4627
405-840-8700

James Mitchell & Co.
9710 Scranton Road, Suite 100
San Diego, CA 92121
619-450-0055

NAP Financial Marketing, Inc.
3755 Capital of Texas Hwy., South,
    Suite 130
Austin, TX 78704
800-451-6094

National Financial
82 Devonshire Street, L4C
Boston, MA 02109
800-752-7053

The Ohio Company
155 East Broad Street
Columbus, OH 43215
800-743-8766

Pershing
One Pershing Plaza
Jersey City, NJ 07399
201-413-3343

Planco
Paoli Corporate Center
16 Industrial Boulevard
Paoli, PA 19301-1605
800-523-7798
610-695-9500

Primevest Financial Services, Inc.
400 First Street South, Suite 300
St. Cloud, MN 56302
800-245-0467
612-656-4358

Proequities Services, Inc.
2801 Highway 280 South
Birmingham, AL 35223
800-288-3035

Pro Value Investments, Inc.
2 North LaSalle Street
Chicago, IL 60602
800-247-2752
312-444-2100

Protective Equity Services, Inc.
2801 Highway 280 South
Birmingham, AL 35223
800-288-3035

Purity Financial Corp.
1224 Benson Court, Suite 1
Manchester, MD 21102
410-848-0409
800-798-0839

Purity Financial Corp.
774 State Road 13, Suite 11
Jacksonville, FL 32259
904-287-0839
800-798-0839

SM&R Financial Services
One Moody Plaza, 14th Floor
Galveston, TX 77550
800-231-4639

Specialized Investments Division,
    a division of Financial Service
    Corporation
2300 Windy Ridge Parkway,
    Suite 1100
Atlanta, GA 30339
404-916-6500
800-352-4372

Spectrum Financial Network
270 Walker Drive, Suite 200
State College, PA 16804
814-231-2292
800-828-5654

Stephens Inc.
111 Center Street
Little Rock, AR 72201
501-374-4361
800-643-9691

T.H.E. Financial Group, Inc.
5010 Ritter Road, Suite 119
Mechanicsburg, PA 17055
800-272-9297
717-766-4551

Robert Thomas Securities, Inc.
Financial Institutions Division
1600 Oak Street
Kansas City, MO 64108
800-752-2657
816-561-5008

Talbot Financial Services
6565 Americas Parkway N.E.,
    Suite 840
Albuquerque, NM 87110
505-880-3000
800-829-5445

T'N'T Marketing, Inc.
1380 Corporate Center Curve,
    Suite 318
Eagan, MN 55121
612-686-5775
800-966-3519

Trade$aver,
    a Division of PNC Securities
    Corp.
630 Dresher Road
Horsham, PA 19044
800-545-7773
215-956-2537

Tradestar Investments, Inc.
5599 San Felipe, Suite 1400
Houston, TX 77056
713-993-2028
800-993-2028

Tri-Merica Securities
    Corporation
1206 Mulberry
Des Moines, IA 50309
800-798-8324

U.S. Clearing Corporation
26 Broadway
New York, NY 10004-1798
212-747-1402
800-221-3524

Uvest Investment Services
128 South Tryon Street, Suite 1340
Charlotte, NC 28202
800-277-7700
704-375-0484

Wall Street Investor Services
17 Battery Place, 25th Floor
New York, NY 10004
800-428-9919

Winthrop Financial Advisory
    Services, Inc.
619 Enterprise Drive, Suite 100
Oak Brook, IL 60521
708-573-4800

Wood Logan Companies
1455 East Putnam Avenue
Old Greenwich, CT 06870
203-698-0068
800-334-0575

Source: *Banker's Guide to Third-Party Securities and Annuity Programs,* 15th edition,
American Brokerage Consultants, Inc. Used with permission.

Index

A

Account monitoring, bank financial advisors, 22–23

Account registration, account application, 184

Accounts handled by bank financial advisors, 22

Account statements, investments, 189

Account type, ownership, and servicing, account application, 185

Accrued interest, bonds, 85

Accumulation phase, fixed annuities, 112–13

Accurate record keeping, value of, 203

Aggressive growth mutual funds, 89

American Municipal Bond Assurance Company (AMBAC), 107

American Stock Exchange (AMEX), 74, 75

Annual free withdrawal, fixed annuities, 117–18

Annual investment evaluation, 203–4

Annual reports, 173

Annuitant, annuity, 118

Annuities; see Fixed annuities; and Variable annuities

Annuities applications, 187–88

Annuity providers to bank customers, 227–32

Asset mix, 39–40

Audited performance, mutual funds and, 95–95

Automatic reinvestment compounding, mutual funds, 96

B

Back-end loaded mutual funds, 178

Back-end surrender charges, fixed annuities, 117

Bailout rate, fixed annuities, 120

Balanced mutual funds, 89

Bank accounts
  business accounts, 68–69
  and FDIC insurance, 60–69
  joint, 64–67
  and short-term, mid-term, and long-term money, 55–56
  types of, 56–60

Bank money market deposit accounts, 59

Bank propriety mutual funds, 213–25

Bank-related variable annuities, 223–34

Bankruptcy risk, mutual funds and, 96

Banks
  discount brokerage of, 182
  and financial advisors, 8, 19–26, 33–34
  investment mechanics of investing at, 184–90
  investment products of, 7–8, 21
  management and broker/dealers active in, 235–40
  and mutual funds, 86–87

Beneficiary, annuity, 118

Bond mutual funds, 85, 91–92

Bonds
  bond terms, 84–85
  corporate, 81–82
  cost of, 177
  defined, 78–79
  as income vehicles, 28

and inflation, 28
market and credit risk of, 80–81
mutual funds, 85, 91–92
overexposure to, 195
stated interest rate of, 79–80
as traded instruments, 79
types of, 81–84
U.S. government, 79, 82–83, 92, 157
Bonus rate, fixed annuities, 120
Brackets and rates, federal income
    tax, 106, 162
Buying and selling fixed annuities,
    116–18
Buy price, mutual funds, 99

C

Capital appreciation, municipal
    bonds, 110
Certificates of deposit (CD), 57-58
    cost of, 176
Certified financial planner (CFP), 24
Certified fund specialist, (CFS), 24
Certified investment management
    consultant (CIMC), 24
Chartered financial consultant
    (ChFC), 24
Choice variety, variable annuities,
    132
Class A, B, and C shares, mutual
    funds, sales charge on, 178
Close-end mutual fund, 88
Commission breakpoints, mutual
    funds, 181
Commissions, lack of, and variable
    annuities, 132
Common stock, 71
Compensation, bank financial
    advisors, 24–26
Compounding interest, power of,
    49–50, 51
Confirmation statements,
    investment accounts, 188–89
Consumer items, basket of, 12
Contingent annuitants, annuity, 118

Contract owner, annuity, 118
Convertible mutual funds, 89–90
Corporate affiliations, account
    application, 185
Corporate bonds, 81–82
Corporate mutual bond funds, 92
Costs, variable annuities, 129–30
Coupon date, bonds, 84
Credit risk, 158
    bonds, 81
Credit unions, 61
Current investments, goals, and
    time horizons matching, 40
Current value measurement, stocks,
    75–77
Current yield, bonds, 85
Custodian risk, mutual funds and, 96
Customer agreement, account
    application, 186
Customer complaints and arbitration,
    bank investment accounts, 189–90
Customer types served by bank
    financial advisors, 22

D

Death benefit, variable annuities,
    127, 132
Death benefits/avoiding probate,
    fixed annuities, 119–20
Deduction on taxes, IRAs, 142
Defined-benefit pension plans, 140
Defined contribution pension plans, 140
Department of Housing and Urban
    Development, 84
Disclaimer, prospectus, 170–71
Disclosure forms, account
    application, 187
Discount brokerage, bank, 182–83
Distributions, listed, prospectus on, 172
Diversification
    and asset allocation, 13, 29–31
    and investment costs, 181
    and mutual funds, 95
    postretirement years and, 158
    retirement and, 149

and variable annuities, 132
Dividend-distributing agent,
    prospectus on, 172
Dividend payout ratio, stocks, 76
Dividends, stock, 70–72
Dividend yield, stocks, 76
Dollar cost averaging, 51
Dow-Jones Industrial Average
    (DJIA), 75

E

Early years (20-40), investing
    during, 43–44
Educational creditials, bank
    financial advisors, 23–24
Elderly, increase in numbers of, 4–5
Embezzlement, 14
Employer-sponsored pension plans,
    140–41
Employment status, account
    application, 185
Expenditure reduction, retirement
    and, 147

F

Federal Deposit Insurance Corporation
    (FDIC), 4, 6, 10, 19
    background of, 60–61
    business accounts, 68
    and deposit and investment
        insurance, 10
    extent of coverage, 61–63
    insurance limits, 63
    items not covered by, 7, 55, 59, 69,
        86, 93, 107, 109, 112, 137–38,
        157, 171, 187
    joint accounts, 64–67
    retirement accounts, 63, 67–68
    single ownership accounts, 63–64
    Treasury securities, 69
Federal income tax
    brackets and rates, 106, 162
    on social security income, 139, 162–63

Federally tax-free money market
    funds, 109–10
Fees, lack of, fixed annuities, 120
Financial advisors, banks
    and financial need, condition, and
        goals, 33–34
    interviewing of, 20–21
    and postretirement years, 152
    questions concerning, 21–26
    selection of, 192
    trust and, 19–20
Financial affairs review, bank
    financial advisors, 22
Financial goals
    attainment of, 41–42
    definition of, 34–35, 40
    and needs determinastion, 21
Financial Guaranty Insurance
    Company (FGIC), 107
Financial needs, retirement and,
    136–38
Financial needs discovery worksheet,
    192–93
Fixed annuities
    accumulation phase of, 112–13
    buying and surrendering, 116–18
    compared with CDs, 117, 119
    compared with variable annuities,
        112, 117
    cost of, 176
    defined, 112
    miscellaneous benefits of, 118–21
    payout phase, 113–16
    and postretirement years, 161
    and probate avoidance, 163, 119–20
    terms connected with, 118
Fixed interest rates, fixed annuities, 119
Fixed payment, fixed annuity
    payout, 115
Flexibility
    fixed annuities, 121
    municipal bonds, 110
Flexible deposits, variable annuities,
    126–27
Flexible payment fixed annuities, 117
Form, bonds, 85

Form SSA-7004, social security
     earnings, 139
Foundation building, investment
     strategy, 27
457 plans, 68
401(k) plan, 135, 141
403(b) plan, 141
Fraud and deception, investments
     and, 14–15
Full-time professionals, and mutual
     funds, 94–95
Fund advisor and custodian,
     prospectus on, 172

G

General obligation bonds,
     municipal, 83, 105–6
Get-rich-quick schemes, and
     postretirement years, 164–65
Gifts as tax avoidance, 164
Gifts to minors, 64
Ginnie Maes, 84
Global mutual bond funds, 92
Global mutual funds, 90
Goals and needs determination,
     bank financial advisors and, 21
Gold mutual funds, 90
Governmental National Mortgage
     Association (GNMA), 84
Great Depression, 4, 10, 109
Growth and enhance-income
     component, investment strategy,
     27–29
Growth and income mutual
     funds, 90
Growth mutual funds, 89
Growth of $100,000 at 7% a year, 144
Growth potential, variable
     annuities, 132
Guaranteed principal and interest,
     fixed annuities, 119

H

Health care needs, retirement and, 149

High-quality corporate mutual bond
     funds, 92
High-yield corporate mutual bond
     funds, 92
Historical performance, stocks, 71, 72
Hot tips avoidance, 202
Hybrid mutual funds, 91

I

Ibbotson, Roger G., 28, 72, 201
Ibbotson Associates, 28, 30, 201
Income maximization, postretirement
     years, 158–61
Income mutual funds, 90
Income shortfall, retirement on, 143–45
Income vehicles, bonds as, 28
Index mutual funds, 90
Individual retirement accounts (IRA),
     63, 68, 123, 138, 141-43, 147
     rollovers, 149
Inflation, 11–12, 28–29, 137
Inflation-beating investments, 148
Initial investment, mutual funds, 95
Insurance, muncipal bond, 107
Insured-municipal mutual bond
     funds, 93
Interest payment dates, bonds, 84
Interest rates and share price,
     relationship between, 80
Interest rate-share price relationship,
     stocks, 80
Intermediate bond mutual funds, 91
Internal expenses, variable
     annuities, 130
Internal Revenue Service (IRS), 103,
     104, 113, 148, 186
Interviewing bank financial
     advisors, 20–21
Investment ceiling, lack of, and
     variable annuities, 132
Investment checkup, value of, 150
Investment choices, needs and, 31–32
Investment Company Act, 98
Investment costs
     bank services, 174

bonds and stocks, 177–78
CDs and annuities, 174, 176
fixed annuities, 176
mutual funds, 97, 178–80
no-load mutual funds, 179–80
payment of, 188
professional advice, 175
UITs, 177
variable annuities, 129–30, 176
ways to reduce, 181–83
Investment evaluation, 203–4
Investment follow through and
    regularity of, 201–2
Investment information sources,
    bank financial advisors, 24
Investment Institute, 6
Investment knowledge maintenance,
    bank financial advisors, 24
Investment mechanics, bank
account applications, 184–86
annuities application, 187–88
confirmation and account
    statements, 188–89
customer complaints and arbitration,
    189–90
disclosure form, 187
payment of fees, 188
W-9 form, 186–87
Investment objectives
account application, 186
prospectus on, 172
Investment philosophy, bank financial
    advisors, 23
Investment plan
adjustments to, 202–3
development of, 196
and recommendations, 195–96
Investment policies, prospectus
    on, 172
Investment products, banks and,
    7–8, 21
Investment pyramid, 160
Investment risk
and earnings increase, 29–31
prospectus on, 172
relationship to time, 47–49, 199–201

tolerance for, 38, 172, 193–94
Investments, and life expectancy,
    4, 153–57
Investments, value fluctuation, 199–99
Investment safety
fixed annuities, 119
and high return reconciliation, 151–52
municipal bonds, 106, 110–11
redefinition of, 1990s, 11–12
Investments appropriate to
    postretirement years, 157–58
Investments rethinking, 42
Investment strategy
compounding, value of, 49–50, 51
diversification and asset allocation,
    31, 29–31
foundation building, 27
growth and enhance-income
    component of, 27–29
investment risk, influence of time
    on, 47–49
life stages and, 43–47
systematic investing/dollar cost
    averaging, 50–51
Investment tips
action now better than later, 191–92
careful advisor choice, 192
financial needs discovery
    worksheet completion, 192–93
investment plan and
    recommendations, 195–96
plan building, 196
rate of return targets, product
    knowledge, and managed
    products use, 194
retirement accounts value
    maximization, 196
risk tolerance determination, 193–94
stocks and bonds over- and
    underexposure avoidance, 195
tax considerations, 196
time horizons establishment,
    194–95
Investors' economic status, municipal
    bonds and, 103
IOUs, bonds as, 78–79

J

Joint accounts with rights of
  survivorship, and probate
  avoidance, 163
Joint and last survivor, fixed
  annuity payout, 115
Joint and survivor life annuity
  with period certain, variable
  annunities, 129
Joint and survivor variable annuity,
  128–29
Joint bank accounts, 64–67
Joint contract owners, annuity, 118

K

Keogh plans, 68, 135, 141

L

Late years (70 plus), investing
  during, 47
Licensed investment consultant
  (LIC), 24
Life and period certain, variable
  annuities, 129
Life and refund certain, variable
  annuities, 129
Life annuity option, variable
  annuities, 128
Life expectancy, 4
  and investments, 153–57
  tables, 155–56
Life stages, investing and, 43–47
Lifetime payment, fixed annuity
  payout, 115
Lifetime with period certain, fixed
  annuity payout, 115
Liquidity
  fixed annuities, 120
  municipal bonds, 110
  mutual funds and, 95
Living trust, 163
Load, no-load mutual funds, 178–80
Lobby-issued annuity insurance, 116

Longer term investments,
  postretirement years, 153–57
Long-term bond mutual fund, 91
Long-term stock mutual funds, 153

M

Managed products, use of, 194
Management experience, prospectus
  on, 171
Marketers and broker/dealers active
  in banks, 235–40
Market risk, bonds, 80, 107
Maturity date, bonds, 84
Middle years (40-60), investing during,
  44, 45
Money market accounts, 58
Money market funds, 59-60, 114
  tax-free, 109–10
Moody's rating service, 106
Mortgage-backed corporate mutual
  bond funds, 92
Municipal bond funds, 108–9
Municipal Bond Insurance
  Association (MBIA), 107
Municipal bond mutual funds, 92
Municipal bonds, 83-84
  attractive features of, 109–10
  and credit risk and rating services,
    106–7
  defined, 103
  kinds of, 105–6
  liquidity, flexibility, and capital
    appreciation of, 110
  market risk of and bond
    insurance, 107
  packaged, 107–9
  and rule of principal fluctuation, 111
  safety of, 106, 109–10
  strategy regarding, 106, 110–11
  tax-free properties of, 103–5
  zero coupon, 109
Mutual fund companies, 77
Mutual funds
  bank proprietory, 213–25
  banks and, 86–87

benefits of, 94–97
cost of, 97, 178–79
defined, 87
distributed through banks, 207–11
load, no-load, 99, 178–80
major types of, 88–94
money market funds, 93
and newspaper fund tables, 99
quotation tables, 100
structural safeguards of, 97–99
structures of, 87–88
taxable, 92
tax-exempt, 92–93

N

National Association of Securities
Dealers (NASD), 19, 190
National Association of Securities
Dealers Automated Quotations
(NASDAQ), 74, 75
National Credit Union Administration
(NCUA), 61, 62
National municipal mutual bond
funds, 92
Needs and goals determination
asset mix checking, 39–40
and bank financial advisor, 33–34
goals attainment, 41–42
goals listing, 34–35
investment choices and, 32–33
investments rethinking, 42
needs discovery worksheet, 34–41
personal risk profile
determination, 36–37, 39
profile-investment matching, 39
time horizon determination,
35–36, 40
Net asset value (NAV), mutual funds,
87, 99
New investment account applications,
184–86
Newspaper mutual fund tables, how
to read, 99
New York Stock Exchange (NYSE),
74, 75

New York Stock Exchange Composite
Index, 75
No-load mutual funds, 99, 179–80
Nonretirement expenses, variable
annuities and, 131
Nursing home expenses, asset loss
and, 164

O

Open end mutual fund, 88
Outliving one's money, 4–5
Over- and underexposure to stocks
and bonds, 195
Over-the-counter stocks, 74, 75

P

Packaged tax-free municipal bonds,
107–9
Par amount, bonds, 85
Payout phase, fixed annuities, 113–16
Pension and retirement accounts
maximization, 147
Pension assets rollover, 149–50
Performance, variable annuities,
124–25
Personal risk profile, 36–39
Personal savings, retirement and,
141–43
Physical care expenses, retirement
and, 149
Postretirement expenses, 138
Postretirement years
and get-rich-quick schemes, 164–65
and income maximization, 158–61
investments appropriate to, 157–58
and longer term investments, 153–57
and probate avoidance, 163–64
reconciliation, safety and high
investment returns, 151–52
and tax reduction, 161–63
Preferred stock, 71–73
Preretirement years, investing during,
45–46
Price, bonds, 85

Price-earnings ratio, stocks, 75–76
Price movements, stock, 70, 73
Prices, corporation value, and profit, stocks and, 70
Principal fluctuation, rule of, 111
Probate avoidance, 163-64
  fixed annuities, 119–20
  variable annuities, 130
Product knowledge, 194
Professional money management, 13-14, 17-19
  cost of, 175
  variable annuities and, 132
Profit-sharing plans, 141
Projected monthly income, $100,000 principal, 144
Prospectus
  highlights of, 170–72
  sources of copies of, 170
  uses and shortcomings of, 169

Q

Quarterly reports, 172
Questions for financial advisors, 21–26
Quotation tables, mutual funds, 100

R

Rating, bonds, 81, 82, 84, 106
Residence, account application, 185
Residential real estate retention, retirement and, 147
Retirement accounts, 63, 67–68
Retirement accounts value maximization, 196
Retirement preparation
  allowance for physical care expenses, 149
  curbing expenditures, 147
  employer-sponsored pension plans, 140–41
  financial need assessment, 136–38
  income shortfall, 143–45
  investment checkups, need for, 150

pension and retirement accounts maximization, 147
pension asset rollovers, 149–50
personal savings, 141–43
residential real estate retention, 147
retirement accounts, 135–36
social security, 139–40, 142, 146–47
tax-advantaged investments and inflation considerations, 148
too-early retirement, 146
value of long-term investments and diversification, 148–49
variable annuities and, 130
Retirement years (60-70), investing during, 46
Revenue bonds, municipal, 82, 83, 105–6
Rights and privileges, prospectus on, 172
Risk
  as applied to investment returns, 48
  bankruptcy, and mutual funds, 96
  credit, bonds, 81, 158
  custodian, and mutual funds, 96
  inflation, 11
  investment, 29–31, 38, 47–49, 160, 172, 193–94
  market, 107
  market, bonds, 80
  overall reduction in with increased return, 159
  personal risk profile, 36–37, 39
  risk/return scale, 37
  time relationship to, 47–49, 199–201
Risk level flexibility, mutual funds, 96
Risk tolerance determination, 193–94
Rule of 72, and investments' worth, 143
Rule of principal fluctuation, 111

S

Savings accounts, 57
Savings and investments, effect of taxes on, 12–13
Savings and loan crisis, 1980s, 4

Securities, safety measures regarding, 14–15
Securities and Exchange Commission (SEC), 59, 75, 95–96, 98, 169, 171
Securities Investor Protection Corporation (SIPC), 14–15
Services and products, bank financial advisors, 21
Settlement date, bonds, 84
Shareholder transaction costs and ongoing expenses, prospectus on, 172
Share price-interest rate relationship, stocks, 80
Short-term, mid-term, and long-term money, 55–56
Short-term bond mutual funds, 91
Short-term money and accounts, 148
Signature, account application, 186
Silverstein, Shel, vi
Simplified employee pension (SEP), 135, 141
Single ownership bank accounts, 63–64
Single-premium fixed annuities, 117
Single-state municipal mutual bond funds, 93
Singuefield, Rex A., 28, 72, 201
Social security, 139-40, 142
  delay in accepting, 146–47
  federal income tax on, 139, 162–63
Social Security Administration, 140
Specialty mutual funds, 91
Spending and investment habits, need for change in, 5–7
Standard & Poor's 500 Index, 49, 50, 75
Standard & Poor's rating service, 106
Stated interest rate, bonds, 79–80
Statement frequency, variable annuities, 132
Stock exchange operation, 75
Stock market decline, 1987, 18
Stock mutual funds, 89, 159–60
Stocks
  common, 73
  cost of, 177–78
  defined, 70
  historical performance of, 71, 72
  and inflation, 28
  measurement of current value, 75–77
  and postretirement years, 157
  preferred, 71–73
  price movements, 70, 73
  prices, corporation value, and profit, 70–71
  purchase and redemption, prospectus on, 172
  share price-interest rate relationship, 80
  stock exchange operation, 75
  tax-deferred, and variable annuities, 125–26
  underexposure to, 195
  where traded, 74–75
Structural safeguards, mutual funds, 97–99
Structures, mutual funds, 87–88
Subaccounts, variable annuities, 123–24
Switching, mutual funds and, 96
Systematic investing, 50–51

T

Tables
  life expectancy, 155–56
  mutual funds, 99, 100
Target rates of return establishment, 194
Taxable bond mutual funds, 92
Tax advantaged investments, 148
Tax deferral
  401(k) plans, 123
  fixed annuities, 112–13, 116
  IRAs, 123, 142
  and postretirement years, 162
  stocks, and variable annuities, 122, 123, 125–26, 131
Taxes
  deductions on IRAs, 142
  effect on savings and investments, 12–13

federal income tax on social
    security, 139
investment use of to reduce or
    defer, 112–13, 116, 122, 123,
    125–26, 131, 196
reduction of, postretirement years,
    161–63
Tax-free investments
    bonds compared with taxable bonds,
        103–5
    money market funds, 109–10
    mutual funds, 92–93
    packaged municipal bonds, 107–9
    switching, variable annuities, 125, 132
    unit investment trusts, 108
Tax reduction through gifts, 164
Tax Reform Act, 1986
Time, relationship to investment
    risk, 47–49, 199–201
Time horizons
    establishment of, 194–95
    financial goals and, 35–36, 40
Tolerance for investment risk, 38,
    172, 193–94
Too-early retirement, 146
Track record, organization's, prospectus
    on, 171
Trade date, bonds, 84
Trading stock, 73–74
Transaction costs, mutual funds, 96
Transfer agent, prospectus on, 172
Treasury bills (T-bills), 82
Treasury bonds, 84, 109
Treasury securities, 69
Trust, and bank financial advisors,
    19–20

U

U.S. government mutual bond
    funds, 92
    postretirement years and, 157
U.S. government notes and bonds,
    79, 82-83
    postretirement years and, 157

U.S. savings bonds, 60
Uniform Gifts to Minors Act, 64
Unit investment trusts (UIT), 93, 94
    cost of, 177
    tax-free, 108
Unmanaged mutual bond funds, 93
Utility mutual funds, 90

V

Value fluctuation, investments, 198–99
Value Line Composite Index, 75
Variable annuities
    bank-related, 223–24
    compared with fixed annuities, 112,
        117, 122, 123
    cost of, 129–30, 176
    death benefits of, 127
    flexible deposits, 126–27
    performance of, 124–25
    popularity of, 122–23
    and postretirement years, 161
    and probate avoidance, 163
    subaccounts, 123–24
    and tax-deferred stocks, 125–26
    tax-free switching, 125
    uses of, 130–31
    withdrawal options of, 128–29

W

W-9 form, account application, 186–87
Withdrawal options, variable
    annuities, 128–29
Worst-time investing, 193

Y

Yield, tax-free versus taxable bonds,
    104–5
Yield to maturity, bonds, 85

Z

Zero coupon bonds, municipal and
    Treasury, 83, 109